Rekindling
the
Flame

Rekindling the Flame

How Jews
Are Coming Back
to Their Faith

SAMUEL OSHERSON

A Harvest Book
Harcourt, Inc.
San Diego   New York   London

Requests for permission to make copies of any part
of the work should be mailed to the following
address: Permissions Department, Harcourt, Inc.,
6277 Sea Harbor Drive, Orlando, Florida 32887-6777.

www.HarcourtBooks.com

Library of Congress Cataloging-in-Publication Data
Osherson, Samuel, 1945–
Rekindling the flame: the many paths to a vibrant Judaism/
Samuel Osherson.
p.   cm.
Includes index.
ISBN 0-15-100633-4
ISBN 0-15-602703-8 (pbk.)
1. Judaism—United States. 2. Jews—United States—Identity.
3. Jews—Cultural assimilation—United States. 4. Judaism—
Psychology. 5. Spiritual life—Judaism. 6. Interfaith marriage—
United States.
BM205.O84 2001
296'0973—dc21   2001024630

Lines from the re-creation of the Shema on p. 274 are
excerpted from *The Book of Blessings: New Jewish Prayers
for Daily Life, the Sabbath, and the New Moon Festival*;
Harper, 1996; paperback edition, Beacon, 1999; copyright
© 1996 Marcia Lee Falk. Used by permission of the author.

"Sheep Passing" by W. S. Merwin. Copyright © 1997 by
W. S. Merwin in the *New Yorker.* Used by permission.

Nemerov: *Debate with a Rabbi.* Copyright © 1981, Howard
Nemerov. Used by permission.

Text set in Sabon
Display set in OptiMarkus
Designed by Cathy Riggs

Printed in the United States of America

First Harvest edition 2002
K J I H G F E D C B A

To my children, Toby and Emily,
that they, too, may find their own way

Contents

Introduction   *The Uncounted and the Discontented*   1

Part One   *Why Jews Struggle with Judaism*

Chapter One   *Who's a Good Enough Jew?*   25

Chapter Two   *The Psychological Resistance to Being Jewish*   45

Chapter Three   L'Chayim *to Life: Overcoming the Resistance*   80

Part Two   *Solutions for Living in an Assimilated World*

Chapter Four   *Composing and Recomposing Judaism in Our Lives*   97

Chapter Five   *Can You Be a Good Jew and Love Handel's* Messiah?   116

Chapter Six   *Intermarried—and Jewish*   137

Part Three   *Finding the Joy in Judaism*

Chapter Seven   *The Psychology of a Vibrant Judaism*   173

Chapter Eight   *Creative Solutions to Careers:*
                 The Real Tikkun Olam   204

Chapter Nine   *Making Judaism Your Own at Home*
                 and on the Holidays   241

Chapter Ten   *Fresh Air in the Synagogue*   271

Conclusion   *The Jew in the Mist—*
                 Being Jewish in Changing Times   303

Appendix   *Starting and Enjoying Your Own*
                 Jewish Discussion Group   318

Notes   325

Acknowledgments   347

Index   350

Rekindling
the
Flame

INTRODUCTION

The Uncounted and the Discontented

Contemporary Judaism faces a crisis, despite its current popular appeal and cultural cachet—it is out of touch with large numbers of those who are a part of it. Many Jews think of themselves as Jewish, but also as *not good enough Jews*. We don't know Hebrew as well as our neighbors in the row next to us in temple. We don't know the history well enough. We search for a deeper sense of significance in our Judaism, feel it's too materialistic, patriarchal, or ingrown. We are variously described as unaffiliated, minimally affiliated, and disaffected. We may call ourselves cultural Jews or secular Jews, but many of us feel like lapsed Jews.

In one recent survey by the American Jewish Committee, 45 percent of the sample was not affiliated with any synagogue.[1] In the 1990 National Jewish Population Survey, among Jewish adults between the ages of thirty and fifty, only a quarter attended services more than once a month.[2] An often-accepted figure is that only about 20 percent of the American Jewish population is actively involved, while an estimated 20 percent never sets foot in Jewish communal settings.[3]

These are the "uncounted"—those who have little contact with traditional, institutional Judaism, and about whose psychology and human struggles little is written. That's understandable, in a way. Rabbis and institutional leaders tend to be excited by, and want to direct their energy toward, those who respond directly to their efforts. The uncertain nature of that large number of Jews who wrestle with their Judaism makes them hard to know. Yet mainstream Judaism often ignores the depth of many men and women's desire to find some revitalized connection to Judaism. Why do people leave Judaism? Why do they return?[4]

Then there are the "discontented." Many of those who *do* attend synagogue don't feel all that engaged. A neighbor recently turned to me during a service and said, "It's not just the Hebrew, the *English* reads like it's translated from the German." As if to echo my friend's words, Rabbi Eric Yoffie, in a recent presidential address to the Union of American Hebrew Congregations, the national organization of Reform Judaism, lamented the "tedious, predictable, and dull" nature of much synagogue worship.[5]

Perhaps Orthodox Jews also struggle and we just don't know it, but among the rest of us there are many with bad consciences and great uncertainty as to what to do with the Jewish part of themselves.

How can we be vibrant, engaged Jews without becoming more traditionally observant? This is the focus of my book. Rather than assuming that "assimilation" means that Judaism is dying, or that Jews who are uncounted or discontented are "not really Jews," I aspire to show the exciting ways that people are creating meaning out of their experiences as Jews in America today.

I am a psychologist and a perplexed Jew who has wrestled with Judaism and who has listened to many fellow Jews give voice to their problems, hopes, and discoveries. I am also married to a non-Jew, and we have been able to create a household that feels "Jewish enough"—despite the dire predictions of those opposed to intermarriage (including, initially, my parents). I am also a parent of two teens—bar and bat mitzvahed and themselves wrestling with what Judaism means to them now that the party is over—and a son to aging parents. I was raised Conservative, by a father and mother raised Orthodox and Reform, respectively, and the observances of my childhood were an uneasy compromise between parents who loved each other deeply.

The 1950s version of Judaism I grew up with in affluent Westchester County, outside New York City, seemed smug and insular, the undercurrent of materialism still painful. After a long period of distance from Judaism—spanning over thirty-five years, from the time of my bar mitzvah until my children began posing difficult questions about faith and spirituality to my wife and me—I reconnected with it. My wife and I joined a synagogue and became involved in the Jewish education of our children. I was invited to join the board of the synagogue but continued (and continue) to wrestle with what Judaism means to me. There are few simple resolutions in life, and reimmersing myself in my Jewish heritage merely opened up new questions about what affiliation and commitment mean (how Jewish is enough?) and how to meld the "non-Jewish" parts of me with the "Jewish."

As a result, I became interested in how other men and women resolve these matters. For the past five years I have been interviewing other Jews and offering seminars and focus groups for those who want to explore Judaism.[6] I have also been reflecting on my work as a psychotherapist with patients who are Jewish, as well as listening to friends and acquaintances in informal conversations snatched from the workday or weekend, over airport lunches or while waiting for our kids at Hebrew school.

Given the number of uncounted and discontented Jews, many of them unhappy Jews, what is the answer to their dilemma? In this book I focus on three answers.

First, *we need to understand that Judaism is a family and life experience as well as a religious tradition.* We need to see Judaism in the context of individual and human development. Judaism has a history and a tradition, it is *a people,* but it is also *persons:* Each of us weaves "a Judaism" out of our unique identifications with parents, childhood experiences, adult transformative moments, and social opportunities.

To really understand Judaism as a *lived experience,* we need to look beyond the tendency to see Judaism in terms of religious groupings. We live in a time when many Jews feel at home in America. In the year 2000 we had a Jewish vice presidential candidate, Senator Joseph I. Lieberman, who invoked Talmudic wisdom, and who brought strength to his ticket because he was Jewish, not despite it. The *New York Times* ran the front-page headline "Senator's Faith Becomes Part of Strategy" and reported on "Mr. Lieberman's Jewishness as a topic not to avoid, but to celebrate."[7] Yet that very success has also posed new dilemmas and questions for American Jews.

In his book *Jew v. Jew* Samuel Freedman argues that the very success of Jews in America has led to a crisis at "the soul of American Jewry."[8] Given the decline in external threats to American Jews and changing attitudes toward Israel, we have less to unite us as Jews. Freedman explores the religious and philosophical differences and the mistrust between Reform, Reconstructionist, Conservative, and Orthodox Jews in America.

The tensions between groups of Jews make for great drama: Jewish neighbors who can't get along because one family takes the Sabbath too seriously, Jews who bomb a local synagogue for sponsoring Americans for Peace Now activities, bitter housing battles in which Reform Jews try to keep Orthodox Jews out of the neighborhood. Yet this lens is also misleading.

Focusing on *groups* of Jews defined by shades of religious belief tends to submerge and obscure the struggle within individual Jews to find meaning and purpose in their faith. Mainstream American Jewry often looks at the sociology of things rather than the psychology, perhaps because we are community-oriented, with a residual memory of existing as an island in a hostile sea of non-Jews.

I am more interested in the struggles within individual Jews. There is great ferment among many people of various Jewish persuasions. Being Reform or Conservative (or even Orthodox) is not as monolithic as it sounds; nor is being "assimilated" or "unengaged." I have met rabbis and congregants who blend Buddhism with Judaism and do not lose the Judaism. I have met interfaith couples whose children are truly Jewish, giving the lie to the argument that intermarriage means the death of Judaism. And as we shall see, it is possible never to set foot in a synagogue and to have a vibrant relationship with Judaism, while some of those who are "actively involved"—board members, presidents of congregations, those who regularly attend services—struggle mightily with the meaning of Judaism in their lives. As one rabbi remarked to me, "Some of the liveliest juice in Judaism is happening outside the synagogue."

Second, to really comprehend Jewish struggle in twenty-first-century America, we need to understand that *Jewish identity is not a task that is settled once and for all in our lives.* Deciding how Jewish to be, and in what way to practice, is a part of the adult's identity struggle. Jewish identity is a moving picture, not a still photograph.

We do not simply achieve a concrete identity in adolescence. Psychologist Erik Erikson, a seminal thinker about identity, noted that each person's identity is being constantly reworked throughout life. As we age and our culture evolves, our identity changes.[9] As we change, so does our Jewish identity. We become more or less Jewish as we and our lives change.

For Jews, as for other minority groups, identity is a complex matter. Growing up in America for many Jews is a matter of growing up with a minority status psychologically, no matter the privilege and status one's family might possess in a community. Being Jewish may occupy a large part of the self or a small part, but it is not always an easy fit. At particular points in our lives there may be some grinding of the gears as we struggle to figure out to what extent Jewishness is a part of us, and at other times our great tradition offers the avenue for solving some of the core struggles of aging. Your not seeming "very Jewish" at one point in time doesn't mean that the seeds for a vibrant relationship to Judaism aren't there, waiting to bloom.

Brandeis psychologist and educator Joseph Reimer points out the implications for Jews of Erik Erikson's insights into identity:

> From some of the existing literature, one gains the impression that adolescence is *the* period during which youth "form" or "develop" their Jewish identity. The image suggested is of a young person making a life-long commitment to live a certain Jewish life style by his/her mid-twenties. While this may be accurate for some Jews, many others in North America will be deciding and re-deciding about their basic Jewish commitments during the coming stages of their adult development.

Most important, Reimer notes, "When a developmental crisis arises at a later stage, an adult can return and recompose aspects of his/her identity, including those aspects we call 'Jewish Identity.' "[10]

Identity is not something given to us in adolescence by our bar or bat mitzvah or Jewish summer camp, but a matter of life-long evolution. The Judaism we create and express changes as we do.

From her recent study of Jewish identity among a sample of 1,504 American- and Canadian-born Jews, Bethamie Horowitz concluded that "60% of the people in the study experienced changes in their relationship to being Jewish over time, suggesting that Jewish identity is not a fixed factor in one's life, but rather a matter that parallels personal growth and development."[11]

What is Judaism? Which raises the question of what I mean when I refer to Judaism in this book—is it a religion, a culture, an ethnicity, a spiritual path, a political movement? It's all those things, and the ways in which people tap into that part of their heritage will differ. We can think of Judaism in terms of identity as nourishment—people knit together pieces of Judaism in various ways in order to develop a more authentic sense of who they are as individuals growing up in particular families at particular points in history. The Jewish identity within each of us is a unique, never-finished tapestry woven of many threads. I have no desire to fall into debates about which "brand" of Judaism is better, about whether the religious aspects wipe out the political voices, or vice versa. We have had enough judgments about who's "correct" or not as a Jew. The more important question is how each of us constructs Judaism in our life. There is not a single right answer. There is room for many choirs in Judaism, many braids to the Havdalah candle that is Judaism.

Does the phrase "personally meaningful" mean that anything goes? What of "historical Judaism"—that great body of text, commentaries, and tradition, beginning in biblical times and continuing to the present?[12] Is it irrelevant? Not at all. Without historical Judaism we wouldn't be wrestling with anything, and most Jews know there is something profoundly important in Jewish history and tradition. The question is how to wrestle with Judaism without feeling debased or guilty or somehow "not kosher," how to experience that history and tradition as more than an angry father saying, "No!"

This brings us to the third point about the Jewish uncounted and the discontented: *the importance of understanding the "undertow" when wrestling with Judaism.* The undertow is the emotions, conflicts, and fears we have when reopening such personally loaded issues as religion and faith in our lives. To debate, question, and worry is a part of Judaism and probably the source of our greatest strength. Searching is so much a part of what Jews are about, as expressed through our uneasy relationship through history to cultures in which we have lived, through our struggles with God, with our very faith itself. The scientific and artistic contributions of Jews to cultures throughout history can in part be traced to our ability to break the frame, to look at things in new ways, which has been a part of Jewish life from the beginning.

Howard Nemerov's playfully wicked poem "Debate with the Rabbi" makes this point clearly. In the poem, Nemerov, a skeptical Jew most of his life, runs through several verses of clever argument and response with the rabbi ("You've lost your religion, the Rabbi said / It wasn't much to keep, said I" and "You should affirm the spirit, said he / and the communal solidarity. / I don't feel so solid, I said"). Finally, the outraged rabbi criticizes the poet's lack of respect and belief: "Instead of bowing down, said he / you go on in your obstinacy." Nemerov's reply ends the poem: "We Jews are like that."[13] Debate and obstinacy define—and unite—us.

Yet we shouldn't make wrestling with Judaism sound easy—it's not. Not because it demands lots of Talmudic study, or going to classes or attending synagogue. No, I think the hard part comes from that undertow within all of us that is rarely talked about: the feeling of being disloyal to the past, of betraying those we love who've come before us. I began this book with a vague sense of foreboding—as if I were betraying my father and grandfathers. The combined weight of fathers, going back to Abraham and Isaac, pushed against me. In my questioning, wanting something different from Judaism, feeling at times so bored in service that the skin on my arm began to itch, was I a bad boy?

A fundamental tension of human life involves wrestling with a divided loyalty to the past—wanting to honor our parents and be different from them, wanting to find meaning in the stories of the matriarchs and patriarchs yet explore a different life of our own, wanting to daven as generations past have always done and to create new prayers for new times. Much of the spice in our lives is rooted in how each of us manages the twin human desires to both hold on and to let go, to break tradition and to continue it. We may feel alone as skeptical Jews but in fact we all have the same secrets.

Often a muted Jewish voice is struggling for expression. It's the twenty-first-century form of the basic human question, one that has always been at the core of the great tradition of Judaism, Do we follow blindly the old traditions or do we find new solutions to ancient dilemmas as Jews?

It's clear to me that many of the uncounted and the discontented are far from "disconnected" from Judaism. In the process of sorting out what Judaism means to us, we often reconnect and link to something positive and good in our lives. It is a hopeful prospect, even though it may anger or scare us.

To provide a sense of the way in which the discontented and uncounted are often profoundly connected to Judaism, let's return to the quintessential Jewish activity—passionate talk and sharing about the meaning of life. Let's take a brief look at a focus group—at who participates and what happens in it.

"Now What?":
The Family Life Context of Judaism

One Wednesday evening in a recent, mild December, eight of us gathered in my small office to tell stories about our experiences of Judaism. It was mainly a group of strangers, volunteers who called me in response to flyers and advertisements. All had professional careers of some sort; several were married with children, one divorced, another not married; all were between twenty-five and fifty-five; four were men and four women.

Several were quite active in their synagogues; others hadn't been to temple in many years. One man, Bruce, gave a picturesque description of his alienation: "Judaism is about oppression for me. It's about slavery in Egypt, and then about forty years in the desert eating this Sheetrock called matzoh, and then it's about the Holocaust and defending Israel."

One woman in the group worked in a Jewish social service agency but felt "pushed away" by Judaism as a religion. She wondered, Is there a spirituality to Judaism? She couldn't imagine the two words going together. Is *Jewish spirituality* an oxymoron?

Yet each person there had been willing to trek in the dark to my office, a place they'd never been to before, and take two hours out of a busy weekday evening to talk about Judaism. Their effort provided concrete evidence of the desire for a connection to Judaism that is not provided by the traditional structure of the religion.

The undertow was palpable from the beginning. I felt a familiar reluctance even as I was grateful to everyone for taking the time to come. I wanted, and didn't want, to hear their stories. It's a familiar lethargy; I've come to welcome a dopey resistance as part of people's spiritual struggles, part of our halfhearted wish to know more about what Judaism means to us. Our minds wander, and we yawn as we approach the topic, as if to say, "Someday I gotta look at this."

At the focus group that night, in fact, Diane, a forty-five-year-old married mother of three who had just come from work (she is a bank vice president), observed, "This is a most interesting event for me. I don't think I've *ever* sat with a bunch of Jews and talked about Judaism. There's a part of me that wants to close my eyes and go to sleep, not because I'm bored, but because there is so much here. There is a part of me that wants to sleep on the whole thing."

We feel sleepy "because there is so much here." Boredom,

sleepiness, agitation, anxiety, anger, embarrassment, and confusion are all part of wrestling with Judaism. To really take Jewish "outreach" seriously, we have to attend to the affective undercurrent of reopening "the Jewish question" in our own lives. Familiar signposts are no longer reliable. We know that there is a lot bound up with our Judaism, our personal histories and experiences of it, but no one wants to be flooded or overwhelmed by what gets stirred up. As we shall see, the dynamics of shame will be very helpful in understanding the resistance we feel to exploring our Judaism.

There *is* a friskiness and excitement that comes from finding yourself in a room of only Jews. Usually watchful, feeling different, part of the minority, suddenly we were not only the majority, we were the only ones in the room! For a Jew, that can be hard to take in—despite the fact that this was about "Exploring Our Judaism," one participant was startled that the group was all Jewish. Perhaps out of habit, she had expected other faiths to be present as well but now felt some relief that it was "just Jews—makes it easier to talk, there's a shorthand."

Talking about why we come to such events can be a tall order in a group of strangers. Writing about it can be easier, and gets us deeper into ourselves. So I often begin the focus groups in an unusual way: after our brief introductions and small talk, I invite participants to do a free-writing exercise that allows us to express why we came here. That night we began with five minutes of free-writing on the topic "I came here tonight because..." Striving for a light touch, I added, "And no copying off your neighbor."

So, we scribbled for five minutes, as I kept one eye on the clock and another on my paper. Then we went around the room and read aloud.

What emerged was a portrait of the fluidity of Jewish identity through the life cycle and the key life influences that shape the Judaism people construct at different points in their lives. I will focus on two major influences: the pressures of specific life stages and the separation-connection process with parents. Each is illustrated in what follows in this sample focus group, culled from many.[14]

Judaism and Life Stages. There is the influence of being at specific developmental life stages, particularly midlife. Penina, for example, shy and hesitant at first, wrote, "I came here tonight because I wanted to hear other people's voices about their explorations and search for spirituality. I get trapped by the push and pull of spirituality and religion—ways to fully embrace my own spirituality without embracing religion—which always pushes me away as I try to explore." At age forty-five with two kids in their twenties, Penina has recently lost her mother, who herself had been ambivalently connected to Judaism. Her father died many years ago. Trying to reconnect with her religion is for Penina a way of both grieving the loss of her mother and moving into a new phase of life. "I'm an orphan now," she told us. And orphans need homes. For Penina, a life cycle loss has generated a desire to take another look at the role of Judaism in her life.

Normal transitions that accompany aging into midlife can lead to a renewed wrestling with Judaism. The arrival, aging, and departure of children make a big impact. The birth of a child can raise anew religious questions we put on hold when we were younger. So, too, can their leaving home. Nagging questions are often derived from the fact that "launching" our kids puts us in a transition point in adult life—we've taken the kids to synagogue, been Jewish "for them," but now they're grown and we're older. In one woman's words, "Now what?" Anne, fifty-five years old with grown children, read aloud that winter night in our group: "I came because of connection. What is my spirituality? Am I paying enough attention to it, has it stopped growing? I've become too connected with my synagogue and its politics and fables. I am hoping to organize my religious life and impulses. Where do I go from here? I learned Hebrew as an adult, began to celebrate Shabbat as an adult, raised my kids Jewish. Now what?"

When Anne stopped reading, she looked up and scanned the room, defiant. Her searching eyes betrayed embarrassment. Here again, the undertow. We'd been together only about an hour and now she found herself revealing how disorganized her "religious life and impulses" felt, how much she'd been living in the forms and rituals without being sure any longer that they actually made sense for her. How lonely it can be to try and once again sort it all out, as an adult, to reinvent ourselves at age fifty-five or sixty-five, overcoming the feeling that as an adult we should *already* have it sorted out. Anne's look seemed to ask, *Do you understand? Am I alone? Who else feels this way?*

Daniel Levinson, a psychologist who studied the adult life cycle, believed that young adulthood is the time for the development of a "first life structure," defined by our initial choices about career, intimacy, and religious commitments, among other involvements. The midlife years are the time for the development of a "second life structure" as these initial choices evolve and change. A beginning or continuing wrestling with the meaning of Judaism may reflect the normal developmental changes of the middle years.[15]

What looks like disconnection may also reflect a return, after some rebellion and experimentation. Some Jews who come to the focus groups have explored integrating Eastern approaches with their experience of Judaism. Rodger Kamenetz provided a rich portrait of "JuBus" in his book *The Jew in the Lotus*.[16] The integration of Jewish spirituality and thought with other religious traditions is a popular topic on the Jewish lecture and workshop circuit.

Carl came to the focus group that evening with a strong Jewish background—he was president of his college's Hillel chapter—but has explored Buddhism and Eastern approaches. He makes it very clear that he doesn't want to be "segregated" with Jews, and is very concerned about the parochialism of much of Judaism. He and his wife have organized "Chranukah" celebrations in their home every December, bringing together Jews and Christians.

Carl has spent much of his life trying not to be "too Jewish." (Many of us in the sixties generation found identity through opposition—to Jewish authority, among others.) Now, however, at age forty-five he has a newborn child and came to the group because "I wanted to hear and learn how to feel my spiritual side in more of my life. I see and feel God in nature, life, birth, and death and forget too often to feel the joy and fascination of the miracles all around me all the time. Most of all when I feel the awe of watching my son's growth from newborn to toddler." For Carl, part of expressing the feelings connected with becoming a father involves reconnecting more fully with Judaism.

Carl wants to find more grounding in his Judaism without losing his connection to other faiths and to his more universal impulse. Having a child, though, has reminded him of his Jewish roots and he wrestles with the question of how to make that part of him real. It's as if he has expressed for years how he is not Jewish, but then the question comes back as, How *is* he Jewish? Saying no doesn't answer the question of who we are, since to really be ourselves we need also to say yes to something. For Carl, the question is, To what part of Judaism can I say yes? Can I be Jewish and love other faiths? The answer is yes, but many of us missed that lesson growing up. Attractions to other faiths, even active participation in Christianity or Eastern religions, can be a route back into Judaism, not necessarily a highway out of it.

We may wrestle with Judaism at any life stage. In young adulthood we struggle to find our own voice, separate from our parents. Uncounted and discontented Jewish young adults are often trying to hold on to parts of their families' sense of Judaism but also to connect it to a wider community. They may feel considerable internal pressure to hold on to their own definitions while feeling scrutinized by community arbiters of what is "correct" and "right." Judy, a graduate student in her twenties, wrote in the focus group that night about this struggle:

"I came because I need to talk, particularly after Yom Kippur and the holidays coming up. My school doesn't give holidays for students, although you can miss class. I always decide to stay home from class; it is my holiday and I always observe it. But for me, my observation is personal. I do not feel that attached to synagogue—certainly not the Hillel service I would attend. Holidays and Judaism to me have always meant more about my family, tradition, the Hebrew, the New Year. I use Yom Kippur as a time of self-reflection and people this year questioned me—people always make comments about if you're just skipping school, taking advantage."

Judy at age twenty-five is attempting to link valued parts of herself to the larger social world and communities in which she lives, while also staying loyal to her family. In our twenties and thirties, we may struggle to make that connection, and may feel orphaned in the world—no longer quite a part of our families of origin but without another "home in the world." The rigidity of some Jewish communities may underline that orphaned feeling for people who do not conform. The question for Judy, as for many adults, is, How do I find a trustworthy sense of my own voice as a Jew, in the face of the internal pressures and social expectations I feel?

This question resurfaces throughout the life cycle. One man in his seventies came to a focus group because "my parents are long-dead, and I am older now than my father was when he died. I have retired from my business, but don't want to retire from life. I want to find some connection to Judaism as I become an elder, as my father did. But I don't know how to do that."

The question of finding your own trustworthy voice as a Jew

can arise at any life stage. This is often true of women who have come to the focus groups and workshops but can be a man's struggle as well. We search for our spiritual voices as adults because what happened when we were children doesn't really fit who we are. For example, Sharon, a forty-year-old woman, wrote, "I came here because my Judaism was hidden for so long, misunderstood, not understood, not seen—sometimes by me but often not acknowledged by others I was close to. I didn't do things exactly the way I was raised to, yet I was sure my spiritual sense was strong. It's how I feel on Shabbat morning singing with my congregation of people who just 'get it' without explanation. I came because this is powerful stuff for me, stuff that was in the dark for so long."

Sharon was raised in a very observant family, but was not allowed to be bat mitzvahed even as the family rejoiced in her brothers' bar mitzvahs over the years. Finding her own place in the temple, after decades of feeling marginalized, is an important part of taking herself seriously and of the development of her own self-esteem as she ages into middle adulthood.

It's one thing to be a boy and to have had performance anxieties about your bar mitzvah; it's another matter entirely to feel it's not important that you have a bat mitzvah because you're a girl. Many women raised Jewish are seeking a more empowered, authentic Jewish voice for themselves. Sometimes it is the growing sense of competence that life brings—becoming a mother or having a successful career—that leads a woman at midlife to want to feel a more potent connection to Judaism. The stories of women who become *b'not mitzvah* (daughters of the commandments) at age forty or even age eighty point to the resilience of Jewish identity, the way that seeds of connection to Judaism often flower later in life.

Some of us grew up without a vibrant, engaging sense of Jewish community because our parents were alienated from Judaism or didn't know what to make of it either. In particular, many men and women born during and soon after the Second World War grew up with a grim, "gray" Judaism. Many of our parents had great difficulty communicating an energetic, meaningful sense of Judaism amid the shock and grief that rippled through the world in the decades after the war.

As a result, many Jewish men and women today feel orphaned from Judaism. They feel clueless—conceiving of Judaism as going to synagogue for the High Holidays but not really knowing why. Some of them need a place to sort things out because they have had a surprising realization: *they are Jewish!* Serendipitous events may spark a Jewish fire. They've known all their lives, of course, in one way, but then have an experience in their thirties or forties—or later—in which they really "get it." James, at age fifty, put it this way: "I realized I was Jewish when I was visiting on a kibbutz in Israel. It was a short visit but I was there on a Friday night and heard from one room near the cafeteria Hebrew prayers and singing. It was a group of older men, davening through the Friday night service. I was drawn to it, by the sounds, the songs. I went in and the melodies and words were so familiar, I could piece them out. The men saw I was familiar with the tunes even though I couldn't sing very many of the words. I realized that anywhere I went in the world I would find this language, these melodies and songs. At that moment I think I really *got* that I was Jewish, in an active rather than a passive way."

James's words caught my attention. Most of us born Jewish know we're Jewish, of course. Yet there's another kind of knowing that seems to be part of the search—from a passive membership, by birth, following the rules without much personal voice, toward a more active knowing, in which we find a personally meaningful Jewish voice that honors our past and our present. Understanding the journey from a passive, uncomfortable Jewish identity toward a more active, muscular engagement—that's what I'm after in this book.

James's parents divorced when he was young, and he lost contact with his father, which broke a link to tradition for him. Yet it is as if Judaism is in his genes—pre-divorce childhood memories were waiting to be touched the day that he walked into the service on the kibbutz.[17] Many of the pessimists about Jewish identity in our assimilationist society don't realize how powerfully connected many Jews are, even if that connection is buried deep down.

Divided Loyalties and Shifting Parental Identifications. One reason that Jewish identity may flower later in life is that our identifications with our parents shift. A major developmental milestone involves changes in our internal sense of our parents. Often our adolescent and young adulthood choices about marriage and career are linked to our separation struggles with our parents. One major task of human development is to see our parents more realistically, not as heroes or demons. In letting ourselves view them as human beings, we allow ourselves more room to become who we truly are.[18]

So, too, with Judaism. Many of the uncounted and discontented struggle with an early experience of sorrow or disappointment that leaves us stuck with childhood images of Judaism. We feel small and powerless in relation to a dominating and oppressive Judaism, as a young child does with a powerful parent. We may feel stuck in battles with our parents about being a "good Jew." Worse, we feel no ability to have any impact on Judaism since it is "out there," somebody else's religion. Rituals and beliefs are frozen in time and inflexible. For these men and women, early cartoonish images of Judaism, reflective of the childhood years, have dominated.

While the experience of a "frozen Judaism" can lead to diatribes (one man once wrote in a focus group about the "100 things wrong with Judaism"—an inverted sort of love letter), often participants give voice to a very poignant struggle to feel more at home with themselves and with Judaism.

Bruce, who had earlier invoked images of oppression, slavery, and years of dry matzoh to describe his experience of Judaism, warmed up considerably when he wrote about why he came to the focus group that evening: "I came here tonight because I need to search for this piece of my heart that disappeared." Later in the meeting Bruce was to write movingly about the large Passover seders of his childhood in the basement of the family home "on Townsend Ave. in the Bronx. The room felt huge and the tables were long. . . . I stood on a chair in my pajamas and read the Four Questions with my yarmulke on and my grandfather glowing nearby and somewhere inside me I can still hear the high pitched voice of the dark blonde little boy and sense the quiet and the importance before we hide the afikoman and sing songs."

There's a concreteness to Bruce's description that places us right back in the Passover seder, and that informs us that in some ways Bruce has never left Townsend Avenue. It emerges that Bruce was abused when he was a child, by the same Jewish relatives he so revered. Bruce's grandparents escaped from Europe and came to America as World War II began. His parents were raised with a fear of "the goyim," which never left the family. As a child in a rural Connecticut community in the early 1970s, Bruce was beaten by his parents when he received low grades in school—achieving in academics may be a primary imperative for an anxious Jewish family adrift in a hostile world. Years later Bruce was diagnosed with dyslexia, a learning disability. He has since become a speech therapist in an urban school system.

For Bruce, sorting out the "pieces of my heart" means coming to terms with his own family and cultural history. "Something is there, dangling in front of me, that makes me want to know why it hurts to be Jewish. Why hide?" Bruce both hides from knowing this and wants to understand it at the same time.

This frozen quality of Judaism also characterizes how many of us, who feel painfully split between the different Jewish orientations of our parents, respond. To keep kosher or not. How often to go to *shul*. How seriously to keep up the old ways, how much to assimilate. In some ways we all grow up in interfaith marriages, as parents struggle to combine various orientations and subtle differences in observance and feeling about Judaism. Family therapist Salvadore Minuchin has observed that families are essentially mutual accommodations to a complex array of rituals, norms, and transactions.[19] Divided loyalties to our parents in our childhood experience of being Jewish can leave us with a cartoon image of Judaism as we age.

To really understand the Jewish struggle today we need to attend to the clash of internal images, often rooted in our divided loyalties to our mothers and fathers. There is rarely, if ever, a single, monolithic version of Judaism alive within any Jew. Different images of being male and female, old and young, strong and weak, a good enough son or daughter to aging parents, a good enough man or woman—all are mixed into the Judaism that we construct at different times in our lives.

What stands out in the stories Jews tell about their search to find a place in Judaism? The death of a parent, the arrival or the launching of children, the reemergence of a long-buried family history, a search for personal significance. Although each story in the focus group is different, they have a common theme: a renewed wrestling with Judaism is entwined with our life experiences, with the charged events happening in our lives. We construct a sense of faith out of our identifications with our parents, the profound experiences we have as children, and the liminal moments we have as adults.

So then how do we, as adults, go about making Judaism meaningful to us? What *kinds* of Judaism are individual Jews creating these days? And what are the psychological processes involved in finding your own sturdy, resilient spiritual voice?

Not just one set on doing it "the way it's always been done," but a voice that is expressive of you, that builds on your past, your present, and your future, that melds what has been with what can be. So many Jews feel like they're not doing well enough as Jews, or that they *could* be Jews if only Judaism were "different," or that they *have* to be Jews and suffer through the worship. On the other hand, there is this great tradition and ferment and opportunity. In this book I hope to build some bridges between the tradition and the discontent.

Let's not kid ourselves—something very important is at stake here: finding a trustworthy connection to Judaism can be the ground on which we resolve vital matters of identity, self-esteem, generativity, and the connection between the generations. In coming to terms with Judaism, we often find ways to make peace with our parents or confront our own shame or anger, and in so doing open up new possibilities for ourselves.

I'm going to chart a psychological journey in the chapters that follow, showing how many of the uncounted and the discontented are creating a joyous, resilient Judaism in their lives. We must begin with the obstacles to a vibrant Jewish identity, the sources of many people's resistance to being Jewish. We can then examine the central questions of Jews today, living in an assimilationist world: can you be a good Jew and participate in other religions? Is intermarriage a betrayal of our Jewish heritage? How does Judaism fit with our work lives?

Part One

Why Jews Struggle with Judaism

CHAPTER ONE

Who's a Good Enough Jew?

No survey of American Jewish opinion that I've come across has asked respondents to answer the question, Do you feel like a good enough Jew? I suspect if there were such a survey it would reveal a substantial component of self-doubt in much of the Jewish community.

Over and over, men and women I've interviewed have begun by apologizing: "I'm not a very observant Jew," or "I am a real ignoramus about Judaism," or "My Hebrew is not very good," or "I don't go to services very much," or "I'm not even a member of a synagogue." There's often a tone in these statements implying that the stories of their lives as Jews are therefore not very interesting.

To really understand the Jewish spiritual search today—its pervasiveness and its depth—we need to understand how two Jewish preoccupations inhibit that search: equating being a good Jew with how much ritual and history you know (e.g., being a good davener) and equating being a good Jew with being a loyal member of the Jewish community. A rule-bound Judaism and "counting heads"—large elements of the Jewish community have internalized these mental equations, a sort of Jewish communal superego. Our individual psyches reflect these preoccupations.

Feeling inadequate is a fundamental part of life: we often feel we are not living up to our potential as a citizen, spouse, parent, or worker—or as a Jew—and such feelings may help us strive to correct things. The gap between the ideal self and the real self is a human experience. Sometimes we *are* inadequate and realizing that is the first step toward doing better.

However, sometimes the feeling of inadequacy leads to withdrawal, a sense of powerlessness, and avoidance of the places where we feel we fall short. For many of the uncounted and discontented, the feeling of not being good enough—an internalized sense of inadequacy—leads them away from spiritual search and away from Judaism, not toward it.

Many authors and observers of Judaism are very judgmental in terms of what or who is a "good Jew." We are good at making judgments about what's "kosher" or not, in terms of observance, belief, marriage, parenting. If you marry a Jew, you're a good Jew; if you don't, then you're "intermarried" and that's a problem to be studied. If you have had a bar or bat mitzvah, you're a good Jew; if not, you're lacking something. Then, of course, there's always matrilineal descent to worry about.... These divisions and distinctions are certainly misleading in terms of identity. Identity is rather like mosaic, a combination of elements, which we each put together in a different way. Many different ways have great integrity.

Good and bad distinctions of all stripes have the added problem of invariably leading to a top-down portrait of Judaism—drawn by institutional authorities, experts, scholars, rabbis, and other keepers of the faith. To really understand Jewish identity today we need a bottom-up portrait—an understanding of how people make meaning of Judaism on their own terms.

The Origins of the Jewish "Not-Good-Enough" Experience

It is important to face the judgmental quality among Jews head-on and to understand it, because it haunts our spiritual search and identity development. The feeling of not being "good enough" as Jews has several sources.

First, there is the internalized self-hatred that many of us feel as Jews. When you grow up as part of a minority culture in an America that is fundamentally Christian, there is an element of turning against the self (see Chapter 2). Whether it's blacks and skin color, or Asians and eye shape, or Jews and noses, there is an impact on the sense of self that comes from feeling different from the majority.[1] As Peter Langman observes, "When it comes to cultural groups, being different seems to be seen as being deficient. The idea of separate but equal doesn't seem to work in terms of majority and minority cultures."[2]

The feeling of defectiveness sometimes turns us against each other. Some of the "not good enough" is the result of Jews turning against Jews—a projecting onto other members of the tribe our oppression and sense of difference. Intragroup quibbling is a common feature of minority life. So we quibble about who's a good enough Jew. Fundamentally, you can never be good enough, because you are Jewish.

A second source of the not-good-enough impulse is the loss resulting from assimilation and the Jewish history of migration. To focus on the rules and to count heads are both ways to manage grief and preserve a version of what has been lost.

Keeping Kosher. For many Jews, the ideal image of Judaism is based on conformity to the rules: knowing the Hebrew, understanding the order of prayer, being able to say the prayers correctly. Judaism is a religion that over its history has developed many rules and rituals, helping to distinguish it from a potentially

hostile environment and to affirm the group identity of its believers. Knowing the rituals and rules is a way of affirming who
we are amid a sea of *them*.

There is, of course, importance to remembering tradition, to
teaching our children the basic traditions and practices of faith.
When we wear a yarmulke, we communicate to our children a
manifest symbol of faith and belief, of hope for the future being
passed along, connecting the generations.

Robert Frost dismissed poets who dislike the rules of traditional form and style by remarking that writing poetry without
conventional meter is like playing tennis without a net. No net,
no Pete Sampras, no Billie Jean King. In the absence of structure
you have no way of becoming who you are within the game.

Similarly, one empathic Conservative rabbi told me that rules
that just come from the rabbi and have no connection to what
you truly believe are indeed quite oppressive. On the other hand,
he said, "you can't be a member of a club and have no rules." He
told me rules of *kashrut* and worship are opportunities to "personally commit yourself to, and live, a fuller life. They are what
you make out of them—a prison or a liberation."

It's not rules per se; for many of us, Judaism became identified with rules without liberation when we were growing up.
It's commonplace to see a historical element to rule-bound Judaism: the post–World War II generations of Jews, responding
to the shock of the Holocaust, lost their spiritual vitality. We
turned to empty rules, and our parents couldn't communicate
the meaning of them so as to enliven what we were doing.
There's clearly an element of truth to this—those of us who
grew up in the 1950s and 1960s can remember the sense of loss
and the horror of the war, even though, as American Jews, we
were safe and protected. As one rabbi, born in 1946, a year
after the liberation of Auschwitz, commented, "It was a great
act of faith to have a Jewish child in 1946; a great spiritual
statement of defiance and courage after one and a half million

Jewish children had just been murdered. I grew up, as many of my generation, with a tremendous sense of the need for Jewish survival."

Such reverberations continue to the present day. One woman said to me, "I can't forget that there was a whole culture lost, which I can't get back except by remaining faithful to what was once there." By holding on to the "old way" of doing it—the strictness, the formality of it—many of our parents were holding on to the lost culture of *their* parents and grandparents. They may also have been wrestling with survivor guilt—the guilt and shame that comes from surviving in comfort in America when others had died or struggled through the displacements of migration and the horrors of the Holocaust.

Our parents, though, held on ambivalently—not sure how to be good Americans and good Jews, wanting to escape the past even as they held on to it. American families fought about Jewish rituals or embraced them, but it was the rituals that were important. One woman remembered driving home as an eight- or nine-year-old with her parents after a seder and listening to her parents mock her grandparents' reverent adherence to every detail of the Haggadah, only minutes after participating in the festival without complaint.

Our families in the 1950s and 1960s were caught between the competing pressures to be good Jews and to assimilate, to recognize the Holocaust and to protect us and themselves from it. It was a Judaism of masks, of evasions, of protections. We got mixed messages from our parents (as many of them got from their own parents), who weren't sure what they wanted, as for many the Judaism of the family stopped at the edge of their suburban lawns.

Yet even when defeated, forces of tradition have a way of holding the moral high ground. During the 1950s, my father—raised Orthodox—wanted to keep kosher and my mother—raised Reform—did not. For years we kept kosher, and doing so was a nod to the old country, to my father's parents and grand-parents, expressing his love for and devotion to them. It was only after my mother went to work and earned money—and more important perhaps, after the death of her old-world mother-in-law—that the revolution happened in our house and we stopped keeping kosher, beginning a struggle between my parents that went on for months. I remember ordering a hot dog at Yankee Stadium during Passover, a hungry, rebellious teen, and was convinced that my father saw me doing so on the TV broadcast of the game. I still remember the terrifying sense of having been seen not only breaking the rules, but, what's worse, enjoying myself when doing so! The "Jewish superego" may come out of the sense of our ancestors looking down upon us, judging us for not following the rules.

The Historical Tensions of Assimilation. What rules to follow. How to preserve the past while living in new worlds. These are, historically, essential Jewish questions. That we wrestle with these questions today doesn't mean we're out of line; it means we are part of historical Judaism.

In an engaging paper on the Jewish joke, German psychoan-alyst Egon Fabian shows how Jewish humor, of the ironic East-ern European, Ashkenazic variety (which characterizes so many Jewish American comedians and writers from vaudeville and Milton Berle to Philip Roth and Saul Bellow to Ben Stiller and Jerry Seinfeld) through the centuries has been about the tension around assimilation, beginning with the German Enlightenment during the second half of the eighteenth century.[3]

Consider a contemporary form of the Jewish joke that circu-lated recently on the Internet: A rabbi from a Conservative Long Island synagogue is on vacation alone in Vienna. He has always kept kosher. Never once in his life has he tasted pork. So, in Vi-enna he decides that this *once*, in a city known for its cuisine, he will know the taste of pork. That night he goes alone for dinner to one of the fanciest restaurants in Vienna and orders a roast suckling pig. It is served with all the trimmings—the pig on an ornate china platter with gold leaf, complete with an apple in its mouth. The rabbi is about to take a bite when he looks up and finds to his horror that, of all people, the president of his congregation back in Long Island is standing beside his table, surveying the scene with a shocked expression. "Rabbi!" the man exclaims. "What is this?" The rabbi responds, "Abe, Abe, can you believe it! I order roast apple and look how they serve it!" Part of the humor in this joke is the way it gives voice to the Jewish impulse to assimilate, to taste what is forbidden. Our laughter releases some of our own internal tension between wanting to obey Jewish law and wanting to stray from it. By putting this impulse in the person of the rabbi, the joke also serves as an equalizer. The rabbi, usually the container of Jewish law, becomes human (and through him Judaism becomes human), as he tries to squirm out of what is obvious.[4]

In each generation the rules and traditions weigh on us as we each try to find our own identity and sense of self in relation to the past and our heritage. So, too, with being a loyal member of "the tribe."

Counting Heads. Judaism is a culture and religion that emphasizes community. We take pride in the fact that Abraham, in making his spiritual search, took his family with him, in contrast to other renowned prophets and seekers for whom the journey was a lonely, individualistic struggle.[5]

On the Web there are many Jewish sites that include a listing of the major cities of the world, along with their Jewish populations. Here in the United States, for example: Miami, 535,000; Boston, 228,000; San Francisco, 210,000; Milwaukee, 28,000. At least *known Jews*. There are many purposes and uses for this list, including helping those who are making relocation decisions to find out how extensive Jewish life is in such places. Yet underneath may lie another impulse: *to know how many of us there are.* In a world where you are a minority and where you have faced significant threats to your cultural survival through the generations, the impulse to count heads is understandable.

Too often, that translates into equating being a good Jew with affiliating and going to a synagogue. We count heads and create categories of Jews, the "unaffiliated" or "moderately affiliated," as if that tells us a lot about the Judaism going on within such people. Within such activities, though, there is a powerful centrifugal force, keeping the emphasis on the group. Some of that force is rooted in reaction to the dangerous world many of us have experienced directly or indirectly as Jews. The sense of us versus them, the need in Judaism to concentrate on marshaling our resources and on claiming and reclaiming a future is powerful. Certainly, this was true after World War II, and through the 1950s and 1960s.

The intensity of this protective "we group" attitude at the cost of individualism during that time was powerfully evoked in 1960 after Philip Roth had won the National Book Award for *Goodbye, Columbus,* a collection of short stories that included "Defender of the Faith," a controversial story about Jewish ambivalence and doubt. Such stories were OK as long as they were confined to a Jewish audience; Roth's sin was that he wrote a best-seller, and showed our dirty laundry to the goyim. He was invited to participate in a panel discussion at Yeshiva University, along with other "minority writers," including Ralph Ellison and Pietro di Donato. The scene turned very hostile, as described by David Remnick in a *New Yorker* profile of Roth: "That night at Yeshiva was a slaughter. The students practically ignored the outsiders, Ellison and di Donato, and focused on their own, on Roth. They battered him, asking him over and over, in one form or another, 'Mr. Roth, would you write the same stories if you lived in Nazi Germany?'... Over and over, Roth answered, 'But we live in the *opposite* of Nazi

Germany!' And he got nowhere...."[6] Remnick continues: "After the program ended and Roth was trying to leave the stage, the students who had been most antagonistic gathered around him, surrounding him, shouting." Later that night, sequestered with friends at the Stage Delicatessen, Roth sighed: "I'll never write about Jews again." A resolution he didn't keep, thank goodness, as such masterworks exploring Jewish self-doubt and resiliency as *Portnoy's Complaint, The Counterlife,* and *Operation Shylock* followed over the years. ("You want outrage? I'll give you outrage!" Remnick comments about Roth's intentions.)[7]

The audience at Yeshiva was mainly composed of Orthodox students, so the reactions must be placed in that context. Yet outrage at Roth's writing was not confined to the Orthodox. Extremists magnify what is within each of us. They provide a window onto the American Jewish emphasis on appearances, on being loyal to the group.

Most of all, one wonders, where did that postwar protectiveness and fear of admitting ambivalence and uncertainty as Jews *go*? It could not be washed away in one generation. These struggles and tensions were communicated in complex ways from one generation to another down to the present day. The tendency to "count heads" even today reflects the pressure to be good, to be loyal, and to not question, for fear that "it's not good for the Jews."

Appearances Are Deceiving

How much Hebrew you know and whether or not you attend services are surface behaviors. We need to look deeper to understand Jewish identity. The misleading nature of external markers for identifying types of Jews is easy to see in the following example of two different Jews who've never met each other: Shelly and Neil.

Shelly is a decidedly unaffiliated Jewish woman in her thirties, a high school teacher of mathematics, married with a young child. She fosters a vibrant expression of Judaism through her family and relationships. Neil is sixty-three, a wealthy businessman, also married, with three grown children and seven young grandchildren. He is a former president of his Conservative synagogue, and has been "always available" for fund-raising and events at "my *shul.*" Yet these days he wonders what Judaism means to him.

Shelly grew up in the Midwest, in a Reform family that only went to synagogue twice a year: for Rosh Hashanah and Yom Kippur. Jewish family life was very strong in Shelly's childhood, but not the religion. She remembers the whole family going for their Yom Kippur break-fast to the local Brown Derby restaurant to eat shrimp and roast beef.

Shelly remembers with great warmth her four observant Orthodox grandparents. Her mother's father was a beloved figure in the family, known for his wit and remembered in family folklore through the "wisdom of Zayda" that her mother would quote from time to time, such as "Never hit a child, that's what the *tush* is for," and "You can never take back a spoken word." Her love for her grandfather is evidenced by a picture of him she still has in her attic: "It's a gorgeous black-and-white portrait of him, taken by a local photographer. He always wore a yarmulke, his hand is visible in the photo holding a book, sitting in a chair. In college my roommate had never met a Jew, and I took her home to visit and we went around to the relatives and they all had the picture of Zayda up and she thought that every Jew had a picture of 'the Jewish Jesus'!"

Here is a woman who is off the radar screens of the head counters and daveners, yet there is a vitality in her words, in the details she includes when talking about the generational threads in her Jewish identity. The same was true when Shelly described her reverence for her father's parents. Shelly's paternal grandfather was also an observant man, and her memory of him captures both her love for, and sense of exclusion from, men's worship. One day when Shelly was about five, she woke up early in the morning and walked into the living room to find her grandfather laying tefillin, as he did every day. "I didn't know what he was doing and I tried to talk to him. 'What are you doing, Grandpa?' He wouldn't answer. My grandmother would say, 'Don't talk to your grandfather when he's doing that.'"

Shelly inherited her grandfather's tallit and tefillin. "Sometimes I'll meditate wearing his tallit," she tells me. "His tallit is narrow and long, it's longer than my arms outstretched. Blue stripes are faded, yellow-gold band around the top. He'd visit and daven in the morning and night. Watching him was a curious experience. I couldn't figure out why he wouldn't talk to me. I'd pull the *tzitzit* and he'd smile but I would be upset. Why wouldn't he talk to me? My grandmother would explain that he was praying and that made it all right. It's a peaceful image of his praying and the bobbing up and down."

With a note of sadness, Shelly observes, "I never learned how to lay tefillin." In fact, she was never bat mitzvahed, since "for girls in small towns in the Midwest, it wasn't the norm back then; only one girl I knew did it when I was growing up." Synagogue worship and the traditional rituals of her grandfathers were appreciated but she was held at a distance from them.

Instead, a major thread in her Jewish identity came from her maternal grandmother and the Judaism expressed through her ways of bringing the family together through rituals—not of Orthodox prayer and davenings, but of cooking, of family celebrations and relationships. Shelly asked me if I knew how to make meat blintzes. "The old kind, made from lungs—they're illegal to make them anymore since lungs are so toxic, but when she visited us the whole dining room table was opened up, with the leaf inserted and she'd just cook—blintzes, gefilte fish. I make our own gefilte fish now, too, because of her. They are so good; after you make your own, even though it's so expensive, you can't eat from a jar of canned gefilte fish anymore. She'd make her own herring, she cut off chicken heads in our kitchen, there'd be shells for blintzes drying on towels and I'd get the ones that ripped. I'd stand next to her while she laid them out in order to get one."

Shelly's grandmother baked her own challah, too, every Friday night, a ritual that traveled down the generations so that Shelly and her husband-to-be made two enormous loaves for their wedding. "We were going to make a challah for each table until friends convinced us we were crazy, so instead we made two big challah, and my mother-in-law made a blessing. It was wonderful."

Many women who have felt excluded from the traditional male observances surrounding the Torah and worship in the synagogue have found in the rituals and observances surrounding food and relationships a powerful sense of Judaism. One fifty-year-old woman described her High Holiday observances as "leaving the synagogue as soon as possible so we women could go home and cook and talk and make the house beautiful and get ready for the men to come home and so do our worship in that way."

Traditional Judaism divides the roles of men and women into "synagogue" and "home" responsibilities. We might be tempted to see one as involving prayer and devotion and the other as involving cooking, but is there not a powerful sense of prayer and devotion in the way Shelly explains in the following description, her way of bringing together people and generations in one of her wedding rituals?

"We also made our own *chuppah* for the wedding. We decided it was cheaper to make our own and didn't want too large a one. We sent twenty-four of our friends a twelve-inch square of muslin with instructions—asking them to make a big square with anything they wanted on it. We got twenty-two squares back; two friends pooped out on us. My husband's friend is a quilter and he got some fabric and sewed it into strips. We found something great ourselves and he sewed it into strips and wove it so the top was over our heads, this weave of gorgeous fabric with the twenty-two squares down the sides. It was the most gorgeous structure. Now it's all folded up, for our house. I want to frame it; it's too large and heavy to display otherwise. The pieces range from people having done clowns, penguins—which everyone knows I like—to a wonderful Star of David, Hebrew sayings, and my oldest and dearest friend sewed in pictures of us as children. The essence of the *chuppah* is that it means community holding, like a house, the community supporting us, extended family of friends, my mother, brother, sister-in-law did squares, so did my husband's brother, and his aunt. The kiddush cup was my uncle's, the candlesticks were my grandmother's, the ones she carried over on the ship when she was thirteen."

Despite the fact that the wedding didn't take place in a synagogue (and that Shelly rarely goes), she has a strong, relational connection to Judaism, one that continues to the present day and is evidenced in her Passover seders, for which she begins preparing days earlier and to which she invites a whole community of diverse individuals who attend each year.[8]

Contrast Shelly with Neil, who is actively involved in a synagogue. He was raised Orthodox by a father to whom he is very close. His father was president of the same synagogue where Neil became president and both still attend. Neil and his wife raised several sons and daughters within the Jewish tradition, and both are dealing with the intermarriages of their children with good humor and patience.

Recently, Neil's father was honored on his ninety-fifth birthday at the synagogue, and Neil felt proud, tearful really, of his father and what his father had accomplished, and very aware of his love for this man. The rabbi and congregation all praised his father. However, as Neil helped his father to the car after the ceremony, the elderly, frail man put his hand on Neil's wrist and whispered, "You should come to *shul* more often!"

Neil realized that he hadn't been attending services very much recently and that on a deeper level "I wasn't sure what I am getting out of Judaism any more." When I asked him if he prays when he's in services, he said, "Well, I recite the words, but they are just words on a printed page. I do like the melodies."

Neil has all the attributes of what some might call "a good Jew," but in fact he is at a time of transition in his Jewish identity, moving from a first (or second or third) construction toward one more fitting for his life stage. Neil is struggling with the fact that he is different from his father, and his kids are different from him, and he wonders what that means for his faith and beliefs. What do I truly believe? And, of course, a much larger question lies beneath: What do I really want from life?

Both Shelly and Neil have a profound and strong Jewish identity. Shelly's Judaism is quite alive and exciting right now, even though she doesn't appear to be observant to those who use affiliation as a measure of Jewish identity, while Neil—who fits the traditional definitions—is actually in a time of change and uncertainty about his Jewish identity.

We need to look at the deeper developmental struggles beneath what we often label in a mushy way as "Jewish identity."

Jewish Doubt and Uncertainty

In reality, even for very observant Jews there are periods of real uncertainty. Faith and commitment are not perfect things we carry around with us all our lives. Instead, we weave many different and changing elements of our experiences into a complex internal tapestry called "Judaism" throughout our lives.

At times, what looks like devotion may be simply seeking a way out of a life dilemma, whereas what looks like lack of devotion may be a profoundly spiritual search. For example, going to visit or live in Israel is considered a mitzvah. Yet for how many people has time in Israel instead been a way to escape from the overbearing family pressures about "being a good Jew"? One man, Lou, remembered his father's demand that he be Orthodox and how hard it was for him to find his own Jewish voice. In the 1960s, when Lou was a teenager, his father forbade him to go on a civil rights demonstration on the Sabbath, despite the care with which the teenage boy made his plans to take Orthodox beliefs into account. Lou had told his father he would walk from the suburbs to the demonstration on Saturday morning, then borrow some money for the bus ride back that evening. His father said no anyway, an act that seemed arbitrary and controlling. The father and son were in the midst of a separation struggle, and the whole episode concerning civil rights was an excellent metaphor for the rebellious struggle of the adolescent! Lou wanted very much to go away to college; his father insisted that he stay at home and attend the local university only blocks from their house. What to do? The quick-thinking boy hit upon a surefire way to find some liberation: "I went to Israel!" Lou told his father that, rather than go to college immediately after high school, he wanted to go to Israel for a year of study and work. His father agreed and Lou began a long process of sorting out who he was and finding his own Jewish voice, very different from his father's Orthodoxy. What looked like devotion was an admixture of escape and search—the beginning of this man's finding an authentic Jewish voice for himself.

Conversely, time away from Judaism may be part of a profound attempt to find oneself. Judith, a rabbi now at midlife, told me about immigrating to Israel for study after college in 1970, part of an undeclared time of investigating her own Jewish identity. When she was a child, Judaism was a shining part of her life. Raised in a busy urban section of Chicago, she was sent to a Jewish camp one summer, where she was astonished by the beauty of the countryside and the opportunity to be out of the city. In that context, studying Hebrew and Jewish history was an activity she excelled at, and she loved it, returning every summer for many years. During the winters, her Hebrew improved and the synagogue became a place where she felt valued and where she found considerable pleasure, particularly in contrast to the stormy relationship of her parents.

Soon after college Judith married, and, largely at her husband's urging, they went to live on a kibbutz. Judith became a graduate assistant to a scholar at the Technion, in Haifa. After a few years of graduate work there, she left Israel in despair, feeling misused because of the patriarchal nature of her graduate department and the attitudes toward women in Israel, especially within the Orthodox religious establishment. She also struggled in her marriage, and a divorce soon followed. Judith came back to the United States and spent several years in poverty work, "exploring the edges of my anti-Jewishness." She stopped keeping kosher and became less observant—"I even started smoking!"

Yet this very rebellion was part of the process of finding her authentic Jewish identity separate from her mother, who was "very Jewish" but also very locked into restrictive, patriarchal views of the role of women. "My mother was president of her local Hadassah, but told me that you have to put the man in your life in the forefront. Her basic worry was that I get married."

Put men in the forefront is exactly what Judith did, and the move to Israel was part of a young adulthood faith construction in which her true spirituality was still subordinate to her husband's. As she wrestled with Judaism, Judith was wrestling with herself and with her mother's anxiety: on the one hand, she kept holding her own desires in check; on the other hand, she wanted a rich and powerful relationship with Judaism, which truly had been the love of her life growing up, "a burst of fresh air amidst all the gray concrete of my Chicago childhood."

Judith was also powerfully influenced by the emerging women's movement in the 1970s. "I had a major epiphany in my first women's consciousness-raising group. But I came home from that meeting and my husband was in a rage that I even went. I made a determination at that point that it was dangerous for me to be too involved with feminism, that it would cost me my marriage." Years went by before Judith was able to look more directly at her life. After her divorce she became involved in a women's group, and then discovered Jewish feminist theology. "It blew my mind that those three words could appear together in one sentence." She joined a Jewish feminist study group and began to incorporate insights of feminism into her life. She believes that feminism "has had a tremendous influence on men and women coming back to Judaism."

Being president of her Hadassah would never be enough for this lively woman, living in a different time from that of her own mother, with more options. Leaving Israel and her marriage was a way of saying no to the subjugation she experienced. Her period on the edges of Judaism was a time of sorting out who she was, leading finally to an application to a prominent American rabbinical college. Judith was one of the first female graduates of the college, and is today a leading American rabbi.

Rabbis who are willing to give you a window onto their own soul-searching are a treasure. Too often rabbis feel too vulnerable within the community to show themselves as human. Community pressure to idealize the rabbi and the rabbi's own confusions about what it means to be a teacher or spiritual leader often lead him or her to portray a cartoon image of the rabbi as spiritual know-it-all, rather than another seeker on the path. What gives Nemerov's poem "Debate with the Rabbi" (discussed in the last chapter) such bite is that he turns the tables on the rabbi, fulfilling many of our aspirations to be out from under rabbis' judgment and more engaged in dialogue. In the poem, the good Jew theme is turned around: the arguer becomes the good Jew, the rabbi, forgetful or ignorant of his own tradition.

Martin, a senior rabbi from the Conservative tradition and the director of Hillel at a large urban university, spoke to me about the problem of authenticity in Judaism and the rabbis' complicity. "Many Jews are Jews because the rabbi said so. This is a serious problem. The rabbi tells the congregation, 'come into *your shul*,' but it's not really *your shul*. He invites you to sit down and stand up. Being Jewish is not living according to what the rabbi says, but according to your own life, your own home."

I asked him if he ever wrestled with feeling inadequate. He answered as a person and as a Jew. "Of course, of course. In every aspect of my life—as a husband, parent, rabbi. As a Jew, too, of course—I've wrestled a lot with the idea of God and the fact that God as portrayed in the Bible is a metaphor projected thousands of years ago, which we take very literally."

What did he mean by God as a metaphor? He replied in true rabbinic fashion—a question to answer a question: "Well, the god of the Old Testament is an all-powerful figure, mysterious and crotchety, who is continually demanding things of you, particular evidence of loyalty. Now, who does that remind you of?"

Perhaps lost in some recent accusations from my teenage son, I hesitantly replied, "A father?"

"No, no," he replied impatiently but not without a touch of kindness. "What father has such power? Fathers are not all-powerful and don't really have godlike power. No, the god of the Old Testament is more reminiscent of a certain Near Eastern despot...say, the Pharaoh." He went on to his own personal struggle. "I've had to wrestle a lot in my life with what I believe about God and the divine. Recently, I've begun to come to some conclusions about what I believe."

Recently! I was aware that this thoughtful, scholarly man, much loved in his community, was approaching seventy. "What about before then?" I asked. His answer was: "It's been a struggle. Judaism is a struggle; living a Jewish life is demanding."

Rabbis who are willing and able to join with you in the struggle can have a tremendous influence on those who are wrestling with Judaism. Their openness can remove some of the shame of feeling inadequate for questioning or not believing in just the right way, which can be a hidden part of Jews' struggle with their Jewish experience.

The Good-Enough Jew

Abraham may have been the first and last good Jew, willing to obediently follow God's command to sacrifice his son. Since then it's been all dispute and argument, which gives Judaism its spine and bite and survival capacity.

We need a sense of the good-enough Jew, different from idealized images. The definition needs to include some recognition of stumbling, unsureness, experimentation, even rebellion. "We have such a wide variety of Jews today that it's unbelievable," one rabbi said to me, excitedly. "There is a whole range of Reform rabbis more observant than Conservative ones; Conservative rabbis who are more experimental than Reconstructionists; Orthodox who sound at times like Reform rabbis. Jewish life is in great ferment."

Many of the Jews I meet don't know about such ferment, having on some level given up on themselves and on Judaism prematurely. There is, though, an enduring love of Jewish life for many Jews who stumble and aren't sure, yet are connected to Judaism nonetheless.

It's time to adopt a more open, inclusive sense of Jewish identity and the lifelong process of Jewish identity-making. One not dominated by obsessive divisions. The idea of the good-enough Jew, rooted in how today we compose Judaism from disparate elements in our lives—identifications with parents, relationships with significant people in our lives, the way that the spiritual impulse is nurtured and expressed in our experiences, including experiences with other faiths—is what we need.

At a university not far from where I live, there was recently a funeral service for a well-known professor emeritus. It was a Jewish funeral service, held in the historical Christian church on campus. Many of the members of the community were surprised that the professor was Jewish. He had never attended synagogue services, and he didn't have a Jewish name. Yet there, for his children and grandchildren to see, was his Jewish allegiance, expressed in these final rites. "Who's Jewish?" the rabbi officiating commented to me afterward.

"You just never know."

CHAPTER TWO

The Psychological Resistance
to Being Jewish

Given the nature of Jewish life today, it's deceptive to speak of "assimilation" as if it were a matter-of-fact option chosen by droves of Jews who simply give up their connection to the traditions and their beliefs. People are more complex than that. We both hold on *and* let go. Many Jews today wrestle with their internal resistances to being Jewish even while seeming to have drifted away from it.

To begin, though, we need to acknowledge the resistance to talking about the resistance to being Jewish. In today's America, where Jews have achieved widespread success, acceptance, and security—where the wife of a vice presidential candidate tells the world she was born in a displaced persons camp—there is also considerable pride in being Jewish. Our history is one of overcoming difficulties. We want to raise our children to feel proud of their Jewish heritage. We don't want to present a weak, self-doubting image to ourselves or to the world. As a result, many Jews resist facing or talking about the wish *not* to be Jewish, *not* to have to carry the glorious yet painful burden of

Jewish history, *not* to be part of a group that is often "the out group," even in twenty-first-century America.

Not too long ago, I bumped into this resistance while giving a talk on the development of Jewish identity to the teaching staff at a Jewish day school. The school is part of a large, sophisticated Reform congregation in a busy metropolitan city. I remarked that a number of Jews that I had talked to over the years had felt some embarrassment, uncertainty, even resistance to being Jewish.

Several teachers nodded in agreement, and then one observed, "I have a way of dealing with that with our first graders. I have trick glasses that reflect Jewish stars wherever the child looks. They put on the glasses and all they see is Jewish stars!" Another teacher offered a different strategy. Self-esteem is an important curriculum topic, she assured the group. How does her class go about exploring Jewish self-esteem? They begin and end the school day singing, "It's great to be Jewish!" The kids love it, I was told.

The glasses, the songs, are useful educational props. And in fact in many ways it *is* wonderful to be Jewish. Yet this is another example of the ways in which we as Jews have difficulty acknowledging and talking about our resistance to Judaism.

The psychological resistance to being Jewish has several sources. One source is shame, connected to a fundamental aspect of Jewish life in America: the tension between being different from and a part of the mainstream American culture, and the resulting experience, for some, of difference as defect.

Shame and Difference

I'm defining shame as the experience of feeling defective or worthless; the painful, if transient, sense that there is something fundamentally wrong with you. Shame carries with it the sense of being exposed, of being seen and unmasked. We may feel acutely self-conscious, painfully trapped in the public eye, wanting to hide or get away from view.[1]

Shame is rooted in loss: the core experience of shame is a turning away, either real or imagined, by those who love us. We experience ourselves as unlovable: ugly, weird, different. We imagine ourselves unable to hold or merit the attention and love of those we count on.

Since shame nestles in the gap between our real self and our ideal self, a potent shame factory originates in the experience of being *different* from the cultural ideal. For some of us, growing up, the experience of the Jewish part of the self can carry with it a feeling of difference that slides into defect.[2]

Making room for the Jewish struggle with shame does not negate the pride many of us take in our Jewish roots, nor the fact that shame is not a part of every Jew's experience.

My experience of the Jewish struggle with difference as a child took the form of what to do with Jesus Christ in music class.

When I was young, Tuckahoe Elementary School, in the suburbs of New York City, was definitely gothic: an ancient, dark brick building with long, narrow windows and angular sections of old copper roof covered with what looked like patches of green mold. Long spikes of ice hung from the roof in the winter and a gnarled old tree presided over the cracked asphalt playground all year round. I don't remember much about what went on inside the school when I was a third, fourth, or fifth grader, but I do remember singing the Christmas carols in music class every December.

How wonderful those carols sounded. There was more gusto in that music than in any of the American songs we sang. "Home on the Range" was bland stuff compared to "Joy to the World" or "Jingle Bells." And compared to what we sang in temple, Christian music was downright, well...celestial. The sense of joy and rapture came across, even, or maybe particularly, to the fresh ears of young children.

Yet as we sang so joyfully, the teacher smiling, the other kids thinking of sledding, Christmas trees, and presents, I faced a problem: *what to do with Jesus Christ.* Even as the wondrous melodies carried us along we Jewish kids knew that a trap lay ahead. Intoning J.C.'s name felt like swearing allegiance. Unkosher, false. Jesus Christ, *our* savior? Whose savior? Not mine. What to do? I remember the day my eyes caught those of Lois, my Jewish friend with the lovely blond hair, my Hebrew school classmate. In that instant she and I knew what to do—we both mouthed the words, without voice, when it came to *his* name. Our embarrassment at singing and not singing produced the uneasy compromise. I was afraid I'd stand out by *not* singing— would the teacher point at me? would some kids ask what I have against Jesus Christ?—and, conversely, afraid I'd stand out *by* singing—in exclaiming my joy at J.C., "our" savior, I would be betraying my parents and everything I was learning in Hebrew school. The idea of such a betrayal produced a visceral feeling akin to what I felt in college when, for the one and only time, I ate pork.

The silent glance and the unspoken resistance to "our" lord made a hidden connection with the other Jews in the room. While all the other kids were singing about Jesus and our savior, we knew something they didn't: *they were wrong.* Maybe they had control of the airwaves and could broadcast all they wanted about Jesus, but we knew they were believers in false wisdom. We knew something secret, about the desert and the Jews and Moses speaking directly to God.

So, our secret was that we were different. There was a smugness to it: all these happy and dumb consumers of the Christian culture and myth were going along, but I was different and so was Lois, the girl I was in love with, beautiful Lois.

Looking back, it's hard to sort out whether our smug, secret Jewish underground in music class at Christmastime—with its sense of being "better"—was sour grapes, or if being different truly was a source of pride. It was probably both. Secret and difference and shame and pride all melded together in an amalgam quite confusing for a seven-year-old.

Many Jews I talk with can remember the Christmas carol experience—the feeling of distaste at singing about Jesus, of feeling on the spot, not being sure what to do. One woman remembered, "In school my parents made clear there was one song we were *never* to sing—'Silent Night.'"

The idea that it's easy to assimilate has often seemed to me simplistic. American society runs on a calendar different from the Jewish one, and the essential cultural references are more Christian than Jewish. The dilemma for the Jew can be, What am I to do with the parts of myself that seem "different," don't quite fit, even if I don't really want to give them up?

There are many reminders of being different when you grow up Jewish. They range from a friend asking about why you're eating matzoh in school in the middle of the week to the more jarring experiences of a classmate asking if you'd take off your hat so he or she can "see your horns," or inquiring whether you "are ready to accept Jesus." Children respond differently to moments like these: some shrug them off, others become more confidently proud of their Jewishness, and others can struggle with an internal feeling of being different and defective.

Shame and Judaism can be wrapped together in our identities in many different ways—around our social status, our looks, our bodies. Nancy, for example, as a child somehow associated being Jewish with being rich. She remembered a particular girl from junior high school—not a friend but very "cool"—who one day visited her house, looked around, and immediately pronounced, "You guys must be rich." For Nancy, her friend's comment was associated with the family's being Jewish and with the idea that Jews are people who handle money, are concerned with money, want to make money. She remembered "feeling very ashamed." Being Jewish, for Nancy, carried with it an embarrassing feeling of being thought of as greedy and materialistic, and envied by other people.

Another woman told me that when she was a child a friend made a comment about another girl having a "Jewish nose." The woman recalled being very preoccupied with this judgment and her friend's negative feelings toward Jews. She remembered wanting to ask, "What's the matter with that? Do I have a Jewish nose?"[3]

Beth, who grew up in a wealthy town in California, where she was a cheerleader and popular in her school—with parents who showed no hesitation either in acknowledging their Jewishness or in being very involved in town politics—remembered the connection between shame and her looks. "There is one place where shame enters in. Growing up in Southern California, all the girls look all-American and I never felt that, I always felt I looked very Semitic." Now she notes the way in which her inner questioning turned her against identification with members of her own religion. "I am a physician who consults to a private girls' school. In my practice I see a lot of Jews, and I have a different style—maybe that is my anti-Semitism—I have a difficult time with Jappy girls, and all their glitz."

Our distinctive features—Jewish noses, hair, body types, whatever they are in each individual case—can become associated with shame about being Jewish, which may feel like the different and secret thing about us. Reading this last sentence in a draft chapter, a colleague replied, "Yes, I totally agree with you. I have so much stuff about this that I can barely see through it sometimes. Some of our struggles about not fitting in socially as a child can have to do with shame about a Jewish appearance in an environment where that was exceptional." Or where Jewish appearance was *not* exceptional but we *felt* odd or exceptional within ourselves. Judaism may become a magnet for whatever part of us feels shameful.

Many Jewish shame struggles are rooted in the shame expressed within our families as we were growing up. The Jewish nose or family wealth becomes a badge of our own shame because of a vulnerability—often unspoken—that one or both of our parents felt. Children's sense of shame is often a mirror of their parents' shame.

Mike, for example, remembered a painful moment: "One day I came home from Hebrew school with a menorah I had made and my mother got very upset—she said that she had sent me to Hebrew school to learn, not to believe." Mike struggles a lot with how much to invest in Judaism, how much to believe, and his struggle is rooted in his mother's struggle. Mike's mother looked down on traditional Judaism as "little more than superstition," and communicated a sense of "dirtiness" about worship, even as she herself tried to hold on to components of that tradition. "We kept kosher in the house, but when we went out to eat Mother made fun of people who didn't eat milk and meat together, who insisted on kosher entrées."

As it turns out, Mike's mother felt considerable shame about being Jewish, connected to a variety of self-esteem struggles in her own life. Judaism for Mike's mother was both a source of pride and the container for her own sense of defect. She conveyed to her son a sense of passionate Jewish worship as a blemish on the self, one that Mike—at age forty—struggles with as he explores what connection he wants to have with Judaism as an adult. Many of the shame struggles we experience as adults have a connection to our parents' shame. Understanding their struggles with Judaism can illuminate our own.

The Shadow of the Holocaust

Individual and family struggles with difference and shame are not the only source of resistance to being Jewish. A powerful set of interconnected and often buried feelings of shame, loss, fear, and anger about the Holocaust may also shape the resistance to "really" being Jewish.

For many, the possibility of a more vibrant Judaism is constricted by the press of feelings of loss and danger associated with the Holocaust.

How even to write about the Holocaust? We bump into resistance, internal and external, even in introducing it as a topic.

One man I know begins dinner table discussions that touch on the Holocaust by asking permission—as an American Jew whose family has lived in this country for generations—to even comment on the subject: "If there are any survivors of the Holocaust present, or children of survivors, is it OK to talk about this subject?"

In fact, those of us who are *not* children of survivors very much feel that we need permission to talk about the Holocaust and its effect on us. The impact of the Holocaust on children of survivors has been well documented, yet in some ways we are *all* survivors, including those of us who did not lose immediate family members.

We may resist being Jewish because of the weight of unintegrated feelings of loss, anger, and shame about the Holocaust. There can be an overwhelming feeling that it is best not to open it up. We resist the sorrow, the danger of being openly Jewish. For the postwar generations, there may be a kind of identity loss that can't really be looked at. Such a fragmentation can be in itself shameful—where do the missing pieces fit into my sense of who I am?

Almost every Jew that I have talked with thinks about the Holocaust, but most have trouble putting into words how it affects them. For instance, over e-mail I received a Happy Shabbos message from Lynn, a Jewish friend, a law professor in her mid-thirties. The message itself was surprising since she had rarely in the past marked Jewish moments. Lynn's immediate family has been in America since the 1890s. We'd been having an ongoing e-mail dialogue about what it means to be Jewish, and this day she mentioned, in passing, the Holocaust. I e-mailed her back, asking her if she thinks much about it and in what ways. Several days went by and I began to worry that I had intruded in some way. Then I received her response:

"I've been thinking about this question since you asked it. In some ways the Holocaust is always present at some level of my consciousness, even if I don't consciously 'think' of it often." Then she provided me some "snippets of thought" about its effect on her: "There must be a reason that I am alive, when so many died." "I have some kind of obligation to the world, to those who died, to be alive and do something useful for humanity." "Why did some of my relatives have the courage or foresight to leave while others stayed?" "What does it mean to us today that those who lived often were those who were less 'religious' or 'traditional'?" "Something wonderful (Israel) emerged in large part from that suffering: do we need to lose so many lives to get a country for Jews?"

Lynn went on to name the deeper loss that comes from thinking about the Holocaust. "As I start writing, I realize I can go on and on." She wrote at length to me about a whole world she feels she has lost: "A world that my relatives came from is gone. People who could have been my distant cousins, my lovers, my teachers are gone. It's like taking away an option. I can't 'go back' to that life. My grandparents came here so I've got to be American." Once she got into it, the subject was vast, and the words didn't come easily; she acknowledged in closing that "I'm not saying this right, but I hope you have a sense of what I mean."

Lynn has a large reservoir of feeling that is hard for her to look at or put into words. People talk of "too much" feeling, of wanting to avoid feeling flooded. Confusion, sorrow, anger, or despair can be internal shame factories, in that they violate the familiar ideal of adults as being in control, having a clear identity, and being able to manage their emotions. Sometimes the uncounted or discontented are wrestling with buried family and personal feelings about the Holocaust.

Growing Up: Discovering the Holocaust. Historian Peter Novick points out that in the 1950s, the word *Holocaust* had not yet been appropriated to refer to events in Europe during the Second World War, nor was it used to refer to the experiences of Jews specifically. In fact, there was not a lot of talk about the concentration camps in the immediate postwar period.[4]

Many of us who grew up in the 1950s learned about the Holocaust in ways that made it a shameful and scary part of our identities as Jews. We knew something terrible had happened, and that knowing had an impact on us as children, whether or not our immediate families were directly affected.

One friend, Susan, says that the Holocaust "was always hanging in the air in my family," never directly talked about but always there in some subtle way. Her father had come over to this country before the Holocaust, but he had lost many relatives in Europe.

"How was it in the air?" I asked, and Susan described unspoken anxiety, communicated nonverbally, one of the most powerful means of communication since it registers outside awareness. Susan related, for example, that her mother became very anxious when her brother was an AFSC high school exchange student in Germany during the late 1950s. "It was tone of voice, short-temperedness, comments about Germans—not much said directly about the Holocaust."

Another woman in the group, Yvonne, who *is* the daughter of concentration camp survivors, said that the Holocaust was always around her "because my parents had tattoos on their arms and chose to live always around people who did. Most of the visitors to our house had tattoos on their arms and when I met an American Jew without Holocaust roots it was a little like, who is this?" For Yvonne, the Holocaust was a constant source of guilt in her family, a burden she couldn't get out from under. "Whenever anyone didn't take out the trash or if there was a whiff of teenage rebellion, my grandmother was always saying, 'How could you do this to us after all we've been through?'" Yet when Yvonne asked her grandmother about what she had been through, the reply was "You only shouldn't know."

Joy Schaverien, an English psychoanalyst and art therapist, explores in her article "Inheritance" how contemporary Jewish identity has been shaped by the Holocaust, particularly what is inherited through the generations. She believes that "for many Jewish people, particularly those whose families have connections with Europe, Jewish identity cannot be easily separated, even today, from the effects of the Holocaust."[5]

Schaverien, whose family had lived in Britain since the early 1900s, offers a personal example: there was an oak sideboard in her childhood home in Britain after World War II, one drawer of which she was forbidden to open. In the drawer were her father's tallit and *kippot* and prayers, which she knew about, but also something hidden: "two books of photographs taken at the liberation of Bergen-Belsen." Inevitably, one day the children did explore the forbidden drawer. Schaverien writes, "I remember looking at the pictures with a kind of appalled incomprehension and fascination. Piles of corpses and half dead human beings looked out at us with empty eyes." She recalls in particular her mother's reaction when she found her daughter had penetrated the secret of the drawer: "The pictures were disturbing but more so was my mother's reaction when she found us looking at them. Although she said little, merely putting them back in the drawer and telling us not to look at them again, there was something worrying in this. There was something unstated that nevertheless communicated itself to us—it was a sense of what it meant to her. I realize now that she was attempting to protect us from the full impact of the horror of the story those pictures told. However, the subliminal message, communicated by the juxtaposition of those prayer books, the photographs and the reactions, was that to be Jewish was dangerous. This unconscious message was conveyed simultaneously with the conscious one of warmth, care, and of belonging."[6]

The fear, the sorrow, the frustrated anger, the shame, the loss was communicated to many of us indirectly—by anxious looks, tone of voice, sudden ends to conversation when "certain subjects" came up. Many Jews looked into that secret drawer as children, through TV or movies. We saw the images of skeletons and emaciated survivors from the camps broadcast on the black-and-white TVs our parents were so proud to own back in the 1950s. How could this not have had an impact on our growing identity as Jews?

In a similar vein, one woman I interviewed, Carol, recalled going to see the movie *Judgment at Nuremberg* as a teenager. "I walked to the theater with a friend. Back in those days it cost fifty cents to get in. I didn't have a clue what I was going to see. As I watched the movie, I realized that I was named after someone killed in the Holocaust. My grandfather came here before the war, but he lost all his brothers and sisters at Babi Yar. I knew all that, sort of, like an abstract concept I didn't need to clarify in any way. But I remember sitting through the movie thinking, this is where I came from, my people."

We had been talking at a table of parents, some of whom were not Jewish but were interested in Judaism. As Carol spoke, a Catholic woman at our table looked visibly upset and tried to console her. "I hope today we're all more accepting."

Carol shot back, "Who's we? I still worry about the Holocaust, that it could happen. I remember my grandmother crying about the death of a relative. I grew up with those experiences, which told me that there are some people willing to shoot Jews just because they are Jews. You pay a price being Jewish. It's a risk."

The resistance to being Jewish may reflect a rejection of being a victim, and the way that being a victim may have been a theme in one's family. For example, Stuart is now a busy financial planner and investment counselor in Houston. He has a family of his own but never attends synagogue. He grew up in the Bronx after the war, and there was a fair amount of bitterness and shame in his house—his grandparents had struggled to make a life in this country and his mother communicated her deep sense of inadequacy, about her body, her looks, and the family's status in the community.

Stuart remembers feeling particularly repulsed by the images from the concentration camps, and the way Judaism connected to standing out and feeling different. With a lot of feeling, he told me, "Who would want to identify with those victims, who stood in line for the boxcars and the gas chambers? I did see the pictures when I was younger, those emaciated skeletons."

Stuart became politically active in the 1960s, working on civil rights, feeling sympathetic to the Black Panthers. "I became an activist, kept a gun in my house, worried about police breaking in, solidarity with the Panthers, but I know some of that was the Jewish mentality—who knows when they'd come to get you, drag you out of your house?"

After his wife became pregnant, the couple wondered if a deeper connection to Judaism would help with the daunting task of raising children. One day Stuart walked over to the new Jewish community center that was about to open in their neighborhood. "It was new and fancy, so I went over and waited on line and it was a long line, winding toward the entrance." Standing in that line, Stuart had a defining moment in his relationship to his religion as he thought, "I'm waiting on line with all these Jews. I left and never went back to the community center or to the synagogue. I have to admit that the image of the Jews lined up on the train platforms, arriving at the camps, was on my mind. The last thing I wanted was to be identified as a Jew, a weak, passive figure, particularly when I was becoming a father myself."

Wounded Fathers

A third source of the resistance to being Jewish, particularly among Jewish men, lies in conflicting images of our fathers, both cultural and personal. On the one hand, there is so much to venerate in our fathers and the world of our fathers. Within Judaism respect for fathers is a central part of our tradition and observance. The Hebrew word for father—*abba*—carries a particular resonance. Yet for many Jewish men and women, conflicts around fathers and masculinity can be associated with a muted or contorted Jewish identity. Part of this is the legacy of the Holocaust, part lies in our history of immigration, part in the social role of fathers in Jewish families.

Many of us have buried feelings about Jewish masculinity connected to the Holocaust. We expect fathers to protect and defend. That may be an unfair burden to place on fathers, but it is powerfully rooted in human psychology and history.[7]

Edwin Black in his article "Could We Have Stopped Hitler?" writes about the "formidable economic war to topple the Nazi regime" mounted by American Jews.[8] He wants to combat the guilt of American Jewry that "we didn't do enough." Reading about the efforts at a boycott by Rabbi Stephen Wise and others, which almost succeeded in bringing Hitler down, I saw how obviously vulnerable Hitler was in 1933. Yet the effect of the article on me is the opposite of the author's intent: it showed me how skilled Hitler and the Nazis were in outmaneuvering the Jews and exploiting our own divisions. The emotional truth was, Hitler outmaneuvered those smart Jews. I thought, *You schmucks, you unseeing schmucks!* It's an unfair accusation, one that I am ashamed of when I realize the fallibility of us all, that few of us would have done any better, but hindsight doesn't hide a deep fury and shame—how could you have allowed this to happen? In Berlin—the city with the biggest synagogue in the world.[9]

The unspoken accusation lurks in the background. As with Freud, whose four sisters died in the camps even as he was able to take his entire office with him from Vienna. "They saved the furniture, but not the people," mused Michael Roth, the curator of the provocative Freud exhibit—*Sigmund Freud: Conflict and Culture*—at the Smithsonian.[10] There is no doubt that saving the furniture was the best that could be done in the circumstances; I intend no accusation here that more "should" have been done. Yet, in fact, the accusation hangs in the air, for the whole generation. *We should have done more.*

Although many, of course, fought in the war, one wonders about the psychic effect on the generations of American Jewish men directly before and after the Second World War of leaving behind loved ones while the Nazi cauldron heats up, then sitting safely in New York or Boston or Chicago or Los Angeles. There's an element of accusation in Roth's passing comment about Freud: "You'd have thought of all people to know about the potential for aggression in man." *You should have known.*

When our parents wouldn't talk about the Holocaust, who was being protected—us or them? In the silence was the attempt to protect the image of Jewish masculinity from the accusation, *You failed.*[11] The challenge for some Jews then is how to identify with a Jewish masculinity that was so smart and so successful, yet unable to protect and defend what they loved.

The internalized sense of masculinity as defective or inadequate is common among minority groups and is rooted in our struggles as sons and daughters to come to terms with our fathers. Fathers are supposed to protect and defend. When a culture is brutalized, the male image within it suffers. As does the female image. Mothers, in their attempts to protect and defend their families, may come to be seen as having too much power, to be too controlling and intrusive in the lives of the children. "Wounded father" and "wounded mother" images abound in African American and American Indian cultures, among others.[12]

Jewish men and women struggle with a "wounded father" and a "wounded mother." Stuart's Holocaust shame about "standing in line" as a Jew is partly linked to feelings about his own father's passivity and his mother's domination in the home. As Stuart was growing up, his father did "OK business-wise" but took a back seat in the home to Stuart's mother in a way that left the young boy feeling too much the property of his mother. Part of Stuart's shame is the feeling that he doesn't really have what it takes an adult male in the world, despite all his "real-world" success.

While there are, of course, many, many reasons why Jewish boys can be—and are—proud of their fathers, and love them deeply, the question of being able to protect and defend is one that many Jewish males struggle with growing up. One of the curses of traditional fatherhood is distance—the father's participation in the family is defined in terms of provider, breadwinner, ambassador to the world of work. Mothers in the traditional division of labor became the "emotional switchboards" in families, linking people together, and exerting enormous power in the minds of the children (and often the husband). This is true in many families, of widely differing ethnic, religious, and class backgrounds. The power of traditional sex roles has for many years washed over other differences. However, in Jewish families, the historical emphasis on intellectual and financial success among fathers may leave them looking very different from the dominant American cultural ideal of "masculinity."

Jerry, for example, told me about "the agony" of spending summers in a Jewish community in the Catskills and watching the Sunday baseball games in which all the men participated. There were a number of great Jewish athletes there ("we had a father there, he was so good we called him 'the Mickey Mantle of the Catskills'"), but what resonated most painfully for Jerry was watching his father's ineptness at baseball, the man striking out or looking clumsy on the field. What was at play for Jerry at the time was his own adolescent worries about his physical adequacy in the world, projected onto his father. For Jerry, going to Israel right after high school and living there during the 1967 Six-Day War was a profound part of his feeling OK about himself as a Jew. Finding that he was "tough enough" was a large step in Jerry's journey to claiming his Jewish identity, and possibly his masculinity.

And what of our mothers? The "wounded mother" inside many Jewish men and women complicates our relationship to Judaism. Mothers have enormous power in the lives of sons and daughters. In many families, children learn about Judaism through their mothers. Whatever injury a mother may have experienced from patriarchal authorities in the synagogue, or feelings of exclusion or ambivalence she may have harbored, can become part of us, sometimes in uncomfortable ways. We may internalize their anger or shame. Many of us who deeply love our mothers have been drawn to the "feminine world" of Judaism—the home celebrations, the food and cooking, all the "gendered sacred knowledge and practices" of women[13]—yet also feel disloyal to our fathers.

Cross-gender relationships—fathers and daughters, mothers and sons—have a special frisson and power to them. There is a special and enduring bond between Jewish mothers and their sons. This bond brings opportunity and burden. Feeling deeply loved by his mother can give a son confidence throughout his life. Yet a son can also carry the weight of his mother's hopes of accomplishment in the world of men. Mothers who have felt constrained by traditional sex roles may look to their sons to complete their unfulfilled longings. The "Jewish Mother's Haiku" captures this expectation: "Is one Nobel Prize / So much to ask from a child / After all I've done?"[14]

For some sons, Judaism may carry with it the oppressive weight of their mothers' demands. "I don't like going to synagogue, all that ritual and instruction—it feels like my mother telling me to put on my galoshes before I go outside," observed Ted. Ted's steadfast refusal to engage with Judaism carries with it the defiant protest of a boy stamping his feet and saying no to an overprotective mother.[15]

For daughters, the "wounded mother" inside may feel critical and demanding, ultimately leading the daughter toward a frozen or alienated experience of Judaism. The daughter may sympathize with a mother's disappointment or sorrow at the way traditional Judaism had excluded or segregated women from worship. In today's world, where active participation in worship and the governance of the synagogue is an option available to women, a grown daughter may feel disloyal to her mother in participating more. She may feel she has gone over to the other side, as does, for example, Joyce, who told me she didn't want to become involved in her synagogue because it felt "too much like a men's club." I was puzzled since I knew that in this particular synagogue many women were actively involved (including the president of the congregation). As Joyce talked, though, the residue of the painful exclusion of her mother became apparent. "It's a club my mother was never allowed to join—for her, Judaism was expressed through her cooking at home on the High Holidays." As a child and teenager, Joyce would leave synagogue services very early with her mother, often with a conspiratorial air of leaving the men to their "business" while the two co-conspirators went home to cook and prepare the house for the after-worship meals. Now the idea of spending more time in the synagogue leaves Joyce feeling both curious and disloyal, eager and angry.

When some daughters try to find their own Jewish voice, there can also be anxiety about *competing* with their mothers. One very competent forty-year-old daughter, Janet, puzzled why she wasn't more involved with Jewish life, particularly given the successful models her parents presented. Janet grew up in a very "Americanized" family—her father a successful publisher, her mother a prominent psychologist—which also had a rich Jewish life in the home. They were active in the synagogue while also living in a very "Waspy" suburb. Janet seemed to have the best of both worlds. Now that she has her own family, Janet agonizes about why she hesitates to join a synagogue—and realizes that it has to do with the very success of her mother in being both Jewish and not Jewish. "She was able to do it all, and I'm not sure I can." Janet's mother was so skilled at this dance, and she feels clumsy at it. Janet, too, lives in a very "non-Jewish community," and she isn't sure she can so gracefully integrate Judaism into her life and family. She doesn't want to try and fail—better to resist Judaism than to face an internal wounded mother, criticizing her for not doing it right.

The Effects of the Resistance on Adult Jewish Identity

Jewish struggles with shame and other sources of resistance to being Jewish have a number of consequences for adult Jewish identity.

Shame can silence us. When we feel too exposed, we want to get out of the spotlight. We may withdraw into the protection of silence. Childhood moments of shame may continue to live within us as adults as pockets of silence. If we harbor an inner

uncertainty about our Jewish identity we may become mute or
silent when called upon to express it in public or even to acknowledge it to ourselves in private.

Talking with Jewish men or women, sometimes you can almost feel the muteness. I was talking over the phone to a friend,
Jane, about her life and experiences with Judaism. A lively, engaging, and thoughtful woman, Jane had contacted me when
she heard I was interested in how Jewish men and women today
search for an authentic faith. "That's been a big theme for me
for a while. I've kept it completely separate from most parts of
my life." Which made sense because I hadn't even known Jane
was Jewish, despite having spent a fair amount of time with her,
both personally and professionally. We were talking over the
phone across the country but it was sunny in both places, so
Jane took her portable phone onto her front stoop while we
talked. "Work, job, children, my partner—all press for priority.
I've been looking for where Judaism fits in."

We were having a rich conversation about Jane's interest in
Judaism these days, particularly her lifelong struggle with wanting and not wanting to belong—from the "joyless" Judaism of
her childhood to the fact that "I belong to a Jewish Reconstructionist congregation and I'm still not sure if I belong." The eter-
nal, wandering Jew.

All of a sudden there was silence on the phone.

Hello? Jane, hello? Had I been disconnected?

Then Jane's voice returned; she apologized, and explained:
"My mailman is coming and he doesn't need to hear this." Another silence, then the mailman left and Jane's voice returned.
When I asked about that she said, "I feel self-conscious, sitting
on the front stoop and trying to formulate a train of thought."
How often in having a "Jewish conversation" at the local
YMCA (who can forget what the C stands for?), or in a parking
lot with a friend, do I feel self-conscious, does my voice get
lower, or do we start to whisper? How quickly do I take off my

yarmulke when leaving synagogue, so as not to be seen as "Jewish"? Do I remove the *chai* around my neck when going into the football locker room?[16]

Shame can also be welded to our adult yearning to experience the more spiritual, awe-filled aspects of Judaism, and to find a closer relationship to God or the divine. We may feel as if we are giving in or losing a childhood struggle not to "surrender" to a more powerful external force.

This "spiritual shame" may be rooted in the sense of difference from our parents rather than from the majority culture. Some of us have grown up in families that distanced themselves from Judaism, particularly its more religious or spiritual aspects. A father or mother may have "given up" on God as a result of great disappointment or loss or their own shame. As children we may identify with their negative feelings toward faith. As adults, then, when we wish to turn to a more spiritual relationship that involves mystery and faith and surrender, we may feel embarrassed or humiliated.

Isaac, at age forty-four, has spent "more time in the synagogue over the past four years than I had in the first forty years of my life." He is very interested in the service, enjoys the sense of community, and explores prayer. He has a son and two daughters, all of whom are approaching *b'nai mitzvah* age, his wife has had a cancer scare ("We dodged the bullet this time, but who knows?"), and he is watching his parents age. His business is very successful.

Isaac has much to celebrate in his life, to be grateful for, and he is more aware than ever of the fragility of life. He enjoys the idea of prayer and that there may be "a force in the world much greater than us, some divinity that we can't really explain." He has found a synagogue that utilizes music, chanting, and meditation—as well as more traditional prayer and liturgy—in its service. So he is, for the first time, exploring what it is like to feel a sense of surrender, of mystery, of awe in his life. He also feels considerable shame. "Given my family, it's hard for me to imagine myself having any kind of special relationship with God, to imagine even that there really *is* a God. Spirituality and ritual in our household were considered lower than superstition."

Isaac's parents raised him in an ethical-humanistic tradition, emphasizing the importance of ethics and values in human life and drawing on parts of Jewish ethics as one source of the moral life. His father had been raised Orthodox, but one event changed that. Just before his father's own bar mitzvah in 1926, a beloved older brother (who had planned to become a cantor) died in a car crash. Isaac's grandfather went into a deep depression. He declared that he "no longer believed in God," and Isaac's father's bar mitzvah was, understandably, a gloomy event. Isaac's father struggled with his own guilt and shame about surviving his more pious and observant brother. Distancing from Judaism was one way Isaac's father (and grandfather, for that matter) managed painful feelings—the more reverent, observant rituals and forms of surrender and prayer to a "loving" God became lightning rods for Isaac's father's own anger (and survival shame) at his brother's death. So, growing up, Isaac lived with comments about the "stupidity" and "superstition" of those Jews who attended synagogue. At age forty-four, as Isaac explores his wish to find a place for exactly those yearnings, he struggles with a sense of shame (along with his sense of joy and curiosity), of being foolish and childlike, of submitting in an unsophisticated fashion, of being merely "superstitious."

As Michael Bader notes, "Jewish rituals and prayers that describe the special relationship between Israel and God as one of loving idealization, awe, and surrender can tap into our reservoirs of shame."[17] Bader also points out that for many of us who grew up in an American culture that emphasized power and control and individual achievement, a return to a wish to experience the more reverent, spiritual—less individualistic—sides of ourselves may produce a sense of humiliation and embarrassment.

As if to illustrate Bader's point, Judy, a twenty-eight-year-old woman who very much valued her independence and who as a child experienced Judaism as very patriarchal, spoke in the following way about her hesitant decision to explore a local synagogue. "I don't want to just *surrender.* . . . I mean, the idea of connecting with God has to be on my terms, not as just a kind of giving in. It's a much more personal decision than that."

Bader considers shame to be a major source of resistance to the renewal of Judaism in one's life, and in fact sees shame-based struggles to be at the root of resistance to the spiritual in many forms. Noting that "there is nothing especially embarrassing about Jewish versions of prayer, God, or religious ritual and worship," he writes, "an understanding of the dynamics of shame can thus be used to illuminate the resistance to spiritual experience within any religious paradigm."[18]

Shame and sorrow connected to the Holocaust may also constrict our Jewish creativity right up to the present day. Some of us may "bland" out our Judaism because we can't manage the sorrow and loss our parents felt. There may be fears of danger, and a prohibition in some families against feeling "too Jewish." We may still be struggling with sorrow transmitted from our parents to us that remains barely named.

I spent a very enjoyable several hours, for instance, talking with Lillian about her attempts at age fifty-four to reinvigorate her Judaism. As a teenager, Lillian's mother and her family just made it out of Germany in 1939, with some heroic and very scary moments. Lillian told me how "bland" Judaism was in her parents' home. Her grandparents kept something alive for her, with their fluent Hebrew, particularly her grandfather's mastery of Hebrew displayed during the Passover seders, combined with the old family china and bright flowers that punctuated such events through the years. Such celebrations broke through what seemed like almost an active demeaning of Judaism in her parents' generation.

The superficial, "bland" Judaism masked a much deeper, passionate, and sorrowful connection in Lillian's family though, which emerged when I asked whether she thinks much about the Holocaust today. "Yes, I do think about it, especially when my kids do histories of the family and we talk a lot about the story of my grandparents." Lillian stopped. There was a moment's silence, and then her eyes filled with tears. "Mostly it's very painful—I mostly avoid it. I'm about to cry just thinking about it—my mother falls apart when we talk about the Holocaust."

Her mother's sorrow—expressed so painfully—looms over her own attempts to find a more vibrant Judaism in her own life. Lillian went on to tell me about the story of Lot's wife as a metaphor for how her family dealt with the powerful feelings evoked by the Holocaust.

"Lot's wife rushes to leave the doomed cities of Sodom and Gomorrah but can't resist one more look back at what she is leaving. When she turned around, she was turned into a pillar of salt. The lesson is that there are times when you have to leave, there are bad people, you have to get out. Well, with the Holocaust, you had to leave, you may have wanted to get your kids out, my grandparents just left, with their brothers and sisters back in Germany, and they couldn't look back a lot. We don't think about that a lot. It's a mystery, hard to look at."

For Lillian, the story of Lot's wife captures the feeling of loyalty to the generation that can't look back at their painful choices. We may fear that we would become paralyzed emotionally if *we* looked back. What does it mean for us to "look back"? It may have to do with opening ourselves to what was lost—that beautiful china and flowers, the fluent Hebrew, the civilization of our ancestors. Was there a taboo about looking back in our parents' generation? If so, to really enter into a more vibrant Judaism means to break the taboo of those we love and want to honor. A dilemma: staying silent and "paralyzed" means to go along with the prohibition, and opening ourselves means to defy those who have already suffered.

Grief and loss, cultural and personal, may mute the Judaism we feel inside us. Jay, a young Jewish father, whose own father had died of a heart attack when he was just a teenager, talked to me at length about his wish to justify his father's life, make up for it, his drive to relive and complete his father's life. After his father's death, Jay's family had not truly been able to mourn the loss. His mother struggled to maintain her life and demanded in many ways that Jay replace his father, rather than mourn him.

So strong was Jay's urge to re-create his father's life that he feared losing himself in the process. He knew all about Jewish ritual and worship, yet he felt he "went through the motions." When talking about his Jewish experience, he kept referring to the "responsibility to the missing." I couldn't get the phrase out of my head after our meeting. He was giving voice to the dynamics of individual grief: when we can't really mourn, we try to ambivalently re-create the lost person, place, or thing. The dynamics of individual grief may inform us about the ways that the Holocaust has shaped contemporary Judaism. Many Jews may also be struggling with a "responsibility to the missing"—Eastern European Judaism.

Jay's and Stuart's comments (the man who walked away from Judaism rather than feel that he is part of a passive "line" extending back to the Holocaust victims) lead to a troubling question: Does the emphasis placed on the Holocaust as the defining event by twentieth-century American Jewry lead to a distorted Judaism, focused around loss, passivity, and ritualized "remembrance," that stifles a creative, hopeful view of the future?

In a recent survey by the American Jewish Committee, a large group of Jewish men and women were asked to rank the importance of a variety of activities for their Jewish identity, ranging from "participation in synagogue services" to "travel to Israel" to "celebration of Jewish holidays." The item ranked the most important to Jewish identity was "remembrance of the Holocaust."[19]

Peter Novick, in his incisive analysis of the Holocaust's role in American life, argues that the Holocaust became primary in Jewish consciousness in part because it fulfilled the need for a "consensual symbol" that would unite American Jews in the late twentieth century, a time when traditional beliefs, rituals, and traditions were fragmenting under assimilationist pressures. Of course, it is important to remember the suffering of the Holocaust and to take steps to ensure that it never happens again. Yet a preoccupation with the Holocaust may not be the best psychological ground on which to make your primary connection to Judaism.[20]

At least some of the uncounted feel impatient with, and oppressed by, the "Holocaust-centered" nature of contemporary American Judaism. The psychology of healing after a loss involves both a remembrance of who and what was lost, and a changing of them, as we take into ourselves the valued parts of the lost person, place, or thing and make it our own, carried forward into the future. A vibrant, positive Judaism means celebrating life today, now, not simply loss and death.[21]

There is one other consequence of struggling with shame and difference as a Jew that is important for us to consider—the link between childhood shame and adult aggression. This link is becoming better understood.[22] One way of managing painful feelings of smallness and inadequacy is to attempt to become big and powerful, to achieve power and dominance over what threatens to humiliate us. I got an insight into how Jews may handle the shame we feel when growing up while talking to Milt, a fifty-year-old proprietor of a computer store, a man who loves exploring the internal workings of software programs.

Poking his spoon thoughtfully into his coffee cup as he

spoke, Milt explained to me the difference between "knowing" you are Jewish and "realizing" it. The latter is much more active, and for Milt, realizing his Jewishness came in a painful moment of difference from those around him:

"Before the fifth grade I knew I was Jewish. There was Hebrew class at the Central Synagogue in Manhattan that I loved. I felt there I could really be myself and play and be silly and have a good time, but it was during fifth grade that I realized that, hey, I was really different in some way.

"We were living in a faded section of Upper Manhattan that had once been elegant. It was really 'the wrong side of the tracks' and not the best place for Jews to live—largely an Irish-Catholic neighborhood.

"I was the only Jewish kid in my public school class. Only two of us were not Catholic, me and a Protestant girl. So they'd let all the Catholic kids out an hour early on Thursdays to study catechism and they'd be leaving the church just as I left the school. I had to walk through the kids to get home. It was not very good—they'd just heard about how the Jews killed Jesus and would call me names and punch me. One day I got into a fight, really didn't know how to defend myself and offered my nose to a kid who punched me and gave me a bloody nose. I ran home. It was pretty awful. No one was home. Both my parents were working. I just cried to myself alone in the apartment."

There was no adult or friend to help Milt contain and manage his sorrow and shame. In a moment of felt inadequacy, suddenly being frightened and helpless and humiliated, feeling *small*—Milt's fantasy turns toward becoming *big*, a common journey, especially for boys who feel they have been shamed: "I used to have a fantasy about the Israeli air force roaring overhead, over Manhattan, nobody getting hurt, just the other kids being very impressed and scared and saying, 'Wow, we better leave him alone.'"

We all deal with shame in different ways. One of the sequelae of early struggles with shame can be compensatory attempts at power and size, as well as attempts to disappear, to float away into the protective fog of our own words or of some nonhuman activity. Milt's fantasy about the sudden appearance of the Israeli air force provides us with an illustration of some Jewish preoccupations with power, with covering or wiping away the painful feeling of being small and puny and under someone else's power. It can help explain why for some Jews there may be more interest in being the aggressor than in identifying with those who are unfairly dominated: it requires a special sense of character to remember one's own smallness and also be protective of others' vulnerability.

Demonstrating that you're big and strong and that you can take care of yourself is only part of the struggle toward a whole identity. Sometimes our attempts at power come out of "identification with the aggressor"—determined not to be the victim anymore, we take on the attributes of those who have abused us.

We can wonder if in fact there is some inhibited aggression related to the Holocaust in all of us. Do we as Jews, so identified with overcoming the shameful "victim" role, disown our own aggression? A rabbi once told me that "we Americans have created these Holocaust museums and brought the Holocaust to America by buying it up from Europe, but it's a false ownership of the Holocaust. It was never *our* experience." He went on, "We identify with some sort of Holocaust chic and obscure our own aggression in the world." He concluded, "We are more likely these days to be the aggressors than the victims, but we don't want to look at that."

Does the Holocaust make us more likely to disown aggression, rather than admit that murderous aggression is a part of us all, perhaps even encoded in the human genome? The tendency of many Jews to see themselves only as innocent victims of aggression, and never as the purveyors of it, can leave many of the uncounted and discontented struggling with how to identify with a Judaism that seems to split the world into a cartoonlike, black-and-white place.

Managing the Resistance to Being Jewish

One of Freud's great insights into the human condition was that the strongest resistances we have to self-knowledge are often the sources of our greatest strengths. In listening to people talk about their shame, sorrow, and many life troubles, Freud became curious about the places where their stories got blocked, confused, or trailed off into silence. He saw such moments as places of resistance to exploring deeper feelings and conflicts. In these places of resistance often lay painful experiences, hard to talk about, certainly, yet also containing the path to greater wholeness and creativity.

The same is true for the various resistances to being Jewish— the shame, the submerged impact of the Holocaust, the wounded quality in our fathers. Not only can each be managed, but, in fact, becoming mindful of them can be the bedrock for a more honest, real Jewish identity.

The Opportunity in Shame. The first response to shame is to avoid it, in ourselves and in our children. Yet the feeling of being in exile, apart from, different from the mainstream culture, is a part of every Jew's heritage. We don't give our children any gift by denying that reality to them, nor do we help ourselves deal with who we are as adults. We cannot "shame-proof" Jewish children and adults; the key is to make a place for open discussion of the "normal shame" of being Jewish in America. Jewish shame can be managed if we recognize its role in our lives. Sweeping it under the rug only reinforces the sense that there is something wrong with us and our need for silence and isolation.

"This may be the first time in history when we have had the opportunity to *choose* to be Jewish or not," one man remarked to me. He meant that the impulse to assimilate, to get away from Judaism, was now a real possibility, in ways not available to past generations. We don't help our children, or ourselves, by criticizing or ignoring that feeling or by admonishing adult Jews to "hold on to their heritage."

As parents we need to be aware of the unconscious messages we send to our children. It is important to reassure a child who is hurt by an anti-Semitic comment, or by the fear of not fitting in, that it *is* good to be Jewish, but it also helps to accept the fact that the child feels that way. Also important is pointing out to our children the extraordinary cultural contributions of Jews throughout history, and reminding them that many of the people they admire are Jewish, from Adam Sandler to Winona Ryder to dozens of Nobel Prize winners to baseball stars Sandy Koufax, Hank Greenberg, and Shawn Green.

However, you don't heal painful feelings of difference by ignoring them or trying to talk children out of them. Self-esteem curricula don't replace an open family atmosphere that acknowledges the tensions of difference.

It is important to talk with our children about how being Jewish means at times feeling different. Being attentive to moments of difference and shame can bring great opportunity, even as they challenge us. When my twelve-year-old daughter, Emily, approached her bat mitzvah, she had also changed schools, moving to seventh grade in a small private day school. So, as she prepared for a very public celebration of her Jewishness, she was also making new friends in a new school. We live in rural southern New Hampshire, not an area teeming with Jews. Her new school was an excellent one, which she clearly loved—a sentiment we shared. In it, Christianity was taken for granted—not in an obvious way, but in a more subliminal one. In late December, for instance, there was not a Christmas service per se;

rather, the kids worked hard on the "Holiday Revels," a creative musical event in which they reenacted the myth of St. George and the Dragon, performed a variety of old English dances, and sang traditional carols and hymns. We loved the event, a major milestone in the school year, but it did have the obliviousness to other traditions that only those who have spent years feeling right at home among "people like us" can feel.

Soon after that event, my daughter and I went to a menorah lighting at our synagogue. The congregants brought their menorahs to the *shul* and placed them all around the sanctuary—beautiful pottery menorahs, elegant silver ones, children's menorahs made from wood or Spackle or clay, and antique ones carried through the generations. As we lit them all, the lights were turned off, making a thrilling sight—the entire room ringed with menorahs, each with candles ablaze.

Driving home later that evening, I was surprised when Emily seemed quiet. She broke down into tears, asking, "Why do we have to be Jewish? I'm the only one in my whole school!"

My heart twisted. I felt ashamed and angry at myself for being Jewish and thus putting that on her. Her shame washed over me (and perhaps mine over her), reminding me of my own loneliness. Given all a twelve-year-old girl goes through, why did I put that baggage on her as well? Part of me wished my wife and I had made it "easier" on her, not worked so hard to help Emily understand her Jewish heritage and history. It slowly dawned on me that the very experience that night of being thrilled by Judaism may have left her feeling more raw and exposed, aware of the way that she was different from the comfortable assumptions at her school, which she also loved.

Yet I also recognized that there was some opportunity in my daughter's question: she was asking me to help her understand herself and her family, to make sense of feeling different from everyone else. So, in the car we talked about being Jewish and what that meant. I told my daughter that I felt that way, too, sometimes—why did I have to be born Jewish? I, too, felt alone and different at times.

Emily was surprised, replying in a way that revealed how hard it is for young children to conceive of their parents' self-doubts. "Oh, no, you don't really feel that, Daddy!"

I assured her I sometimes did. And I told her that I suspected that most Jews felt similarly at some points in their lives. I came away from the conversation grateful for the dialogue with my daughter, and aware that one source of the pain that emerges whenever we feel shame is our attempt to keep it a secret.

Humor and irony can be very valuable, too. They may communicate more than stern platitudes. One woman remembered with pleasure her father's response to a moment in her childhood when the family was painfully aware of being different within their community. Adele's parents had moved to a wealthy Westchester suburb of New York City in the 1950s, when she was still in elementary school. There were a few Jewish families living there at the time, but because Adele's last name didn't sound Jewish, and because she had blond hair, few people seemed to realize her family was Jewish. Her father was a physician who practiced locally and was clearly welcomed in the town. However, not long after moving in, the entire community encountered a painful anti-Semitic event: one day, many Jewish families found dead rats in their mailboxes. Since they were not identified as Jewish, their mailbox had no rat.

Adele's father was outraged at this event, and at the apparent lack of outrage in the community itself. So he wrote a tongue-in-cheek letter to their local paper in which he acknowledged the fact that many of the Jewish families who had moved into the community had received a welcome present of a dead rat, which he took to be a local custom, and so he was very upset... very upset by the fact that as a Jewish family they had not received one. *Where was their rat?* he wanted to know. *And why hadn't they received one?* He asked for directions to the town office where they could pick up their rat. With a provocative humor Adele's father modeled for her a way of dealing with difference and being Jewish.

As Jews, we can also be more aware of the role of shame in the lives of many people, not only Jews. Sylvan Tomkins, an influential psychologist who has helped shape our understanding of shame, wrote that "the nature of the experience of shame guarantees a perpetual sensitivity to any violation of the dignity of man."[23] Helping our children understand the role of scapegoating in human life and the impact of feeling unheard or being in a minority can be important goals for Jewish parents. We can teach our children about the ways that Jews participate in such dynamics as well, rather than portray Jews as simply the victims of shame-based behaviors. Jews are no strangers to scapegoating and humiliating others.

Resolving the tensions of feeling different is not just a task for our children—adults are often on a parallel track. We may need to respect and make room—in synagogues and outside them—for the tension and ambivalence that being Jewish today brings with it for us as adults. That means allowing more discussion of the urge to be not-Jewish and respect for the dilemma itself. The fact that these issues become heightened in our awareness every December offers us a yearly opportunity to do so.

Menorahs and Christmas Trees. Is there any time of year when difference and otherness is as piquant for American Jews as it is in December? In many synagogue discussions, the emphasis is on how to "Christmas-proof" your family—what to say to your kids when they ask why you don't have a Christmas tree, or when they ask why little Johnny got more presents when he celebrated Christmas than they did at Chanukah. To answer such questions parents can point to what's good about Judaism—you can explain the meaning of the tree and how it represents an understanding different from the Jewish experience of the world;

you can talk about all the good parts of Chanukah that Christians *don't* experience. These are all excellent responses. And you can make room for the experience of difference and yearning that our children—and we ourselves—experience. Yes, there is some difference, it's not *all* great being a Jew, and there are some sacrifices and costs to being Jewish, but they are part and parcel of being Jewish.

Most of all, we can admit to our own internal ambivalence. We *can* explore ambivalence without losing our Jewish identity. In fact, acknowledging ambivalence often leads to a stronger, more authentic Jewish identity. Often the "December Dilemma" discussions become so heated because they tap our own mixed feelings, our wish to participate in the Christmas revelry and to remain loyal to our own traditions. These kinds of discussions quickly become polarized because many of us feel guilty and ashamed, as if they are signs of being a not-good-enough Jew.

Sometimes ambivalence in a discussion leads somewhere important. I saw that happen at one synagogue discussion entitled "Menorahs, Christmas Trees, and Chanukah Stockings." There was considerable embarrassment expressed within the group about being attracted to Christmas carols and wanting to have a Christmas tree at home. Some members of the congregation did have Christmas trees; some whose spouses had converted to Judaism spoke with a shameful but gleeful tone of how great it was to go to visit in-laws on Christmas and decorate the tree. Other participants were outraged that "any Jew would have a Christmas tree in their house!"

Finally, one of the men, who was devotedly Jewish but had admitted to enjoying Christmas when it was in someone *else's* house, exclaimed, "Look, Chanukah is all about fighting for your faith and standing up, and that's wonderful, but, you know, Christmas is about peace and getting along and silent night and the wonder of everyone loving each other." The Maccabean impulse is to defend our boundaries and fight for our identity, and it is an important and honorable one. Yet he said, "I would just like to have the experience in Judaism of not having to fight all the time."[24] He was articulating the wish to acknowledge similarities and connection between people, not just the differences, and that was a feeling he missed in Judaism. The love of Christmas expressed this more universal, connected impulse in a way that he had not yet been able to find in Judaism.

His comments that night led the group into a discussion about how we all shared the yearning to be part of "humanity" and not just Judaism. One person said that when the 2000 Census asked for her religious orientation and ethnic background, she wrote "human being" in response to both. That led into a discussion about the very community-oriented and nonjudgmental nature of Jewish tradition.

By not shaming each other, and by making room for our divided wishes to be both similar to and different from the mainstream culture, we were able to talk more honestly and openly in our group, and to feel *more* Jewish, not less.

CHAPTER THREE

L'Chayim to Life:
Overcoming the Resistance

To discover a positive, joyful Judaism, we must get past the painful images of Jewish suffering and passivity that are our inheritance. How do we do that?

For those of us to whom the Holocaust seems an endless stream of images of Jewish passivity and shame, it can be helpful to explore more active, realistic, textured images of what the experience of those fateful years was for many individuals. Too often, discussions of the Holocaust revolve around unrealistic "heroic" images of Jewish resistance or horrific stories of suffering and despair. Often the reality presents a more nuanced, interesting picture.

At a conference for mental health professionals entitled "Remembering the Holocaust: Until What Generation?" I had the opportunity to listen to a thoughtful observer of the Holocaust experience.[1] Dr. Anna Ornstein, a well-known child psychoanalyst and a survivor of the camps, spoke about the process of mourning and recovering from the Holocaust. A short, older woman, Ornstein still retained her German accent, speaking rapidly and clearly.

She criticized the "survivor syndrome" literature, observing that by emphasizing the psychological difficulties of Holocaust survivors, we have ignored the remarkable range of coping strategies they have adopted. Ornstein wasn't trying to make survivors look nice or make them into heroes or paint a pretty picture. Rather, she wanted the audience to see the Holocaust experience without blinders.

Ornstein talked about the way in which we block emotion and constrict thought in response to trauma. In extreme trauma we become "musclemen," rigid and armored, suppressing our feelings and thoughts—essentially shutting down emotionally in response to overwhelming pain. However, she was interested in the way that these defenses help us get through extreme situations. She spoke of how "disavowal"—a state of extreme emotional detachment—makes survival possible.

Again the pictures of the Jews in line at the camps came to mind, the ones that cause so many of us such shame and self-disgust: the pictures of the Jews marching to the camps, lining up for their own death, and the oddly calm, passive look on their faces even at the moment of their execution—a look that enraged and shamed me. Why did you not fight back? Why did you not scream and yell?

Ornstein pointed out that the capacity to detach might in fact be part of the process of affirming life, not death. Listening, I began to think of this proud seventy-five-year-old woman as "Anna," not Dr. Ornstein. Anna was a teenager when she was in Auschwitz, and she explained the way the prisoners handled the smoke that came from the crematoria as an example of detachment—the "heavy black smoke and the sweet smell of it" in Auschwitz. She said, "We all smelt it but the meaning was disavowed by most of us, though not all. We did it to retain a safe space. We fooled ourselves: 'Oh, something is burning, who knows what?'"

That dumb, numb look on the face of the Jews in so many

photos, standing in line at the camps, waiting to be shot in the Palmiry Forest outside Warsaw, about to be gassed at Auschwitz, waiting for whatever fate dealt them—the look that so enraged Stuart—was not blank passivity; it was a way of trying to survive amid an overwhelming reality, one beyond human imagining.

Anna, who lost her father in the camps, continued to talk to us about detachment, psychology, and survival by describing two different psychological levels of function inside the camps. Prisoners had to devote their attention to (1) the world outside them, to know where the next blows were coming from, as well as where and when to get the bread and water essential to physical survival, and (2) the inside world, to some preservation of an internal sense of the wholeness of the self. How did the Jews in the camps preserve their sense of self and their sense that the world had any meaning and continuity and history? To lose that would be to go mad, making physical survival moot.

The example Anna gave was going to the latrines. "The guards didn't go with us there," so it was something of a play space, if we can think of one in the camps, "and we would engage in little exercises. My mother or one of us would ask, 'Who remembers such and such a character in a novel? How does this poem end?' My mother loved novels and helped us out with questions." In the camps, mothers and daughters talked of poetry and novels, of love and loss. This way of playing was vital—it meant the affirmation and direct transmission of values, tendrils of ambition and hope for the future being kept alive.

Anna talked about the small groups that existed informally in the camps, groups with three or four members, providing a setting where hostility, generosity, caring, and loyalty could be expressed and developed. "We found ways to fight and reconcile and love and hate, with an intensity similar to any family." Dealt nearly the worst hand life could give them, people went on, found ways to keep going with hope.

At the break after Anna's talk, I went out to the lobby to see an exhibition of writing. "Tales of Slavery and Deliverance" is a collection of one- to two-page memoirs written by Anna about her experiences in the camp. Leaning over the display table, I read about the day she got her tattoo. It was given by a young German Jewish girl, well fed, wearing a uniform, whom Anna had watched doing her job on other young girls' arms. Observing closely, Anna could tell that the girl was a skilled tattoo artist, and she would do a really neat, tidy job. To her delight, Anna was right, and on that day she received a clearly numbered tattoo, one she felt good about. It was a joyous day for her: the tattoos meant that they were not going to be killed; giving them a number meant that the Nazis wanted them to live. How ironic that the very act that was meant to dehumanize was interpreted as proof that they would survive.

After the war, of course, Anna's children wanted to know about the tattoo, and she would tell them and they would express sorrow and feel bad about what their mother had gone through, but she writes that she would "apologize to my children but tell them it was a hopeful day."

Instead of the shameful "passivity" many of us attribute to Jewish behavior during the Holocaust, Anna pointed to personal courage and the humanness of the experience, to ways in which people were making meaning and finding strength through experiences that were designed to remove all dignity and traces of humanity. These resourceful people found ways to invest hope and life into the darkest of days. I had inwardly scoffed when one of the conference organizers asserted that listening to Holocaust survivors reminds us of both overwhelming suffering and the overwhelming capacity to survive and procreate, of the fight between death and life within us all that can lead to ways of saying *l'chayim* to life. Thinking of the young girl who finds joy and hope in the selection for a tattooing, I finally understood.

Here is a fundamental Jewish question not adequately addressed either in Holocaust studies or in Jewish education of the young: how in the face of death do we say yes to life? The Holocaust may, fundamentally, be about affirmation, not just remembrance. So often the emphasis in teaching the young is on the suffering and the horror, not on the "yes" in the lives of those who lived through the Holocaust.

The passivity we saw in those pictures and stories existed only in outward behavior. To survive, one had to get along with the SS "and one's Jewish superiors." But there was nothing passive in terms of the state of mind. That was very active: Not to fall asleep in line, or sit down when exhausted. Not to eat all at once a piece of bread that needed to last all day. Here is real heroism despite Jewish suffering. Here is the adaptive capacity to retain hope even in the face of despair.

If many of us carry around distorted images about being Jewish—the image of the corrupted, weak Jew or the noble but defenseless Jew who needs a strong protector (the ultimate seduction of *Schindler's List*) or visions of power and domination as the antidote to victimhood (the Israeli air force, triumphant over all enemies)—then the road to healing does not begin with heroic tales of Jewish resistance or with the power of the Israeli air force but with a more careful look at Holocaust survivors, and a respectful listening to their stories.

If we can understand who they were, maybe we can clarify who we are and feel less resistance to finding a more joyous Judaism in our lives.

Finding a more vibrant Jewish identity is often connected with coming to terms with our fathers and mothers. Fathers are mysteries to their young children, and as adults we may need to try and see them more fully. This can happen in many different ways; it usually involves a deeper understanding of their lives, of what it was like for them to be sons to their fathers, to live through the prewar years, the war years, and the postwar years.

It's a matter of constructing a more coherent narrative in our minds about our fathers as Jewish men. Sometimes details and minor events can mean a lot.

Laura offers a particular dramatic example of learning more as an adult about her father. She is a forty-year-old woman living in Portland who has had a very ambivalent relationship to Judaism, partly based on her parents' conflicting attitudes. They wanted her "to know about Judaism, but then be really a secular Jew." Her mother's negativity toward Judaism was clear; her father, though, seemed oddly distant and unengaged. It was hard for her to read him.

One day, when Laura was in her late thirties, she got a phone call from her father; he told her that he had learned that his brothers were still alive. Laura hadn't known that her father *had* any brothers. Her father had come over from Europe in the 1930s and believed that his two brothers had been lost in the war. But it turned out that they had escaped to Russia and after many years emigrated to Israel, where, again after many years, they reconnected with their American brother. He had never told his daughter or wife about these relatives, locked as he was into sorrow, isolation, and denial.

Then Laura and her parents visited Israel. Laura saw a much more passionate, involved connection to Judaism in her father—and Laura herself began to investigate what Judaism meant to her. Although her mother's hostility to Judaism didn't change, seeing her father's connection led to some internal shifts for Laura. After many years of being "a secular Jew," last year Laura held a seder in her home; she is also experimenting to determine which forms of Jewish worship speak to her.[2]

What of coming to terms with our mothers? Many of us suffered because of overbearing, pushy Jewish mothers. If we were shamed by passive fathers, we were also surely oppressed by Jewish mothers who ruled the roost. It is no accident that many of the communal arrangements of the kibbutz movement (e.g., shared meals and shared child-rearing) originated from the pioneers' desire to get away from confining and stressful family experiences.

Coming to terms with mothers involves seeing them as real people, struggling with their own hopes, fears, and disappointments in life, rather than as impossible heroes or terrifying demons. Jennifer, for example, had for many years stayed away from Jewish life. Although she was raised Jewish, Jennifer's mother had viewed Judaism as an embarrassment—"It was like it was some sort of stain she didn't want to get on her." From an early age, her mother had struggled with her self-esteem; part of the darkness she felt about herself had to do with her very Semitic features, and her equating Jewishness with ugliness. Growing up, Jennifer felt drawn to many aspects of Judaism—the music, the warmth of it—but felt tethered to her mother's antagonism toward it. To be "too Jewish" at home was a risky proposition for Jennifer, threatening to bring scorn or sorrow from her quick-tongued mother. For Jennifer, part of her path was coming to see her aging mother more fully—hearing about her embarrassment at standing out as one of the few Jews in her community, learning about her grandmother's insecurities, which were heaped onto *her* daughter. Jennifer came to feel less dominated by her mother's "wounded" quality, even as she understood it better. Jennifer is today very involved in the musical life of her synagogue, playing the guitar during services and enjoying herself in ways that she wouldn't have predicted when young.

Often we are unable or unwilling to connect directly with our own fathers and mothers. It is also possible to listen to other men and women, and to see the heroism and failure that is embedded in so many of their lives. Dr. Ornstein's talk provided me with the image of a courageous, honest woman.

When a man talks openly and honestly about the struggles in his life with aggression, sorrow, shame, and identity, it is a mitzvah. Sometimes that happens not with our own fathers but listening to other fathers talk honestly about their hopes, fears, and struggles.

I learned this at the same Holocaust conference where Dr. Ornstein spoke. Her presentation was followed by a man talking about shame, anger, and Jewish identity. While he focused on the Holocaust, he spoke to the central tensions in the lives of Jewish men today.

Dr. Maurice Vanderpol is a tall, elegant man who speaks with only a light trace of his native Dutch accent. The title of his talk at the conference was "Survival and Resilience," but in fact he spoke mostly about his teenage experiences in Amsterdam, hiding during the war. After the war he immigrated to this country and became a distinguished psychiatrist and psychoanalyst. His openness and humility made me also think of him by his nickname, Ries, although we had not yet met.

Ries's father, a salesman, was trapped in southern France when the war began and was not reunited with his family until after the war. Ries and his mother and brothers went into hiding, helped by a Dutch Christian woman who had been their housekeeper.

Ries spoke about the humiliation and shame of being seen and treated as nonhuman. When you are hiding in someone's house, depending on them for protection, all avenues of escape are useless. All you have is your imagination. He spoke of the shame he still feels, over fifty years later, at being dependent on a former housekeeper for his life, and he spoke of his guilt at allowing himself to be put in such a passive position.

After the war Ries struggled with the question of whether to continue as a Jew or not. In Holland his family had been very assimilated, snobbish, and both embarrassed by and critical of poor Jews. Yet when he came to America for his education, he wondered about how this country felt about the Jews. "I lost all contact with my family in Amsterdam, I was shocked by the newness here, and was totally focused on making it as a Jew in America." He talked movingly about "the quest for belonging and respect from others." Then he said, in words that may be true of many immigrants, "Who had the energy to take care of the past and present simultaneously?" He didn't think about the Holocaust or his family in Holland and he put off connection to the past amid his desire to be connected to the best, the most prestigious. He earned his undergraduate and medical degrees at Harvard University and became active in the most prestigious psychoanalytic and medical institutions in Boston.

Many years went by, with much career success and little involvement with Judaism, until his sons were in their teens. "I began to tell my family they were Jews, and about my war experience." When his sons were as old as he was during the Holocaust, Ries had to confront parts of himself that he had sealed off in the past. "I got past my phobic avoidance of Judaism and the Holocaust to a deeper integration of self."

Finally, here was a man talking about his inner life, and coming to terms with humiliation. The simple directness of his talk felt like opening a window, letting in the fresh air. Hearing and seeing Anna and Ries, both well-known figures, talking about not only their experiences but also their psychological struggles, their heroism, and their cowardice, was very moving. It was as if members of my own family had finally opened up and talked.

I didn't have any close family members in the camps, but the whole experience of the war and the Holocaust was taboo in my family. My parents, my aunts and uncles, are all very caring, loving people—all of the men were in the service, but even asking about the Holocaust meets a wall of silence. Whenever I bring up the subject, my father looks like he wants to lie down with cold compresses on his head. Neither of my parents has seen *Schindler's List*. When I was a kid, we spent so much time talking about battles in the Pacific at my home; "Victory at Sea" was a favorite show to watch with my dad. Why did we speak so little about the European theatre—was it because it meant thinking about the Jewish experience, and those camps it took so many years to liberate?

For Ries, it was going to see the movie *The Pawnbroker* in the 1960s that cracked things open. Watching Rod Steiger portray a survivor who had repressed all his feelings, Ries felt as if a mirror had been held up to him. He began "an acknowledgment of my Jewish identity that led me to mourn my favorite grandfather, who introduced me to Judaism. There was a fear, which is still true, that if I began to talk of him, I would never stop crying."

If our parents tried to protect us by not talking, we tried to protect them by not asking. And into that silence demons rush. Maybe our fathers can handle their sadness. Maybe we can ask questions and tolerate failure and shame and move past it. Maybe we don't have to protect our fathers so much, and maybe we as Jewish men can also accept sadness, failure, loss, and shame as a part of life, part of what it means to be human—maybe we don't have to spend so much time warding off such feelings by being armored and in control and keeping silent. Much of that shut-down quality haunting men every day comes from fear of talking about our fathers' wounds and hurt and shame.

Ries talked of his guilt and shame for losing contact with his family in Holland, for not protecting his family while his father was away. Hence his emphasis on the "best" achievements and his demand for outward success, goals which are not uncommon among Holocaust survivors.

When Ries's daughter was sixteen years old, the same age as his wife when she entered Terezin, the teenager sat her mother down and said, "You've been through terrible things. I want to know exactly what happened."

The daughter's courage in asking and his wife's in answering must have affected Ries, too, since that was around the time he started to talk more openly with his fifteen-year-old sons, breaking through "the fear of breaking down and embarrassing myself."

As Ries ages, the Holocaust experience shapes his experience as an "elder" in the community. Praise for his work as a psychiatrist carries with it guilt at his personal success after so many died in the Holocaust, a fate he escaped. Yet feelings about dying are mixed up with feelings of persecution: thinking about dying brings with it feelings he remembers about the fear of, at any moment, being selected for the gas chambers if he was caught hiding. (The word *selected* is powerful for children of survivors—one survivor's daughter fainted in medical school when asked to "select" a rat to sacrifice for dissection in her first-year class.)

Ries went on to talk about aggression and being a Jewish male. "The passive acceptance of being protected during the Holocaust didn't help me become male. I went from being a normal, angry, rebellious teenager with healthy aggression to being a recluse. Hiding at first was a defiant act, an aggressive stance. But it evolved into a passive hiding, listening to the Allies on the radio and learning Russian."

Ries also told us about the postwar period when he denied being Jewish, even to himself, and "the rage I felt at Jewish men like my father and grandfather and leading figures of the Jewish world who were ineffective when I needed them. They were not able to show me as men how to survive in a difficult time. I couldn't channel my aggression into fighting and so went into hiding rather than displaying the aggression my father and grandfather said they had showed in dealing with anti-Semitism in individual lives before the war." So the shame was double-edged: his father and grandfather had not lived up (to even their words) and Ries had not lived up to the image they had provided before the war. It was as if the Holocaust punctured his image of masculinity, deflated it, from the strong stories of the prewar fathers to the ineffectuality of these men when they were really needed.

He-brew. So, how do we reclaim a convincing, sturdy, trustworthy sense of our Jewish masculinity? By understanding our fathers' struggles—by paying careful attention to their strength, endurance, nurturance, and struggles to live both with their aggression toward and their caring for those they love. And by finding caring, strong images of Jewish male strength and endurance that we can focus on and carry in our minds.

Ries, in closing his presentation, provided a window onto this process and offered us such an image of how love can be brought down through the generations, even in a family that resists part of its Jewishness. He told a story about Alex, his eight-year-old grandson. One day his grandson asked for a bedtime story, and Ries told the boy that he could have a choice between a story from his grandfather's days as a medical intern in the emergency room, riding an ambulance in New York City during his medical training, or a story about his great-grandfather, whom the family called OpahMo.

The boy, of course, picked the macho ambulance stories. After Ries was done, though, Alex said he wanted to know about OpahMo. Ries told him how before the war he loved to play in the kitchen of his grandparents' apartment, and one day they bought him a little teakettle, which he used to play with endlessly. At his bar mitzvah, his grandparents gave Ries a special present: the teakettle was bronzed, and they had put a red carnation in it. Ries treasured this gift, and hid it from the Nazis under the floorboards of his house. "After the war, I survived and the teakettle survived, but OpahMo did not."

There were a few moments of silence from the then eight-year-old Alex. The boy was not being raised traditionally observant, and he asked, "What's a bar mitzvah?"

Ries explained that a bar mitzvah is a ceremony where a Jewish boy turns thirteen and is considered a man.

"Can you drive?"

"No, but you get lots of presents."

The boy then asked if he could have the teakettle as a present from his grandfather. Ries said he'd think about what he wanted to do with the kettle, now that he was older. After that, Alex invited his grandfather to come into his school class and talk about World War II and the Holocaust.

Now Alex is thirteen and he won't be officially bar mitzvahed, given that the family ambivalence toward Judaism is still alive, but it is a special birthday, and Ries told us, "I've wrapped up the kettle and wrote him a letter about it."

In doing this, Ries is able to keep alive the good memories connected to his grandfather, and to tolerate his love for this figure who also had seemed to fail him at the crucial time, when he was so needed, during the dark days of the war back in Holland. Ries is remembering and connecting, affirming his love despite his sorrow and anger. "The kettle goes back five generations."

Then I thought about recent images of Jewish masculinity. We have the Israeli army and air force, who won't be intimidated by anyone; we have the Jewish motormouth intellectual, filled with chutzpah, who bullies his way verbally through the world; we have billionaire moneymakers who become the power brokers to kings. But where is the image of the nurturant, generative Jewish male who is able to bring his healthy aggression and his loving impulses to bear in his fatherhood and family relationships? Where is the image of the Jewish man who makes the honest effort to find his way through conflicting human impulses of harming versus nurturing those he loves, of denying versus accepting the past, of accepting the failures of those we depend on and loving them nonetheless?

Ries's efforts to give voice to such human struggles was a good start toward such an image, and his willingness to pass the teapot (containing his love for and sorrow about his own grandfather) along now to the younger generation was also a good symbol on which to build up new, trustworthy images of Jewish fatherhood and masculinity: Jewish men able to face their limits, their failure, and their shame, while also feeling alive and connected to past and future generations, life-giving even while acknowledging the darkest side of our experiences.

For many of us who feel uncounted and discontented as Jews, the road to a more vibrant Judaism may not be better Jewish "adult education" or outreach that focuses on convincing us that "it's great to be Jewish" or teaching us the correct way to daven.

Rather, we may need to understand and let go of distorted images of Judaism that were part of our parents' experience, or are our inheritance from family shame and loss connected to being Jewish in the twentieth century.

Judaism as a way of saying *l'chayim* to life? To life in contemporary America? If we're not blindly tied to the past, how do people come up with solutions to the challenge of being a different kind of Jew who is also firmly rooted in Jewish tradition? The next part of the book explores how that happens.

Part Two

*Solutions for Living
in an Assimilated World*

CHAPTER FOUR

Composing and Recomposing Judaism in Our Lives

Judaism is more than a sociological concept or a religious observance; it is a state of mind. Neither group labels (Reform, Reconstructionist, Conservative, even Orthodox, or "assimilated" or "purist") nor the stereotyped markers of being Jewish (how much Hebrew you know, whether you go to synagogue) are able to capture the vitality of Jews today.

We need to stop seeking external behavioral markers of Jewish identity and start understanding how Jews internally construct their sense of "being Jewish" and express that subjective feeling in the world. A much more resilient and flexible picture of what it means to be Jewish can emerge. For many of the uncounted and discontented (even those who are traditionally observant), Judaism is a work in progress.

Identity is rather like a tapestry, a combination of threads woven together, which we each create in a different way. The threads of that tapestry are our treasured and heartfelt experiences, carried forward within us: growing up in a family, being an adult, the *felt* experiences of joy and pain lived with those we love. Some of our experiences we cast away, some we hold on

to. One woman referred to her Jewish identity as a Degas painting—"warm images and colors, not always a clear picture." She
went on to tell me about the importance of her grandfather
singing "Chad Gadya" at Passover seders—a powerful sensory
image that is one thread of her tapestry of Jewish identity.

Anthropologist and educator Mary Catherine Bateson has
pointed out the role of "creative makeshift and improvisation"
in our lives, showing the many "individual efforts to compose a
life, framed by birth and death and carefully pieced together
from disparate elements."[1] What are the disparate elements that
we draw on throughout our lives to "compose" and "recompose" Judaism?

Five elements stand out. There are, first of all, the felt experiences of our childhood, the sensory, bodily, often nonverbal
experiences encoded in our warm, treasured memories of the
songs we sang around the seder table or the feel of a father's tallit in *shul*. Then there are the aspects of our parents and grandparents we carry forward with us into the future. Some qualities
with which we have identified may shift and change as we age.
A third thread in many people's lives is unexpected "tipping"
events that influence us, such as a powerful chance encounter
with a rabbi or the experience of a Jewish summer camp. The
fourth thread is the key adult relationships in our lives and their
influence on us. And the fifth thread consists of the marker
experiences in our adult lives, leading to shifts in our own attitudes and values.

We draw on each of these disparate elements in different
ways throughout our lives. The importance of watching your
mother light the Sabbath candles on Friday night back when
you were seven years old—the magical flicker of the match, the
way the candlelight glowed, the changing tone of your mother's
voice as she quietly said the blessings, the mysterious way her
hands moved to "gather in" the flames—may only be remembered after the arrival of one's own children, watching one's

wife perform the same ancient ceremony. Or a chance encounter with the rabbi in the supermarket, an encouraging comment he makes that affirms who you are, may lead you to again try and reconnect with Judaism, to go to a Friday night service after years away from the synagogue, to find that things have changed dramatically and for the better, since your childhood.

Those who are constantly striking frightening notes about the "survival of Judaism" and want to pack the Hebrew school curriculum with facts and information—making it a heavily cognitive experience—would do well to look at the powerful sensory, bodily experiences of Judaism in the lives of many of us, which can be the seeds for later flowering. Without the sensory, emotional engagement, no amount of cognitive force-feeding will "save" Judaism. Sometimes the bodily, felt experiences of wonderful moments in the synagogue when we were children are at the core of our Jewish identity.

For example, David is fifty-five years old, now an American citizen, born and raised in Argentina by parents who had emigrated from Europe during World War II. Despite the fact that Argentina has a large Jewish population, David's family did not emphasize their Jewishness. They belonged to a synagogue in Buenos Aires, but were not very observant. David recalls that the synagogues were arranged by ethnic origin: Turkish, Spanish, German. "Ours was the German one. The men and women sat separately, so it looked very Orthodox even though it really wasn't." Their synagogue was housed in a wooden building, and "it was a cozy place, down to earth." For David, being Jewish back then felt "like an obligation and that was all." He didn't go to Hebrew school, although he was bar mitzvahed, having been tutored privately by the rabbi.

Secrets and silence about Judaism pervaded David's family life. His parents had made a perilous escape from Nazi Germany and several members of the family who had survived the camps joined them in Argentina. "I have no idea what my parents believed about Judaism. Coming from the Holocaust they must have had a lot to say. Their families both left in the late 1930s, my mother later than my father." His mother was one of the "last-boat-out" émigrés and was lucky to have made it. "But all of that *never* came up." David's aunt (his mother's sister) didn't make it out of Germany and was a survivor of the camps. She stayed with his family for a while after the war. He remembers being fascinated by the tattoo on her arm, but they never talked about it. "It was just avoided. We never had a discussion of what that all meant."

David recalls his mother making fun of the Jews who paid for lavish bar mitzvahs; there was distaste for Jews who chose to "stand out." The harsh experience of escaping the Nazis and emigrating seems to have taken a bigger toll on his mother than on his father. He remembers his mother as critical of very religious Jews who she felt were very dogmatic, and judgmental. In fact, she was confused about her own Jewish identity. "Understanding the mechanics of Judaism was hard as a kid—kosher always seemed so ridiculous; my mother made fun of it. She served ham and cheese in our house, but looked down her nose at people who ate ham in a restaurant. What was that about?"

David's father became a successful businessman in Argentina, and seems to have simply "kept quiet" about Judaism. Whatever ambivalence he felt, he kept to himself. He was accepting and supportive of his son but he operated with a great deal of secrecy—since bribery was part of the business lifestyle in Argentina, much of his business dealings were hidden from his family. There were many shady dealings with money that were taken for granted, but not discussed. As a teenager David was aware of his father's wheeling and dealing, and struggled with what was "moral" and "proper." Although he was close to his father, none of this was discussed. "There was the attitude as well of 'I'm a man and so I don't have to talk about stuff in my family.' That was to get me into a lot of trouble once I married."

However, while David's father didn't talk with him about either Judaism or the moral dilemmas of the business world, there always seemed for David the *possibility* of such conversations. His connection to his father was hopeful.

David entered young adulthood identified within himself as a Jew but he says, "I didn't know what it meant to be Jewish." Eventually David came to America for college and medical school. "When people asked me, I identified myself as a Jew. I didn't feel German, Argentinian, and I knew I was not American. I was most comfortable around other Jews."

He married a woman with a considerable Jewish upbringing, from the Bronx. "She grew up so differently from me. She felt like the whole world was Jewish. She didn't feel like an outsider as a Jew, yet she, too, struggles with Judaism and what she wants from it." His wife, Selena, grew up in a very Jewish environment, speaking Hebrew, attending Hebrew school, and she didn't like the insularity of her "too-Jewish" upbringing. So both husband and wife wrestled with the question of Jewish identity, and what they wanted for their children. "Different growings up, similar questions," David observed.

David's "macho" attitudes have caused him pain in his marriage and in his medical career. Despite ample skill as a surgeon, he struggled in his group practice with his tendency to override others' opinions and to make decisions without consulting other doctors. His continual grousing led the other members of his practice to buy him out when he was forty, "a shocking and painful experience."

When his father died, seven years ago, David's marriage and career nose-dived, and he decided he needed to look more fully at himself and what he wanted from life. He realized that he missed his father very much. "I never quite mourned my father's death for years after he died because I couldn't face it. Today I feel essentially sad because my father is not around. I miss having a father figure in my life. There's nothing I want to ask in particular, just to have the conversations we never had: what kind of conflicts did he have about his wife, his work? We actually were very close and little was unresolved with him, thank goodness, but it would be nice to have that support mechanism."

David sees a connection between the loss of his father and the emerging role of Judaism in his life. After his father's death, David and his wife began to turn back toward Judaism. They "went shopping" by looking at many different synagogues and joined a local one, where they are now very active. His wife had helped lead the way. "What was and still is embarrassing to me is that I don't know the choreography of Judaism." David meant that he didn't know when to stand, when to sit, the order of the prayers, what they mean, what to do if called upon during a service. For many men the feeling of not knowing is doubly humiliating. Since men are "supposed" to know and be able to perform, going back into the synagogue after years away means feeling like both a failed Jew and a failed man. If you're given the honor of being called up to open the ark, what do you do exactly? You don't want to step forward and open it before you should.

"At the temple my wife has helped organize a course called 'Jewish Choreography,' which is all about when do you sit, when do you stand, what to do when called up for an *aliyah*. I don't know any of that and I feel very uncomfortable in the synagogue." Despite his fears, David has become a valued member of his congregation, helping to organize workshops for the Temple Brotherhood, working with the Strategic Planning Committee, and joining the PTA of the Hebrew school that his children attend.

David clearly finds in Judaism the moral curiosity and instruction that he wishes he had gotten from his father. "Judaism for me is about community, about establishing connections, and being able to have a place to go to have discussions and be interactive. To talk about Torah and values—why does it say this at a particular place in the Torah?" His father embodies the *hope* of that guidance, in comparison to his mother who, David recalls, was "harsh, judgmental, and dogmatic." With his mother, "if you questioned things with her, she would either walk out on you or attack you."

Judaism also offers David a way of providing his sons with a "corrected" version of what he got from his father—moral guidance. "My wife and I want to create an environment where we can talk with the boys about values. Say a waiter miscalculates the bill and gives you back ten dollars incorrectly. Do you keep it or return it? If you don't talk about that with your kids, they may think it is OK to keep the money. And Judaism has a lot to say about that!"

At one point I asked David if he ever thought about his parents during synagogue services. He told me, "Sitting next to my father in the synagogue, I remember his furry tallit bag. I'd be next to him, leaning into him. I didn't really know what was going on—I didn't speak the language, but it is a very pleasant, warm memory of being with him." David's father was actually the "safer" parent in his family ("I always felt warmth from my father; I'm still not sure about my mother, I could talk for hours about my relationship with her") and that safeness was expressed through the warm feeling of his father's tallit in synagogue.

David's tapestry of Jewish identity is woven of threads of his wife's prompting, of his childhood *felt* connection to Judaism, and of the marker events of professional struggle and becoming a father. The central point, though, is that at age fifty-five, David's changing relationship to Judaism is built on the remembered feeling of his father's tallit on his cheek, of sitting next to his father in *shul,* and of sitting with the rabbi of his bar mitzvah, who took a special interest in him. Through all the years of his "exile" from Judaism, David's deeply felt childhood experiences were like seedlings waiting to bloom into his adult Jewish identity.

Our childhood sensory memories of Judaism are a key part of the Degas painting that is Jewish identity and can override more negative experiences, blooming—sometimes surprisingly—at any age. In the last chapter, for example, we met Laura, who had struggled a lot with her mother's shame and father's family secrets about Judaism. At age forty Laura was considering what led her back into a more involved relationship with her local synagogue. She realized it was the music. Despite a difficult childhood experience of Judaism, she says, "I did get lots of warm colors and feelings about Judaism." She loved in particular the singing in her childhood temple. Then at college Laura joined Hillel and remembers with great joy and warmth the free-singing, which happened because most of the students there didn't really know the Hebrew. "We did all our services ourselves, and just a few weeks ago it came back to me when I was in temple listening to the cantor's music, which I love, that we did this wonderful, free-form singing in college—it was jazz, completely free-form melodies that we made up either on the spot or ahead of time. I felt liberated and so free, to get up there and sing whatever I wanted without worry about what the notes meant."

Laura was a music major in college so she was used to worrying about the notes in other contexts, but at the Hillel services she let herself go. "In my house I worried about being too spiritual, inviting my mother's scorn, but at the Hillel I could just sing with joy and freedom." This is a great example of the way that sensory, felt aspects of ourselves can become rekindled to become part of the self, part of the mosaic that is Judaism within us. The music, the feel of the tallit, the sound of prayer, and the comfort of a community draw people back, build on childhood memories—and it doesn't take many such memories for a person to reengage with Judaism.

The threads for the Judaism we weave within ourselves come in part from our parents. We also wrestle with identifications with our parents that do not quite fit us anymore. For example,

Sheila, a busy law professor who is taking a sabbatical year to read and reflect, is exploring her commitment to Judaism. She is striving to make a place for the more heartfelt, sensuous parts of herself after a childhood identification of Judaism as a cognitive, argumentative enterprise.

At the hotel restaurant where we met for breakfast to talk about an early draft of this book, Sheila began with a challenge. She told me she had read the manuscript and was angry because I had written too much about "faith." For her, "Judaism is about social action." She proceeded to tell me in detail about the social history of Judaism and the "commitments to political and social reform that are at the core of the Jewish experience."

"Judaism as I learned it," Sheila explained, "was a way of understanding the world. An epistemology, outlook. Faith is about a higher power, which we didn't talk about very much."

Argument was in the air; I felt defensive. What I didn't realize until later was that, in those first few minutes, Sheila was showing me what dinner was like for her as a girl in her family, where meals began with assertions and ended in disputes. The split between Sheila and her family is one of social action versus "faith." Judaism was the lightning rod for this split. Sheila's family came from a radical tradition that abhorred religion. Her parents were political activists—they worked on political campaigns, taught literacy to blacks in the sixties. Her grandfather was arrested doing labor work; her great uncle fought in the Spanish civil war and was a labor organizer. "We celebrated Passover as the suffering of all mankind."

Over our coffees, Sheila confessed, "I do have a spiritual side." In fact, for years she has been exploring and experimenting with different aspects of Judaism. She loves the singing and prayerfulness of the Orthodox community, which she often visits on weekends:

"I was very attracted to the Orthodox in college—hanging out with them, finding the *spirituality* I craved. One Rosh

Hashanah my boyfriend at the time took me to visit an Orthodox community in the Catskills. I have goosebumps still, it was
so intense. I remember the rabbi singing, 'I'm a humble messen-
ger, please don't blame the congregation.' He was crying while
he sang. It was so much about devotion, humility . . . *reverence*."

With the word "reverence" Sheila seemed to finally discover
her own language for talking about Judaism. She stopped talking at this point, almost as if she was shy, hesitant about expressing this part of herself. She went on, "In my tradition there
was no reverence." Then she connected this search to growing
up in her family, where there was a lot of love and connection
but also a sharp distinction in her mind between what felt
"masculine" and "feminine." "In my family, there was no
sacredness—we'd do all these things, my parents were work-
aholics. No one ever stepped back and asked *why?* Everything
is in *doing,* no one was into *being.* There was little joy, everything was so dutiful."

At the dinner table, all the attention went to her brother and
father, who argued all the time. Sheila's mother was their audience. Where was the place for her "girlish, feminine" passions?
She remembered a particularly difficult time in her family.
"Everything in my family always needed to be mediated with
words. . . . My older brother was in high school and he got really
radicalized in the 1960s. It was the worst period of my life.
Every single dinner was an argument, he pushed the envelope in
every way, always arguing and always logical. I would just sit
and eat—that's when I got fat. My aggression went into law
school, being very logical and verbal, like in my family. To be
heard in my family I had to be verbal and logical." Judaism embodied a painful split within Sheila, as to what parts of herself
to express: action, being aggressive, not receptive. The underlying struggle was around her self-image as a female: to be good
enough as a girl meant to be quiet and helpful, but to be really

valued by her father and brother (and, possibly, her mother) meant to be aggressive and assertive.

The argumentative, cognitive approach to Judaism that Sheila remembers in her family reflects a struggle within herself about what is more valued: her logical, rational abilities or her sensual, physical, bodily appetites. "I always felt I didn't fit in with my family—that I was the more passionate, right-brain person. I became a lawyer, but am more sensual and physical than a lot of the people I hang around with!"

Smiling, Sheila remembered a moment during a visit to Israel that captures this more mysterious, hidden part of herself. "It was *Shavuot,* June—I can't even remember what *Shavuot* celebrates but this was back before the beginning of the Intifada. Back then all the Orthodox Jews walked to the Western Wall before the sunrise, everyone walking down the old streets silently. It was like receiving the Ten Commandments. Some secular Jews joined them, too—thousands and thousands came together in the middle of the night, dark, silent, so all you heard was the sounds of people walking, with purpose, not to the death camps but something different, *choosing to be Jewish.* I always need to embody my experience—that's how I felt different from my family who just like to sit and talk. In Jerusalem that night there was the walking."

A few years later, a friendly rabbi provided Sheila the permission to wrestle and struggle with these questions, explaining that he, too, struggled with Judaism, and encouraged her to look at different ways of being Jewish.

Today, Sheila still doesn't go to services very often, but she belly dances and finds in that experience part of the bodily Jewish experience she holds so dear. She has explored modern Jewish mysticism and the role of fertility cults in early Jewish history. She is trying to define a way of being a full-bodied Jewish *woman.* In doing so, of course, Sheila is also building on the passionate parts of her parents—the mother who "adored classical music," the father who loved fiery debate. In recomposing Judaism, Sheila is redefining herself as a Jewish woman who can revel in her body and in her reverent impulses, as well as in her sharp intelligence, skepticism, and debating skills. The threads of Sheila's Jewish identity are akin to the threads we all share and to the struggle to weave together our hearts and our heads, our belief and our skepticism, our minds and our bodies.

In different ways, we all weave our parents into our composition of Judaism. Sometimes we struggle with "divided loyalties": one parent may have been very passionate about Judaism, another less so. For a mother, Judaism might be "superstition," whereas for a father, it might be "a wonderful tradition." I have heard so much struggle from people about conflicting experiences of Judaism with parents that it's amusing to listen to the worries of those who feel "mixed marriages" will lead to the end of Judaism. In the contemporary world of choice and scrambled sex roles, where wives are no longer clones of their husbands' values and husbands do not conform to a single male stereotype, we *all* to some extent come from mixed marriages.

The people we meet and are influenced by as adults are a third thread woven into our Jewish identities. As we saw in David's case, the desire and support of a spouse, for example, can be a "tipping point."

Ronnie's family, for example, had a very ambivalent relationship to Judaism. An overbearing grandfather left Ronnie's father angered by the "dogmatism" of Judaism, and they lived in a part of the country—Texas—that put a premium on assimilation, which left him further estranged from his faith. He changed the family name in the interest of his advancement in his law firm, and at one point toyed with converting to Protestantism. Ronnie's mother was less conflicted, at least in the home. She observed the Sabbath by lighting the Friday night candles and provided Ronnie with a clear sense of being Jewish.

Ronnie went to college with a very subdued sense of Judaism. "I never went to synagogue and there was a Jewish sorority interested in me—ironically, given my father's struggles, they identified me as Jewish because of my name!—but I never even visited it, not even for a party."

After moving to Los Angeles and developing her career as a graphic artist, Ronnie fell in love with Gary, who came from a family with a strong Jewish tradition. His parents were warm and welcoming to Ronnie, and she developed a close relationship to them. Gary wanted a Jewish home, in which their kids would go to Hebrew school and Jewish holidays would be observed in a celebratory fashion. "The warmth of Gary's parents and his enjoyment of the holidays opened up a whole new world to me—I had never realized what a *warm* place Judaism can be," reflected Ronnie. They joined a synagogue, and she has become a member of the board; their children were bar mitzvahed over the past several years. Marrying into a family with a strong sense of Judaism, in which family life is a valued part of that commitment, touched off Ronnie's own longings for a deeper connection to Judaism after her childhood. Building on the happy childhood moments meant that she was able to weave a fuller Jewish identity that tapped into her potential. It's easy to imagine Ronnie falling in love with someone whose childhood and adolescent relationship with Judaism was parallel to her own, which might have meant for Ronnie a very different Jewish identity in adulthood.

The vital moment of happenstance that can shift and redirect our lives is the fourth element in our Jewish identity. A college student who has recently graduated and is struggling to make her identity in the real world moves into a house with a really warm, welcoming group of Jewish roommates, one of whom reaches out to her. As a result, the student begins to attend Hillel more regularly. A father for whom synagogue is synonymous with "dutiful and joyless" drops his son off for Hebrew school one Sunday. He finds bagels and coffee in the vestry and meets another father he has rarely talked with before. Over coffee they talk about how "boring" they find the services and what they wish was there. On the next Sunday they talk again and invite some other friends, and soon there is a Jewish discussion group meeting regularly that will eventually transform this man's experience of worship and influence the direction of the synagogue.

Or, consider Geraldine, a thirty-year-old woman who was raised Catholic but felt spiritually homeless—neither truly happy nor welcome as a woman in the church—who moves into a house with several housemates, one of whom is Jewish. One day there is an accident—Geraldine cuts herself while repairing the wall in her room. The Jewish housemate, a man who happens to be an emergency medical technician, fixes the wound with care and concern. Geraldine wonders if his kindness and trustworthiness might have something to do with his being Jewish. So, she attends a service at a local synagogue, becomes interested in Judaism, takes some adult education classes, and finds herself drawn to the profound moral concern of Judaism, to the richness of the tradition, to the beauty of Hebrew. She talks at length with a friendly local female rabbi about conversion, and eventually decides to do so. A few years later she is a valued and active member of her local synagogue, spiritually homeless no longer. What if she had not moved into that house, and not met the housemate who became the portal into Judaism?

Or, a woman who is a lesbian and not sure about how to fit into Judaism attends synagogue sporadically until one day she is at a local amusement park and sees her rabbi wearing a T-shirt with the inscription "There's One in Every Minyan." That affirmation of gay and lesbian identity provides the welcome she needs to feel at home in her synagogue and to start talking with the rabbi about her spiritual search.

The marker events of life are the fifth thread in Jewish identity. The key events of the life cycle—marriage, birth and aging of our children, aging and death of our parents—become the threads that get woven into our Jewish identity, in different ways for different people.

We experience the major milestones of our lives in our own individual ways, often as a private blend of our hopes, wishes, and fears. Our parents age or die and we want to say all that needs to be said, but what is that? How do we do it? How do we make sense of our relationships with them? We all answer these questions in our own ways, but the rituals and 5,000-year-old traditions of Judaism can provide a means of making sense of life events that we hardly paid attention to when we were younger.

Sidney, for example, compared his relationship to Judaism at age fifty-five to the rafting trip he once took down the Grand Canyon with his wife and teenage children. "We spent a week rafting along the Colorado River through the canyon and when you do that you see time and timelessness. The river has cut a vast swath through layers upon layers of rock—Tapeats Sandstone is 570 million years old, the black Vishnu Schist and pink Zoroaster Granite are about 1.8 billion years old. You float along and feel the enormity of time and of effort and begin to feel comfortingly small and just *a part* of something much larger and vast, of something that makes all your petty human frailties and preoccupations much less important, simply part of the vast flow of life and the universe."

Sidney went on to connect that feeling to Judaism: "It's like the Grand Canyon, 5,000 years of tradition, the time it took to produce it, the wisdom over time." He told me about the peacefulness of saying the mourner's Kaddish for his father, and the wonder of his daughter's bat mitzvah. The role of time in his own life became clearer. "I look on Jewish ritual now in ways I never did when I was younger. When I was a kid, all the rituals were really just sort of boring and things you did because you had to. I think that feeling continued until my own kids began to grow up. And then when my father died. Well, Judaism is a way of connecting and reconnecting the generations." For Sidney, Judaism offers a way to find meaning in the separations and changes that aging brings—through its rituals, it reconnects him to the younger and older generations.

Harvey grew up in Ohio, in the industrial town to which his grandfather had brought his young family from Czechoslovakia before World War II. The family had an active Jewish home, and Harvey was particularly close to his grandfather. Yet for Harvey, being Jewish also marked an uncomfortable difference from his friends, a difference symbolized by his grandfather's strong Czech accent, which contrasted with the Polish accent more common in his community. In high school, Harvey fantasized about not being Jewish, and resisted being bar mitzvahed. In college he felt very much in the grip of "wanting to hide my being Jewish. I really wanted to seem like everyone else." His name didn't "give away that I was Jewish" and he admitted with embarrassment that he joined the campus Newman Center, even at times going to Catholic services. "It *was* a great place to meet girls." Throughout his adolescence and young adulthood, his rebellion against Judaism was part of a process of separating from his family and feeling more like his own man. Then his grandfather died. Harvey began to think more about his love for this person with whom he had spent many wonderful childhood hours. It was to his grandfather's house that he often returned after school, and together they would read the comics or watch TV for a while before his grandfather helped him with his homework. It was his grandfather who had helped him learn the Hebrew for his bar mitzvah. At age forty, Harvey had matured—established himself professionally—and could now acknowledge the gentleness and kindness of both his grandfather and his father and his profound love for the Judaism they embodied. "My grandpa's accent seemed to me to be a sign of his courage—coming over to this country, knowing it was time to leave Czechoslovakia before the disaster happened. If he hadn't done that, I wouldn't be here." The rabbi who officiated at his grandfather's funeral seemed to Harvey an interesting, welcoming man, and he went to talk with him, beginning a series of conversations that have helped him clarify his own Jewish voice.

Two recent, evocative books—*Kaddish* and *The Talmud and the Internet*—underline how loss can lead to taking another look at tradition and observance. In *Kaddish,* Leon Wieseltier's exploration of the deep resonances in Jewish mourning ritual provoked by the death of his father and his resulting yearlong journey of exploration transforms his Jewish experience. Wieseltier found that the thrice-daily recitation of the mourner's Kaddish, faithfully observed, meant that he "could not succeed in insulating the rest of my existence from the impact of this obscure and arduous practice. The symbols were sweeping into everything. A season of sorrow became a season of soul-renovation, for which I was not at all prepared."[2]

In *The Talmud and the Internet,* the death of his beloved grandmother leads Jonathan Rosen into a deep appreciation of the meaning and role of the Talmud after a boyhood in a literary, cosmopolitan Jewish home where "there was no Talmud on my parents' bookshelves, for all the groaning Judaica." Despite Hebrew school and a bar mitzvah, for years he felt "forever a tourist in a place that, weirdly, was the one region where, metaphysically, I was meant to be native."[3] The comfortable life and death at age ninety-four of the grandmother he did know leads Rosen to thoughts of the grandmother he never met, murdered by the Nazis in 1939. These losses raise for him essential questions about his Jewish identity:

When I think about my two grandmothers, I find myself thinking symbolically. Worse, I find myself fearing that these two grandmothers cannot exist simultaneously in the same world, even though I am equally a product of both of them. The world of European calamity that my paternal grandmother represents seems irreconcilable with the lucky life of American ease that my maternal grandmother embodied. How do I inhabit my murdered grandmother's world without losing myself in a tragedy I did not experience? How do I live inside the comfortable life my American-born grandmother bequeathed to me without feeling I am somehow betraying history, ignoring the larger voices of suffering inside?... The Talmud bridged the world of the destroyed Temple and the communities that sprang up in the aftermath of that destruction. Is there a bridge for me?[4]

Profound life experiences lead to recombinations of Jewish identity; as we age and change, so does the Judaism within us.

The Resilience of Jewish Identity

What do we learn from these stories? First, that our relationship to Judaism is a lifelong process of change. Second, that good early memories—even only a few—are bridges back to Judaism for later in our lives. We may return to Judaism guided by positive memories that we build on. Third, that one good relationship with another Jew can have a "tipping effect," leading us toward a new and different relationship with Judaism. It may be a rabbi or a buddy, or it may be a small group of fellow seekers who get together for coffee and bagels and talk on occasional Sunday mornings. Think small—often you can talk more freely and openly, be more honest with each other, in small groups rather than in the large forum of the synagogue or even of a class.

There is a wonderful mystery to how identity shifts and changes, but what stands out is how profoundly people are working on their internal tapestries, weaving childhood moments back into their adult senses of self, linking back to something positive in their Jewish pasts, finding ways to encompass the vital experiences of the present within the fabric of the past.

Most important, different compositions of Judaism can involve a loosening of internal stereotypes and blocks, a greater creativity that comes from being less controlled by childhood cartoon images or fears or resentments. Developing an authentic Jewish voice allows for a new personal creativity and playfulness (a theme explored in many of the chapters that follow).

Rather than being something precarious and easily lost, Judaism is a very resilient component of a person's life. Let's examine the resilience of Jewish identity as it meets the assimilationist challenges of American life today, as embodied by attractions to other faiths and intermarriage.

Chapter Five

Can You Be a Good Jew and Love Handel's *Messiah?*

We live in a multifaith world and come into daily contact with other religions. Can Jews connect to other faiths, even *love* other faiths? For many Jews, profound experiences with Christians have allowed them to find a way back into their own Jewish experiences. Yet Jews often talk of good experiences with Christianity and Christians in an embarrassed way, as if it were taboo.

My friend Jules, for example, is sixty years old, an educator who describes himself as "an ignoramus Jew" because he doesn't read Hebrew very well and doesn't know much about the prayers in the synagogue. He was pivotal in starting a synagogue in the town where he lives, but no longer attends, because he finds the politics oppressive. Yet the depth of his continued connection to Judaism is evidenced by his initial reaction when we began talking. "Oy vey, Judaism—I could talk about that for hours!" After we talked for some time, I asked him, "Have you ever had an important experience with Christianity?"

Jules didn't hesitate. "Oh, yes, yes!"

He told me about his work at the start of his career as a counselor in a youth home run through the New York State Department of Social Services. Jules had been part of a staff of counselors that included a Catholic priest and a Protestant minister. "Most Saturday nights we would be on duty, responsible for making sure that all the kids got back by curfew, and every once in a while one or another of us would have to drive somewhere to get a kid and bring him back to the place. It was like trying to keep track of a houseful of cats. But for large portions of many Saturday nights all was quiet, and the three of us would sit around the table in the kitchen and I'd help the other two write their Sunday sermons and homilies for the following morning. We had great conversations about the good life, and redeeming the world, making a difference, about faith and God."

The tone in Jules's voice as he talked of his interfaith group contrasted dramatically with the tone as he spoke of the synagogue. There was a free flow of goodwill and connection that he had lost, or perhaps never found in Judaism.

As Jews we are much more aware of Christianity as a threat and of the importance of maintaining boundaries. "There has been such an accretion of historical horrors that I couldn't feel good about myself if I said that I was attracted to any part of Christianity," observed one Reform rabbi. And of course he is right—many Christians have throughout history behaved horribly toward Jews. "And many still do, and more will continue to," he added.[1]

But some Jews find a spiritual and religious resonance in other religions that they can bring back into their Judaism. Through Buddhism and Christianity in particular, many Jews have gained an insight into reverence, calm, and faith, and a way of praising the world that they could not find in Judaism. Then they weave what they have learned back into their Judaism.

Jews may use other faiths as ways to grow spiritually without losing their "Jewishness." They may find role models for reverence or spiritual passion that they couldn't find at first as Jews. They may find a quiet and mindfulness that was not present in the noisy, highly verbal world they knew as Jews. Christianity or Buddhism can become a safe "holding environment" in which Jews can work out painful religious experiences from childhood, which allows them ultimately to return to Judaism, as the following stories illustrate.

Edward: Church Music
and Jewish Faith

Edward is thirty years old, handsome and trim, and works as a music teacher in the Chicago public school system. He grew up with a passionate connection to Judaism, but it became muted over the years. "Judaism meant nothing to me for a very long time. When I was young, it meant a great deal."

Edward particularly remembers the power and thrill of his father's loving relationship to Judaism, particularly to the music. "When I was four or five years old, my father went to morning minyan every day. He loved it. Some days he'd take me. I was very proud of him. He was there in his tallit. He was the king. I loved the music; it all seemed so mystical."

Edward's family belonged to a particularly beautiful synagogue, with a special magical quality, "built to evoke Mount Sinai, it just keeps going up to the sky." Edward admired his father's competence in the synagogue. "I loved that my dad knew everything. He put on his uniform for *shul*—his dress-up shirt and pants—and just knew where to go, what to do, whatever was happening in service. I'd think, 'This is my dad and his buddies!' None of my brothers and sisters was interested; it was something special between me and him."

Then Edward and his family encountered difficult times.

First, Hebrew school was a disappointing experience. "In third grade I started Hebrew school. It was awful, a waste of an afternoon. My friend Jeremy brought a little electric clock and he'd put it on his desk and count how much time till we could go home. I'd ask, 'How much time left?' He'd reply, 'You don't want to know.'"

Edward's father struggled with business reverses and began to withdraw from the synagogue he so loved. "After my bar mitzvah, my brothers and sisters—all younger—got virtually no religious education. Judaism just disappeared from my family. My father was having work problems and my parents struggled in their marriage and I think he needed to jettison Judaism just to survive."

Edward's father blamed Judaism for his setbacks in a way that he was never able to clarify to his son. As we talked, Edward and I both wondered if in fact his father withdrew out of shame at feeling like a failure (as a businessman, particularly) in the eyes of the middle- and upper-class congregation in which he had been so prominent. Edward speculated, "This may sound strange, but I suspect my father blamed God for the difficulties in his marriage and in his legal practice. His thinking may not have been very rational, but he may have believed that if he were an observant, committed Jew, he should be rewarded. He may have concluded that it was pointless to continue as an observant, synagogue-going Jew if such commitment had no positive effect on his law practice or his marriage."

Whatever the reason, Edward became a "bar mitzvah dropout." Yet something very important happened at his bar mitzvah: he discovered he could sing. "I didn't know that before. I learned my haftorah part very well, and my family was amazed—they had never heard me sing before." It meant a lot to Edward that his father was impressed. "He said, 'I never heard a bar mitzvah boy daven like that before.'"

The connection between music and Judaism lay dormant in

Edward's life for years. After the bar mitzvah, Judaism played "no role" in his life. "It was an embarrassment. I'd go to Woody Allen movies, and I respected him, but why did he whine all the time? Why would he say that he's a Jew, identify himself in that way, but then present the most horrible, weak, powerless image?" The Woody Allen image of the neurotic Jew may have hit too close to home for a teenager who had watched his father shrink from a confident, vital member of the synagogue to one who struggled at work and had to leave the *shul* because he wasn't doing as well as many of his buddies.

Years went by with little connection with Judaism. Edward pursued his career and continued his interest in music. When he was twenty-eight, something significant happened. "I was looking for a choir to hone my skills and I called friends and found a church choir in a local suburb. It's the best in the area. I called the choir director, who said, 'Yes, Edward, we're a choir and we sing Bach and all but we sing in a religious context.'"

Edward had the good fortune to find a minister who welcomed his interests and also respected his religious heritage. "He knew I was Jewish more than I did!"

Edward told the director that the religious context wouldn't bother him, but after a few months he felt some dissonance. "I realized I didn't fit in in many respects. I could sing Psalms and prayers, but not speak them. The Christian context was too much. One day the minister asked if I could read the prayers at a service and I thought about it and finally said no. He asked why not and I told him that I didn't want to trivialize Christianity—I told him that I took his religion seriously and respected it and didn't want to trivialize it by my (a non-Christian) reading it."

Edward was fortunate to encounter a pastor who didn't trivialize Edward's religious heritage. "At this church there was a pastor, who was very liberal—he stood up for gay rights even under community pressure. After several months I went to see him in his study. We talked for several hours. I told him that coming to the church put me in touch with my Judaism. I had a hunger for what I was missing. I also had some envy: Christianity was so loud and present and the church was so big! Here were people who were not afraid to sing out! Bach, Mozart. I see everything through a music lens. Who have we? Schönberg, Copland, many secular composers."

In this Christian context, Edward was finding the desire to sing out as a Jew and give voice to the Judaism that had become muted as his father's silence took over. One day the pastor asked Edward if he would like to give a talk about Passover at the children's service on Easter. Edward agreed and began to read up on Passover. Harold Kushner's book *To Life,* with its chapter on Jewish-Christian relations, gave some legitimacy to Edward's time in the church. For Edward, it was also powerful, meaningful, to have another man be so open about his love for Judaism. "It was wonderful. The book is a primer by a man who says at age fifty-five, Here is what Judaism means to me. I felt Kushner as a kindred spirit."

Yet it was really around music that Edward found his Jewish voice, and it was Christian music that kindled a process that went beyond Christian themes right into Edward's own experience of Judaism.

"Kushner wasn't enough," Edward told me. "It was still the music. Jewish music in my experience was so disappointing. 'I Have a Little Dreidel' doesn't compete with the Hallelujah chorus. One day I was at Tower Records, looking for Jewish music. I didn't want *klezmer* music, I was looking for something choral. I came across a CD by the Male Choir of the Great Synagogue in Moscow. They're a bunch of cantors and they had made several CDs. Their singing is so spectacular! They were doing what my father and his friends were doing back when I was four or five years old, only better! They sang with confidence, not singing in an apologetic manner, no thin reedy voices 'mumbling in Hebrew faster than I can think in English,' to quote Julius Lester."

Edward had found the equivalent of his wonderful, passionate Jewish experience davening with his father and his buddies in the *shul,* the experience he had lost. Edward told me that the Moscow choir was full of feelings, not like the church choir, which was so serious and heavy. These men were just as passionate as anyone singing the Hallelujah chorus, but the sheer musicality and talent were distinctly Jewish; there was nothing Christian about their style. As a musician himself, Edward strives to be clear about this. "I'm not sure I could define a 'Jewish' choral sound. As musicians, the Moscow choir are as accomplished as some of the best Christian or secular choirs I've ever heard. But there is something in their 'over-the-top' sentimentality, their extreme emotionalism, that, to me, simply sounds Jewish."

His description of their singing echoed his emergent Jewish identity. "The singing didn't have a desperate tone. There was extreme emotionalism but nothing to do with complaining, no masochism or doom and gloom, and it hit me one more time: their emotionalism was presented in such a confident manner. The opposite of the Woody Allen image. I knew Jewish women could do that, but not that Jewish men could. I grew up with a mother and two sisters who are highly intelligent, strong-willed, and confident. I have never had trouble believing that Jewish women could be that way. But I'm only beginning to learn that Jewish men can be that way."

Edward went on to become an active member of a Reconstructionist synagogue, where (surprise!) he is a leading contributor to the musical and choral elements of worship, which are a big part of the worship. In a recent letter, Edward wrote to me, "Yes! I lead Friday night services occasionally (and I want to do much more of that), and I've been hired to conduct the volunteer choir in the High Holiday services this year."

One Hundred Acres:
Christian Contemplation and Jewish Reverence

An encounter with an accepting, non-coercive elder of another faith can have a profound impact. It can allow us to locate within ourselves a place of reverence and devotion, to connect with the grace and majesty of life, which may have not been nurtured in our rush toward adulthood. An elder who respects your path, who may even learn from you, can validate feelings you didn't even know you had and give you a space to explore them. This can launch you back into a trajectory toward Judaism. It is the essence of a transformative dyadic relationship and it can happen with Christians as well as Jews.[2]

I had such an experience when I was a graduate student at Harvard in 1970. It was an intense time to be a student at Harvard (is there ever a relaxed time?): the Vietnam War protests had been heating up, Kent State was on the horizon. And beyond that, Harvard was its usual pressure cooker self, where opinion and winning arguments were at a premium. My then girlfriend and I drove north out of Cambridge toward New Hampshire one snowy winter weekend, not knowing where we would wind up. Over dinner at a country restaurant, we asked a friendly waitress if she knew of any place nearby to stay. "Well, you can try the monastery." She ignored the looks on our faces and made a quick phone call, confirmed that they had room, and gave us directions. We drove miles down a lonely country road and wound up at an isolated old New England farmhouse, welcomed by a barking dog and a young man who assured us the dog was friendly. The place was dark and very quiet. He showed us to our room, and then went to sleep himself.

The next morning I woke up to a sun-filled house where, downstairs, I encountered an elderly man, trim and white-haired, weaving at a loom. It was Father Paul, who had helped start 100 Acres Monastery, coming from Pennsylvania, where he had worked with the Berrigans. He explained to me that yes, indeed, this was a monastery. Several monks lived there, and they supported themselves in a variety of ways—including weaving. They welcomed visitors, and any donations in return for room and board were appreciated. In fact, they often took in people with nowhere else to go in return for contributions to the maintenance of the community.

Over the years I returned at least ten times to 100 Acres, for the quiet it afforded. I stayed in the reconverted barn, where the upstairs had been fashioned into a ring of comfortable, small rooms. In each room were just a writing table, chair, bed, and end table; the walls were painted a soft white, reminiscent of monks' cells, while down below there were thick couches, comfortable chairs, a crackling fireplace, and bookshelves lining the walls. Several times I brought chapters of my doctoral dissertation there to work on.

100 Acres was one of the first places of spiritual quiet and calm I had found as an adult—contrasting at that time with the fast pace of Harvard Square and the constant need to prove myself in graduate school. One day after a Catholic service he had led, Father Paul told me, "The service is like a dance, and I always love doing each of the steps even after almost fifty years." He spoke with such reverence about the details of devotion. It was the first time I had heard someone close to me describe the visceral, bodily meaning of religious ritual. Jewish worship had always felt a chore, distant from me, something I did out of duty, but hardly a dance. If it was, then I was always tangled up in the steps! I was to remember his words when I learned more about the order of prayer in Jewish worship, when I reflected on the meaning of a tallit and yarmulke. 100 Acres was one of the

first places where I felt a connection with quiet and contemplation. Years later, when I ventured back into a synagogue, it was the quiet, calm, and loving connection of 100 Acres that I suspect I was seeking, in a context closer to my own heritage.

Buddhism: Taming the Angry Jewish Voices Within

Buddhism has inspired many Jews who are attracted to a non-materialism and mysticism that is not often found in suburban temples. The Buddhist emphasis on mindfulness and meditation can open us up to a new world within ourselves. It may bring us back to Judaism, especially if the Judaism of our youth is jarring and invasive, silencing the authentic voice within us.

In *The Jew and the Lotus,* Rodger Kamenetz explores how fluid and permeable the boundaries are between Buddhism and Judaism. In a chapter entitled "Buddha's Jews," he shows how many "JuBus"—people who follow a Buddhist practice but were raised Jewish—actually hold on to many parts of their Jewish identity. The late poet Allen Ginsberg, for example, was at the center of the American Buddhist movement and defined himself "as strictly a cultural Jew," yet could "reel off the blessing over bread at the drop of a hat."[3]

For some Jews, such as Ginsberg, Buddhist study becomes the center of their spiritual practice. Leah, a forty-year-old woman, believes that Judaism "is cultural, there is very little spiritual content." Leah's husband finds a great deal of beauty and richness in Judaism, and their children have both been bar mitzvahed, "but for me Judaism is the food and sound and smells, and the holidays with my husband and kids."

Leah grew up in a house with considerable violence, which has forever tinged her experience of Judaism. "My grandfather was a grocer and a cantor, very religious—supposedly—and admired in the community. He had a white robe and yarmulke, he'd go to the Catskills to study and pray, but at home he beat his wife and children. I saw from a very young age the hypocrisy, and it was very difficult."

For Leah, Zen Buddhism offered an experience of spirituality and connectedness that Judaism has never been able to provide. Buddhist practice allows her to "tolerate" synagogue services. "My Buddhism is Zen, which involves daily meditation practice, twice a day, plus about five times a year a retreat with my teacher. It's a formal and strenuous practice and it informs everything I do, including my Judaism. Buddhism gives me a sense of what's holy. It's rare that I go into a synagogue, except for family events such as my niece's bat mitzvah. I don't go on the High Holidays. When I do go, Buddhism helps give me a spiritual frame for what's going on in the synagogue. I transliterate from Buddhism into Judaism." The feeling state that Leah has discovered through her Buddhist practice replaces the harshness she felt in Judaism, the mix of violence and hypocrisy and prayer she knew as a child. "When I see or hear the word 'God' in synagogue, I substitute from my Buddhist practice. I'll tell myself that when the prayer was written that's the best they could do. All the sexism and the patriarchy and the exhortations about defeating all our enemies, and the good-guy-versus-bad-guy stuff. I try to put it into its cultural context, to understand what they were trying to say at the time, thousands of years ago."

Zen meditation has helped Leah find her spiritual experience and center. "What's holy is the visceral, not a visual image. There's a palpable presence or energy I have discovered from Zen meditation, which I assume anyone in any religion or culture would feel. A bodily sense. Zen practice has helped me to feel it. It's very visceral. I'll feel that I'm growing roots out of my tushy when I meditate. I'll feel very rooted to the earth along with the sense that my body is expanding out into the world and that is the same for all beings. That rootedness and felt connection with the world is very precious to me. It's not based on theology, but on my experience. That's why I sit a lot—I felt it in meditation and now I feel it more in my everyday life. For twenty-five years I've been doing it, and I have a long way to go. My measure is my daily life—that I can keep a calm center while my daughter dyes her hair green, or when I'm stuck in a traffic jam on my way to work."

For many Jews, though, Buddhist practice and spirituality lead them back to Judaism. Lynn is a forty-five-year-old mother of three young children, a psychologist, and married to a man who is a "Jewish atheist." Lynn's grandparents barely escaped the Holocaust, coming over from Germany in 1941; they lost many relatives. The Holocaust "makes me want to cry; my mother cries whenever the topic comes up."

Within Lynn's family the sense of loss was very real, although her immediate family survived. The anger and sorrow at what was lost, and the guilt at having survived, resulted in very conflicting signals about being Jewish. "The Jewish piece was more like an Impressionist painting—images and sounds most of all, but not a clear picture."

The family was very assimilated, but her grandparents were quite conversant in the details of Jewish observance. "I remember my grandfather at seders singing 'Dayenu' but nobody ever taught us the meaning of all that. That's the impressionist theme—not clear images but warm colors. I hardly knew what the seders were all about. I just remember people dressed up, flowers, and good music."

In Lynn's own childhood home, there were very few happy sensory impressions. "My mother sent us to a horrible Hebrew school; my brother was bar mitzvahed but just barely; I wasn't and didn't want to be. I wasn't interested, felt it boring. . . . God seemed more weird than sex or money in our house—we never talked about the subject. We went to temple—if I can call it that—on the High Holidays at a community center in town. We belonged to a temple but the High Holidays were in the community center, which was enormous—it was a place where they played basketball games during the year before thousands of people. So that was the Jewish thing with my parents. It was ridiculous."

Yet the powerful sensory memories of her grandparents remained with Lynn. And, in fact, her father continued to hold on to a passionate, suppressed connection to Judaism, which Lynn found out about during her second year in college, away from home. "The first High Holidays there I had gone to a synagogue in town, taken a bus to get there and decided the next year not to bother. Well, I mentioned that and my father threw a fit. I was shocked. We were talking on the phone and I mentioned that I hadn't gone to temple on the High Holidays and my father yelled at me. 'What! This means something! You can't forget your Jewish heritage!' That was a turning point for me. I can still hear him shouting, 'You have to go, you have to go!' In eighteen years he hadn't said anything about God, religion. So after that I went, even though I didn't know why."

The residue of her family's history—the silence, the shouting, the shadowy images—lived within Lynn and meant that Judaism was a place she both couldn't leave and couldn't get comfortable within.

Lynn married a man who thinks of himself as a secular Jew. "He's an atheist, grew up with Christmas trees. There's tension between us as I get more involved these days with Judaism. My mother's really an atheist, too—he and she laugh at me. They keep buying me the book *The Year Mom Got Religion*. My whole family laughs at me!" Lynn reveals, with humor in her own voice. "My mother says to him, 'You should have married an atheist.' My husband says, 'I did—what happened?' "

What happened is that after her grandmother died, Lynn found herself more interested in Judaism and all that was represented by this kind, caring woman in her life. What Lynn did, though, was to explore the meaning of quiet and calm in her life—some of the feelings associated with her grandmother and now found in Eastern approaches. She began to do yoga and Buddhist meditation, finding the peacefulness and calm of these body-centered and mindful practices appealing; they provided her some space to listen to herself and better understand what she was feeling.

Then, something else happened. In part for their children, Lynn and her husband joined a synagogue with a rabbi who could really listen and respond to her. "He's very important, as a role model, because he's an unbelievably kind and helpful person. Always giving classes on Tuesday nights. If there's someone asking dumb questions or is really annoying, he knows how to answer, handle them with grace and compassion."

When I asked Lynn if she prays in temple, she replied, "Not enough, but yes. I go to synagogue once a month, with mixed feelings. Our temple is becoming very big. The bar mitzvahs are such productions. I do love the *devar Torah*. Our rabbi gives out stories and commentary for us to read during the service; then we discuss the material. That's great, but the Hebrew is very discouraging. I tried to learn it but can't."

However, the Buddhist emphasis on meditation is a practice that appeals to Lynn, and finding a version of that within Judaism has been very important to her. She has found a version of Jewish meditation through a different rabbi, one that involves the study of text and meditation on it. "I don't know what prayer is, but meditation is fulfilling. Part of it is being in the rabbi's presence—a power he lends to us. His *shul* is not a fancy place. We sit in a little dinky classroom in a small suburban temple. It's not even pretty! Turn down the lights, sit in the circle, that's all a part—all together, guided meditation through the *S'ferot,* the mystical text of the Kabbalah. Once he talked about losing your ego—getting to this place, I don't even have the vocabulary, I don't know how to speak to you about it! It's about another consciousness—so open and quiet and connected to, I want to say God, but even the words—putting the words to it trivializes it—it's another way of being, on a nonverbal level."

As she spoke, Lynn gave a clear picture of the way that she has found in this form of Judaism some of the richness and color and warmth of the Degas painting that was the Judaism of her childhood. The trip back to Judaism was through yoga and Buddhism, which helped her balance the tensions she experienced about her Jewish heritage.

Rabbis, too, may find that learning about Buddhist practice lends ideas and energy they can take back into Judaism. Rabbi Sheila Peltz Weinberg is the rabbi of the Jewish Community of Amherst congregation in Amherst, Massachusetts. Sheila graduated from the Reconstructionist Rabbinical College in 1986 and was rabbi of a congregation in Philadelphia before moving to Amherst. Sheila has become very active in teaching meditation to Jews and is now a popular presenter at Jewish retreat centers such as Elat Chayyim. She combines feminist and traditional practices in her services and is particularly interested in how to introduce mindfulness into the Jewish context.

When I asked Sheila how she became interested in the intersection of Buddhism and Judaism, she laughed and said that, in fact, she is interested not so much in Buddhism as a religion, as in the practice of mindfulness. "I am interested in meditation. I was first attracted to the idea of silence."

After joining the Amherst community, Sheila felt "mind-tired" and needed a respite from the noise and animation. A former president of the congregation told her about the Insight Meditation Society in Barre, Massachusetts, about fifty minutes away. The Insight Meditation Society operates a retreat center for the intensive practice of insight meditation. Complete silence is maintained during retreats at all times except during teacher interviews.

A year went by before Sheila signed up for a ten-day meditation retreat. "I went for spiritual renewal," Sheila says, and the non-Jewish nature of it was part of the attraction. "I was exhausted from being a teacher all the time in my community, and I wanted some anonymity, to be out of the very public role of the rabbi."

It was Sheila's first experience of meditation for any extended period. "It was very challenging. Really hard to be in my own mind. I saw things about my own mind that frightened me, upset me, things I didn't like about myself."

But the direct, nonauthoritarian nature of the teaching impressed Sheila, particularly the respectful way that the learning was rooted in the students' experience of meditation.

Mindfulness meditation, also called insight or Vipassana, is based on the teachings of the Buddha. It involves focusing on an accessible object, such as your breathing, sounds, or bodily sensations, bringing your attention back to focus as it wanders, paying attention to when you drift away. Joseph Goldstein, one of the founders of the Insight Meditation Society, advises that "at times other objects will arise—physical sensations, thoughts, images, emotions. Notice how all these appearances arise and change in the open awareness of mind. Often we become distracted, lost in the display of experience, no longer mindful. As soon as you remember, come back to the simple state of awareness."[4]

Sheila found the experience difficult at first. "There was a lot of physical pain, sitting for hours and meditating. When you carry tension in your body it manifests in different parts. And I wanted to be a good girl and do it just right."

At night the teachers would talk and pull things together from a Buddhist context and Sheila would "translate it for myself into something Jewish." For example, the Buddhist notions of open awareness and compassion, Sheila could find in Jewish theology because "I would hear the teachings of God as compassion and mercy. The experience of awareness and compassion is an aspect of God. I can personalize it, experience it as being held by the divine. How does the divine work? When we love someone, that is the attention and present, the power and force of really listening. For me, this connects to many of the words and intentions of Jewish prayer.... You don't have to be at a retreat—any time we pay close attention to our experience, it's a spiritual exercise; we become alive or awake."

Sheila found the experience of meditation very powerful. "It allowed me to see my own heart in a new way. It becomes harder to project all your stuff on other people. The silence of meditation allows me to see myself."

Within Buddhism, the mind is seen to breed hatred and desire, constantly creating stories and fantasies. Within Judaism, there is a mystical tradition, which says that we are always fabricating ways of seeing, that we feel separate from the world but are really a part of everything. Sheila quoted the Hasidic saying "Where is God? God is where you let God in."

Mindfulness meditation found a home within Sheila's strong Jewish framework. "The life of the Buddha is interesting, but I didn't need another story of spiritual inquiry or of religion—I already had mine, called Judaism."

In her synagogue services Sheila incorporates mindfulness practice. "In Buddhism there are the sutras, but we have the Torah, and in any Torah portion you can be mindful of its meaning for your experience. The Torah is also just trying to get you to wake up. Take the story of Noah, which we recently read in *shul*—what is it that remains in the midst of turbulence? Your own awareness, the still point of your awareness is that ark, and how can we be mindful of that?" Sheila finds within Judaism the centrality of focusing on the here and now of your experience, not getting lost in the fantasies and desires the mind breeds. "Shabbat is teaching about what *is,* about resting in your experience. Or consider *teshuvah*—return, return to the object of our attention." Returning to the object of our attention is the essential strategy or technique used in meditation.[5] "Ultimately, the clarity of mind and the insights into reality allows wisdom and compassion to arise," Sheila notes.

Over the years, Sheila's exploration of the uses of meditation and silence has expanded, and she has helped to develop workshops and conferences for Jews who have left Judaism, who are involved with Buddhism, and who return to Judaism, working with such fellow teachers as Sylvia Boorstein.[6] In addition, she has developed a meditation retreat for rabbis, using mindfulness training to provide rabbis with techniques and confidence "to see more clearly their connection to all life and to God."

Meditation has become an increasing part of Jewish service. In one large synagogue in New York City, the *Yizkor* service on Yom Kippur always includes a guided meditation in which each congregant is invited to close his or her eyes for ten minutes, locate a loved one who is lost, and "talk to them." One woman who lost her mother as a teenager remembered the profound experience during one such guided meditation of connecting with her mother, truly feeling the longing and loss she had ignored for many years, a recognition that led to several positive steps in her life, including taking greater control of her career. There is an ancient tradition of Jewish meditation and mysticism, in the Kabbalah and elsewhere.[7] Yet for many Jews who carry childhood scars from their Jewish experiences, exploring the Buddhist heritage provides a way of coming to appreciate one's own more fully.

Providing Our Children with a Broader Jewish Identity

Many of us remember helpful and important moments of connection with other faiths. We may remember with fondness decorating other people's Christmas trees, going from house to house singing carols, reveling in the sights, smells, and sounds of being in a cathedral. Many rabbis also have important moments of connection and inspiration with other faiths. One rabbi said to me, comparing an Eastern and a Jewish retreat center, "You know, I'd much rather spend a weekend at the Kripalu Institute than at Elat Chayyim!"

A friend of mine who loves the grand tradition of Western music asked her rabbi a scary question: "Is it OK that I really love Handel's *Messiah*?" His response: "You can enjoy it, but don't believe it." Years later, she reflected to me, "At least he didn't leave me feeling even guiltier." Maybe we can feel less of that guilt, explore our connections with other faiths, and gain appreciation of Christian and Eastern approaches to spirituality.

Consider Steve. His son's public school second-grade teacher insisted on a class project, "Christmas around the world." Steve's son was the only Jewish child in the classroom. When Steve protested, the teacher offered to have the boy sit by himself and read alone during the project time. That was unacceptable, and Steve went to the school principal, feeling as if he was trying to deprive the Christians of Christmas. The principal was "sympathetic" but didn't put his foot down with the offending teacher, so Steve took his son out of school for those several weeks and homeschooled the boy until January. But he felt that the experience colored his son's school year and subsequently transferred his son to a private school, still predominantly Christian, that displayed more sensitivity to issues of diversity among its students.

Later that year Steve and his son were driving through the city square at night and there was a big Christmas tree, ablaze with lights. His son remarked, "Dad, I don't mind Christmas trees in the square."

"Why?" asked the father.

"Because both holidays celebrate light, and I like that in the winter."

"That's exactly right," replied Steve.

The father and son then talked about how both Christian and

Jewish traditions really celebrate the winter solstice, the darkest time of year. They talked about darkness, what it was like for people before electricity, and the joy and hopefulness they might feel as the days lengthened after the solstice. This fear and hope is shared by Jews and Christians everywhere.

"I also told my son about differences: that the lights were in the temple and that if the Maccabees hadn't won, there would be no Jews today."

Steve felt irritated when his son liked the tree so much, but he also recognized the opportunity to talk with his son about bridging differences rather than falling into an "us versus them" mentality.

A key for parents and teachers in the modern world, suggests Jewish educator Joseph Reimer, is to think about how "broad" or "narrow" a Jewish identity we develop instead of how "strong" or "weak."[8] Reimer argues that all world religions, including Judaism, divide the world into good and bad. The question today is how to be "a defined person within a given community" without also "embracing an ideology that divides the world into 'we' versus 'they.'" This is the great gift of Mahatma Gandhi, who at midlife struggled to give up a Western identity and remake himself into an Indian without dehumanizing the West or dividing people into hostile categories.[9]

How do we build toward a more inclusive Jewish identity? A starting point is not only to hold on to our story as Jews, but also to see the validity and importance of other life stories and our connection to them. We are, in other words, all God's children. More open discussion of the connections between Jews and non-Jews might leave many Jews feeling less alone in the synagogue and strengthen Jewish identity, not weaken it.

Strengthening Jewish identity means also to welcome *ourselves* into the Jewish community, to recognize the extraordinary variety of Jewish pathways rather than to split Judaism into an "us versus them" mentality, in which only certain kinds of knowledge and observance are really kosher. Some of the most painful devaluations of Jews come from other Jews, who are very clearly Jewish-identified, but in a narrow sense.

One area where Jewish identity can be strengthened is in interfaith marriages, which is ironic, given that the topic is a nightmare for many traditionally observant Jews.

CHAPTER SIX

Intermarried—and Jewish

There is so much anxiety—I'm tempted to say "hysteria"—about intermarriage among contemporary American Jews that it is difficult to separate the reality from the fantasy. Intermarriage may, in fact, be a source of strength for Judaism. It can make real contributions to the spiritual lives of the partners, and it can certainly result in a strong Jewish identity among their children.

American Jews have come to tolerate intermarriage but not to embrace it. In the years since 1987, when Paul and Rachel Cowan published their thoughtful and encouraging book, *Mixed Blessings,* intermarriage has become ever more common. Many synagogues have a large proportion of intermarried couples, and it's not unusual for board members and presidents of synagogues to be in interfaith marriages.[1] Yet the undercurrent of discomfort that the Cowans address in their concluding chapter remains: "As a whole the Jewish community has not yet decided whether to treat interfaith couples as problems or people."[2] In discussions about marriage and the future of Judaism, too often the "intermarried" or the "outmarried" become faceless symbols of Jewish anxiety, fear, and ambivalence about assimilation.

Intermarriage presses on the most primal of human concerns: personal and cultural continuity. When a child marries outside his or her faith, parents can experience the loss of an imagined future in which the children and grandchildren are part of an unbroken line stretching back in time. The parents may feel agony and self-reproach: *What did I do wrong? How will the children be raised? How can I hold on to my child and be loyal to my heritage?*

"Nothing is whole / that is not first rent / and out of the torn / we make whole again," Marcia Falk writes in her alternative Aleynu.[3] From the tear that an intermarriage brings, I believe wholeness can come—for the spouses, for their families, and for Judaism. If we can see intermarriage clearly, beyond the stereotypes, guilt, and shame, we can find the answer to cultural continuity.

Those of us who are intermarried often feel apologetic or embarrassed among other couples (the really Jewish families) in the synagogue. Reform Judaism has left the matter up to the individual rabbi, but many Reform rabbis will not perform interfaith marriages. In one large study, fewer than half the Reform and Reconstructionist rabbis interviewed indicated that they would officiate at an intermarriage (48 percent of Reform and 38 percent of Reconstructionist). Of the total group of 710 respondents, 14 percent would neither officiate nor refer the couple to another rabbi.[4] A Conservative rabbi can lose his or her membership in the Rabbinical Assembly for officiating at an interfaith marriage. The dire intermarriage statistics from Jewish agencies continue to predict the end of Judaism in America.

What these statistics cannot count are the numerous interfaith couples who raise their children Jewish and the many others who provide their children with a profound sense of being part of the Jewish tradition. For example, among the five men and women in my small monthly Jewish discussion group, four have spouses who are not Jewish. In three of those marriages, all of the children—a total of five—have been bar or bat mitzvahed. In the fourth, the daughter has attended Hebrew school and has told her mother that she plans to raise her own children Jewish, even though there was no bat mitzvah.

Perhaps intermarriage is not the impediment to the survival of Judaism it is billed to be. In fact, I have seen many intermarriages that are a source of strength, both for families and for Judaism itself, giving children a rich sense of the possibilities of faith and belief in the world. Interfaith marriages make demands on both parents and children and can be "a confusing, frustrating experience at times," as one Jewish man, raised by a Jewish mother and Catholic father, put it. However, *all* relationships can be confusing and frustrating; the real difficulties should not be whitewashed, but neither should they be taken as terminal diseases.[5] In fact, interfaith marriages often can be a way *back into* Judaism for spouses who have had ambivalent or broken relationships to our faith. And non-Jewish spouses can be adept at helping raise a Jewish child, participating fully in Judaism without converting.

The key is how much as parents we are able to enter into our children's struggles with faith. Wrestling with Jewish identity is not something that occurs only among children; adults, too, struggle to determine which rituals and observances and beliefs really matter to them. There is often a parallel process that goes on between parents and children, each struggling to find a trustworthy, authentic Jewish voice. There are many opportunities for parents and children to engage in rich dialogue about the meaning of belief, tradition, and ritual. The parents' willingness to support *and participate in* the questioning and uncertainty and discovery that interfaith marriage brings with it can be the bedrock upon which a child's Jewish identity rests.

In intermarried families, both spouses at some point confront again the developmental issues around separation from their parents that were alive at the time they chose to enter into the marriage. Often that moment arrives when the children are born. How the Jewish member of the marriage handles the return of that ambivalence and his or her own resistance to Judaism shapes what happens to the children.

Some of the most lively, juicy conversations I've had about Judaism have been with interfaith couples, many of whom are actively engaged with Judaism—in large part because they've *chosen* Judaism, rather than simply dutifully following age-old family patterns.

Arthur and Ada:
"You Have to Let Your Children Lead You"

Sitting with Arthur Cohen and Ada DeWolf in the comfortable living room of their home in Bridgton, Maine, is a pleasant experience. They enjoy conversation, are good hosts, and are clearly happily married. Arthur and Ada are the parents of Barbara, bat mitzvahed three years ago, and Selena, who looks forward to her bat mitzvah in a few years. Arthur is a high school biology teacher and Ada is a third-grade teacher.

There was an informality and give-and-take to our conversation. I've known them for years and enjoyed the chance to get to know more about their marriage and the decision to raise their children Jewish.

When we began, Arthur suggested that the stereotype of Jewish men marrying non-Jewish women to escape their Jewish mothers didn't seem to characterize him. His mother, Arthur advised, was not "suffocating." Ada then added, "No, but your father was." As is true for many men, Arthur's struggle to find his Jewish voice is connected to his wavering loyalties to his father.

To Arthur, marrying a Jew didn't seem particularly important to his parents. Raised in New York City by two Jewish parents who emphasized an Ethical Culture value system,[6] Arthur remembers considerable putting down of Judaism as a religion. He rarely went to synagogue. His father, who was brought up in a liberal Jewish home and bar mitzvahed, had a vitriolic and sarcastic attitude toward religion, which he saw as superstitious and politically unsophisticated. "What was valued in my childhood was diversity—part of my values and my family was not to think about Judaism in a narrow way as 'the chosen people,' but to connect to people as people." He concluded, "My marrying a non-Jew was not a rebellion, but a more neutral choice in terms of religion."

Ada, too, came from a background that was relatively hostile toward institutionalized religion. Her mother was raised as a Mormon, and Ada remembers stories about her great-grandmother traveling from Kentucky to Utah in the mid-1800s pushing a handcart, "a real connection to the pioneer spirit of the Mormons." Mormonism didn't "take" for Ada's mother, who eventually moved back East and married a Protestant man who was not very religious. They decided to raise their children without religion. "Growing up, I heard a lot about how religions were poison, brainwashing, indoctrination." Ada remembers celebrating lackluster Christmases, and "Easter ended by the time I was ten." She has no memories of ever attending church with her parents. "Christmas felt very materialistic—there was no family tradition of people getting together. It was just Santa and the tree and some presents—all our attention was focused on the gifts; very little on each other and our family being together."

Arthur eventually moved up to Maine, where he and Ada met and married. Prior to marrying, Arthur remembered an awakening interest in Jewish holidays and in reading about Jewish history. "I was keenly aware that wherever I lived—even in rural Maine—the people I'd connect with were those the most like New York Jews." However, "I really didn't start thinking about *being* Jewish until I got married." But it became serious after their first child, Barbara, was born. At Ada's suggestion, they celebrated Chanukah for the first time when their daughter was two.

Why Chanukah, why Judaism? As in many interfaith families, the impetus for the Jewish exploration came from the non-Jewish spouse, and again as is often the case, from the mother. That the arrival of children is the goad for interfaith couples to struggle with religious belief is a truism (in dramatic fashion, the Cowans call parenting one of the "time bombs" in interfaith marriages), but for many couples, parenting causes their own spiritual struggles to begin again, after a period of dormancy. For Arthur and Ada, Chanukah was a good way of testing the Jewish waters, because it is so strongly family-centered.

Arthur remembered that when he was a child, his family did not celebrate Chanukah; they celebrated Christmas and exchanged presents (although he does not remember a tree in the house).

And so, Arthur and Ada did celebrate Christmas for a while, but the experience made him cringe. Arthur would do household chores and pay bills on Christmas Day. Soon after his marriage began, Arthur realized his strong Jewish identification. When he became a father, resonant memories of his childhood experiences became more available to him. Arthur remembered the hours he spent in his grandfather's delicatessen, the wonderful smells and sounds, the stories his father told of being a delivery boy there, the conversations with the colorful waiters and waitresses. He remembered the Passover seders, which his uncles officiated and his parents enjoyed, despite their reservations. He recalled the strong "Jewishness" of growing up in New York City, the arguments and disputes around the dinner table, the kosher delicatessens he loved, and even the family meals at a local Chinese restaurant and "the Jewishness of those meals," where his family seemed the loudest, most argumentative (his childhood embarrassment became a source of pride).

"Having lived in Maine for fourteen years, I thought of my-self as a hip, alternative lifestyle kind of guy, not particularly connected to Judaism, but then things changed. Even so far re-moved from New York City and Jewish culture, whenever vis-iting I had the feeling of comfort, of belonging and the sense of place. One semester after we married, I went to NYU for some advanced teacher training and the school closed on the High Holidays. I thought to myself, 'Oh my god, this is wonderful.' I realized I had missed that, and it seemed like I had come home. A tribal sense of belonging. It was a very powerful emo-tional connection to my ancient faith and history, not an intel-lectual one."

So when Ada suggested Chanukah, Arthur responded, de-spite his ambivalence. Luckily, they started at the same point in their explorations of Judaism. Arthur "knew little" about Chanukah, as did Ada. "We were on an even keel."

Ada was attracted to Judaism and enjoys it still, although she has never converted. "My memories of Christmas were so un-happy, and Judaism felt very warm and intellectually stimulat-ing. Growing up, the absence of religion was not a big deal for me, but what *was* hard was the undercurrent of the absence of relationships—my parents didn't have lots of friends who'd come over and do things. It wasn't an ethic of the family doing things as a group."

The Jewish ethic of family appealed to Ada. Both laughed when remembering one of the first Passover seders Ada attended with Arthur's family; every child was paraded in front of the adults and performed in some way, whether it was playing the violin or reciting Hebrew or reading from the Haggadah. Ada confessed to being a "bit nauseated" by the way the children were put center stage in Jewish families. But the accompanying warmth and demonstrativeness of Arthur's family eventually won over Ada.

She also found an intellectual stimulation that was missing in her life, and she offered a teacher's view of Judaism: "It has so many interesting stories about interesting issues. Look at the Passover meal—how well suited it is for exploring ethical issues within the family. There's no analogue in Christianity—there's nothing more interesting than the story of Christ, but do many Christians at home talk of the resurrection and its meaning in the same way that Jewish families explore the meaning of the Exodus, slavery, and liberation? I doubt it. Maybe in church, but not at home."

In Ada, Arthur also found a loving ally in his struggle to find his own Jewish voice, distinct from that of his father. She described how she "would get pissed off at my father-in-law's controlling behavior. I'd tell him to shut up." She did this in a caring way that didn't create antagonisms in the family; in fact, her willingness to stand up for ritual and faith became an inspiration to Arthur, who clearly appreciated his wife's defending him against his father's criticism. Never before had someone validated those feelings. Ada helped him create a "safe space" within which to explore his spiritual side.

Arthur and Ada's religious evolution might have stayed at that level, except for two things: "our kids led us," and they encountered a rabbi who welcomed their explorations and encouraged their participation in the synagogue. Ada remembered being very interested in her older daughter's efforts to look deeply at life, "her take on God, the world, death. She would really talk to me about these things and she'd really put it out there. 'Why did our hamster die? Where do dead animals go? Where do people go when they die?' I was paying real attention because I felt that was so lacking in my own childhood."

For Arthur, though, his very lack of spiritual answers to his own questions made it harder to focus on his daughter. "It was embarrassing not to have the answers. As a parent, I'm supposed to know, but it felt like I was good at teasing out their questions, but then didn't have the answers." So, what Ada and

Arthur did was to encourage their children to think and learn for themselves, and for their parents. "But the kids led us—first our youngest, then our oldest." Both children told their parents that they wanted to go to Hebrew school. This upset Arthur, who had never been to Jewish service, "except for some bar mitzvahs of friends back when I was thirteen."

A fortunate thing happened—the local rabbi and his wife put their kids in the play group that Ada started when their younger daughter was one year old. Arthur and Ada got to know the rabbi socially, and eventually he put together an interfaith group at the synagogue, which he invited them to join.

The group changed their relationship to Judaism. It brought together eight couples, husbands and wives from their community. Arthur recalled, "The group had a tremendous impact on me—it was a wonderful group of people, and the discussions were far-reaching, beyond interfaith and Judaism, to talking about how we grew up, what we wanted from life, our careers and marriages, parenting issues. It was through the group that I realized my primal connection to Judaism. I felt myself connected to thousands of years of Jewish history."

The group was another safe place where Arthur could explore his ambivalence about Judaism and see that people he respected shared his mixed feelings of uncertainty, incompetence, and attraction. He could admit to uncertainty and not feel too ashamed; he could get some answers, but not feel too inept, and he could feel OK as a man exploring spirituality.

The group helped Ada understand her own spiritual struggles and Arthur's. "In the group I realized how hard it was for Arthur to celebrate Easter or Christmas and not hard for me to celebrate Jewish holidays. He had always been part of the minority in this country and has had Christian symbols thrown in his face, rituals he doesn't feel a part of. No wonder he'd walk away from the Christmas tree after an hour and start paying bills! I had grown up as part of a majority in this country and I think that makes it easier for me to embrace Judaism. I just don't have that much baggage."

When their younger daughter, Selena, was in elementary school, she said she wanted to attend Hebrew school, and on the way home from a cousin's bar mitzvah said she wanted to have one when she was thirteen. Both children enrolled in Hebrew school.

When Barbara was in fourth grade, she asked if they could stop having a Christmas tree and celebrating Christmas altogether, a request that was fine with her parents. She told them, "It is cheating to have a tree, wanting it both ways."

Selena, though, didn't want to stop. So Arthur and Ada offered their youngest daughter a compromise. She could pick two of the things the family used to do: having a Christmas tree, having "big" presents under the tree, or having stockings with little presents. Selena decided that year she wanted the tree and stockings, and to leave out the big presents. The next year, she could choose one thing, and she chose the stockings but no tree. The next year they didn't celebrate Christmas, and they haven't since.

Clearly, non-Jewish wives can raise Jewish-identified children. Frequently, in fact, it is the woman who pushes for some attention to religion. Arthur and Ada both mentioned a prominent doctor and his wife with whom they are friends. He's Jewish; she's not. "Do you celebrate Passover?" Arthur asked him one day. "Yes," his friend replied, "but Mary really makes me do it."

Many fathers absent themselves from a more vital religious dialogue with their children because they are ashamed of not knowing and of their ambivalence. A rabbi once remarked to me that many fathers in interfaith marriages don't come to temple, despite raising kids Jewish, because they can't admit that they—smart, successful professional types—can't read Hebrew, don't know their Jewish history. The rabbi, a woman, observed wryly, "It's more appropriate for the mothers to come to temple or church and not know—that's been women's role in organized religion for generations."

Coming to terms with the spiritual issues in an interfaith marriage is part of becoming an adult. Arthur felt himself stretched in this way by his older daughter's bat mitzvah. "I had such ambivalence, so many worries about pleasing other people, my father a lot, I suppose, and what if I couldn't? Two weeks before her bat mitzvah, I was furious at Barbara—she was not doing the speeches well enough. I looked at my anger and admitted to myself that I was angry because my parents would have been angry—they would have put that kind of pressure on me. And I felt that I had to relate to people in ways different from before, to take responsibility in all the ways that I shirked. It was my coming out as much as hers. I had to give a speech to my daughter at the bat mitzvah, I had to take responsibility for the food, I had to say something at the party, really being present—I was declaring myself to the world as a Jew and as an adult."

Arthur's father did berate his son when he spent more time in synagogue: "How can you go in there and do that stuff, the davening? Have you ever read what they're saying? Do you believe that stuff?"

And Arthur made clear to me that he still was "somewhat repulsed" by a lot of what happens in services. He particularly dislikes the constant references to "Our Lord" and to a masculine god who sits in judgment of mankind. What drew Arthur back into the synagogue was the sense of community, the strong ethical stance of his synagogue (Arthur helped organize an event in which a Palestinian lecturer came to the synagogue to talk about the Israeli-Arab peace talks, along with a presenter from the Israeli embassy), and most of all the desire for a personal community of dialogue and interaction. "I most like to feel like we can talk in our synagogue and express what these symbols and rituals mean to us as people." He feels now that "you can be an observant Jew without a definite belief in a personified god."

Sociologist and religious observer Robert Bellah cautions that interfaith marriages can result in children having an "ambiguous" religious identity.[7] Yet listening to Arthur and Ada and their children, I sense the vitality of people wrestling with freedom, choice, and authenticity. Arthur says, "Part of me wishes I was just brought up well versed in Judaism, without doubts, and that I married a Jewish woman, and it'd all be cohesive. I worry sometimes I just school my children in ambivalence."

"Which might not be the worst thing in the world!" I replied. Arthur laughed and said, "Even if I was brought up in an observant, Conservative family, it'd be similar. I am who I am."

Barbara, the older daughter, has said that she wishes her parents had always gone to services ("you guys just told us to go"), because then "we wouldn't have the burden of making the decisions." But is that such a bad thing—to help your children understand that adults are constantly making choices? That living as an adult means wrestling with ambiguity and uncertainty and making choices nonetheless, without easy answers? That these days we are all "Jews by choice"?

I once sat next to a sixteen-year-old girl at a friend's seder. Her father is Episcopalian, her mother Jewish. We discussed Judaism and Christianity. Smart and engaged, she knew a lot about both faiths. "Do you think of yourself as one or the other?" I asked. She replied, "I haven't decided yet. It feels good not to have too much pressure and see what these different religions are like." She was clearly not caught between her parents and felt the gift of being able to "try on" faiths and to explore what they meant for her. She will have the space to sort out what she feels and to make her choice an authentic one for that time in her life.

Of course, not all children at all ages appreciate ambiguity. The key is to not leave your children to struggle on their own.

For Ada, it was crucial to listen to the kids and what they were really saying they wanted. She and Arthur let the kids "push us into stuff we were not familiar with, but then we took charge of it. Once they chose, we had standards—you have to go and do the work. Each year they had a choice about Hebrew school. But if their choice was to go then they had to meet our standards." She admits, "It's a dicey line, letting them lead and then setting the standards."

Arthur and Ada put in a lot of effort to make sure that Judaism and spirituality are a family matter and not just another after-school chore, and they have brought it into their home, as well. They've had Passover seders for the past ten years, using a familiar family Haggadah and with the same guests and the same traditions.

Tom and Yvette:
"Judaism Speaks to the Buddhist in Us"

As I sat at Tom and Yvette's daughter Emily's bat mitzvah, listening to her chant her Torah and haftorah portions so confidently, her thoughtful *devar Torah* explaining what the passage meant to her, closing it all out by playing the saxophone, followed by her younger brother Josh leading the congregation in a version of Adon Olom, I marveled at what a journey Tom and Yvette had been on, and how the family—led by Emily, really—arrived at this wonderful event.

When I first met Yvette, she was angry at Judaism—its patriarchy, austerity, and lack of compassion. She was much more attracted to Buddhism (still is), despite having been raised Orthodox. When she was a young girl, the tragic, too early, accidental death of her father, with whom she was very close, left Yvette angry at God.

Yvette's husband, Tom, was raised Catholic by his mother. His father was an atheist who was hostile to organized religion.

"The way they saved their marriage was that we could be raised Catholic but not participate in Sunday school. At age sixteen we were to decide, and I remember my father saying, 'Maybe they'll know better by that age.'" One of Tom's sisters is a Catholic nun in Brazil, another sister converted to Mormonism, and Tom follows the Buddhist path. Tom's elderly mother was too ill to attend Emily's bat mitzvah, but she wrote a loving, encouraging letter that was read aloud to the congregation by Emily's aunt. It begins, "Here I sit, the Catholic grandmother, writing a letter to be sent to my Mormon daughter to bring to my Buddhist son's Jewish daughter's bat mitzvah. Who would have thought it!"

Who indeed? Yet out of this soup of religious seeking emerged a Jewish daughter. How did this happen? When Tom and Yvette first met, at a Halloween party in 1983, they spent hours talking about religion—Buddhism. Tom, a mathematics teacher, had spent time in the Peace Corps in Nepal and was following Theravada Buddhism, a very strict, orthodox form of Buddhism. Yvette was at that time a follower of the Tibetan teacher Chögyam Trungpa, centered at the Naropa Institute in Boulder, Colorado, who offered a more expressive, Reform-minded form. "We had an interfaith Buddhist relationship in the beginning!" Yvette joked.

In the early years of their relationship, Buddhist meditation and study formed the core of their spiritual practice. However, for both Tom and Yvette, "the religion question" was not settled.

One year Yvette gave Tom a Christmas present of a weekend retreat at a progressive Catholic monastery in New England. While showing the new guest around, the brother escorting Tom mentioned, "This is the room where we have services for all who want to attend." He added, "During Eucharist, everybody moves up to the altar." *"Everybody?"* Tom asked, explaining that he was no longer Catholic. "Sure," the brother replied. With tension in his throat, Tom went on. "I'm not Catholic anymore, but I would like to receive communion. Would that be OK?" The brother replied, "That's between you and God. You are welcome here." At that point, Tom started to cry. At communion, Tom found himself crying again. There was a warmth and connection for him in Christianity that he missed in the more impersonal Buddhist practice he still valued. "I had been very cut off, and felt at that communion like I was getting family back into my life." He remembered from his Peace Corps days that in Hinduism there is a clear love of other faiths, with the clarity that there are many ways to express your spirituality. Exposure to Hinduism led to the study of Buddhism. "Having found Buddhism, I felt now that I didn't have to give up Christianity."

Yvette, on her own spiritual path, disliked the "claustrophobic" Judaism of her childhood. Her parents were Holocaust survivors, and she observed, "I was so rebellious—I wanted to prove that just because my parents were Holocaust survivors, it didn't affect me. I went to a small college in the Midwest, where I was the 'token Jew.'"

Before meeting Tom, Yvette went to social work school and took a new course that was being offered for the first time: "Social Work Intervention with Survivors of the Holocaust." In families of Holocaust survivors, she learned, one of two things happens: "you either talk about the Holocaust all the time or you never talk about it." In her family, no one ever talked about the Holocaust, "but it was always present"—the fear of the outside world, the use of guilt as a childrearing technique ("How can you do this to us after all we've been through?").

Reading about the lives and families of Holocaust survivors, Yvette realized that much of what had happened to her had happened to other families. She no longer felt alone. At dinner one night, her mother asked how school was going and Yvette told her she was taking a course on the Holocaust. "I waited nervously for her reaction. There was silence." Then, shyly, her mother said, "Well, if it'll help your education, I'd be willing to tell you about some of my experiences." So mother and grown daughter talked for the first time about her mother's experiences in the underground in France during World War II and her father's experiences in a concentration camp.[8] Yvette's mother has since become a speaker for Jewish organizations, and her videotaped interview is in the archives of the United States Memorial Holocaust Museum.

So, Tom and Yvette were each finding ways to make some peace with painful or cutoff parts of their religions of origin, and they were supporting each other in the process.

Still, in the first few years after the birth of their daughter, Emily, and then of their son, Josh, there was little Jewish experience. Tom and Yvette helped start a small Buddhist meditation group in their town—on the third Sunday of each month, a family potluck followed meditation, and the parents paid attention to all the children's spiritual education; there would be a grace of some sort and a ritual such as bringing dirt from the local park into the family backyard and planting seeds. Tom and Yvette also explored the local Unitarian church, an experience their young children resisted. The family eventually stopped attending, not feeling spiritually nourished by it. They have continued an annual tradition of an Easter egg hunt with four or five close neighboring families, followed by a brunch.

However, from the time she was very young, their daughter, Emily, would not let the issue of religion drop. "When she was four years old, Emily asked me one day, 'Mommy, what am I?' Confused, I asked her what she meant. She mentioned several friends: 'Well, Elena is Catholic and Selena is Jewish. What am I?' I gave her what I thought was a perfectly reasonable explanation: 'Well, Dad was raised Catholic and I was raised Jewish and now we are Buddhists. We want you to know about many faiths. When you're older, then you can decide.'"

Emily replied, "OK, but what *am* I?"

At age four the young child needed a concrete, here-and-now answer, not an abstract explanation or one that talked about "later." Emily was doing work on her own, though. When she was eleven, from the backseat of the car one day she asked a question:

"Mom, could I check out Sunday school?"

Her heart in her throat, Yvette asked, "Which one?" worrying that her daughter had the local Catholic church on her mind.

"Synagogue, of course!" Emily laughed.

Emily had had very little exposure to Judaism for the first ten years of her life, although she had been to three or four seders at a neighbor's home. Her maternal grandmother, who had come over in 1944, played a big role in her life. Emily loved to sit and talk with her grandmother whenever she visited. Then as she got older, Emily went to the bar and bat mitzvahs of several older cousins. And she had several friends in the Sunday school of the synagogue. At her bat mitzvah, Emily explained, "Talking in the kitchen one day to my friends Emily and Rachel, and hearing about how much they enjoyed Hebrew school, all they did there, made me want to attend."

For Yvette, Emily's desire was a source of great pride, and also some conflict. Frankly, she loved the idea that her daughter would accentuate the Jewish part of herself but she also was aware that she and Tom had agreed that their children would make no decisions until they were older. And she wasn't sure how she herself would handle the idea of participating more in a synagogue. She had three reactions: "Damn it!" "Wow!" and "Oy vey!"

Yvette went home that day and told Tom that "we need to talk." Although Tom was not at all drawn to Judaism (finding it "preoccupied with the letter of the law, a lot of nit-picking about how you do this or that, rather than the spirit of things"), he also knew that he would never stand in the way of Emily's spiritual explorations, just as his parents, particularly his father, had not stood in his way.

Deep down, for Tom, as many non-Jewish parents, this decision produced several different kinds of anxiety. He worried about his daughter confronting anti-Semitism in her life if she emphasized her Jewishness. He also had to do a gut check as to what kind of anti-Semitism he harbored within himself. As he returned to his Buddhist practice, where he learned to breathe in and lean into his fears rather than flee them, Tom also connected with a deep fear of losing his family. One day he said to Yvette, "What if Emily decided to identify as Jewish and Josh followed and then the three of you shared in that experience—how would that impact on us as a family if the three of you share something that I'm not interested in?"

The fear of loss—that a beloved child would be swallowed up by Judaism and separated from the non-Jewish parent—can be a profound source of resistance in interfaith marriages.

Tom and Yvette managed their fears by learning more about Judaism and staying connected as their daughter explored this part of herself. When they interviewed the local rabbi, they were pleased to find that her approach to spirituality was similar to their own.

"She listened carefully and respectfully to my concerns that religion was really indoctrination and that at age thirteen, Emily was really too young to decide about these matters," Tom remembered. "When I finished, the rabbi said she agreed with a lot of what I had said and explained that her primary goal was not to convert our daughter. If she decided at some point to be Jewish, fine, but the rabbi said her real goal was to help Emily discover her spiritual roots, to own her own self more fully."

Hearing that the rabbi respected spiritual search and that a bat mitzvah was not simply a narrow-minded matter of "rescuing one more child for Judaism from an interfaith marriage,"

Tom felt freer to explore what Judaism meant to *him*. "All this might not have happened if there had been a different rabbi," he observed. Of course there were difficult moments and strong disagreements between rabbi and parents, between parents and child, between rabbi and child, but the underlying sense of respect and dialogue helped sweeten some of the hard times.

Tom decided he wanted to learn Hebrew so it would feel less foreign. He joined a regular class at the synagogue and found himself excited by Hebrew. Having learned the Sanskrit alphabet while working in the Peace Corps in Nepal, Tom was fascinated by the similarities between Sanskrit and Hebrew letters. He obtained some tutoring so as to be able to read the prayers and recite the *aliyot* correctly. Looking back, this was a huge step for Tom, and for Emily. She was very proud that her father would do that: "She took it as a symbolic act of affirming my love for her."

The law of unintended consequences sometimes produces moments of grace. As a teenager, Emily is separating from her father, with whom she had always been close. "At times it feels like she wants to reject everything I stand for, but the bat mitzvah bridged some of that rift between us. I still recall how she put her arm around me when we were standing on the *bimah*."

According to Tom, his daughter "understands connection in some ways better than I do." He very much wanted to find ways to stay connected to Emily as she found her way within Judaism, and she helped him do that. "She was very wise and made clear she wanted me involved. For example, she asked me if I would crochet her a yarmulke for the event. How could I make the yarmulke that she wore and not participate fully in the event?" The child's making clear that she wants and needs both parents' involvement is very important.

The non-Jewish parent may worry that they have no role. That can be the source of the anger and fighting that accompanies the bar mitzvah preparation. A hidden hurt or wound may be expressed by anger. Tom observed that "after a fight, my tendency was to disconnect and hers was to connect. Once, I remember, we got into a bitter fight about some matter and I would not talk to her. Hours went by. I went and put the TV on. She came into the room and sat next to me and then she leaned over and put my arm around her shoulder. WOW! I realized that she was not going to let the bat mitzvah or her adolescence disconnect us."

The key for both parents was their ability to let their daughter be *different* from them. They quoted Kahlil Gibran at the bat mitzvah: "Your children are not your children. / They are the sons and daughters of Life's longing for itself. / They come through you but not from you, / And though they are with you yet they belong not to you."

This was true for both parents. Yvette had to let Emily do her bat mitzvah *her* way, to be imperfect and perfect in her own way, to wrestle with the studying in her own way. Tom had to let Emily explore a faith different from his own, a world he didn't know very well, and endure the separations that implied.

In her speech Yvette linked childbirth and bat mitzvahs. She described dancing while waiting for labor to begin and dancing that morning, thirteen years later, at 6:30 A.M. in the hairdresser's salon where mother and daughter had gone to have their hair done. With these images Yvette acknowledged the "birthing" going on at the bat mitzvah—the birth of her daughter as an adult and perhaps also of Yvette's changed relationship with Judaism.

Yvette was never bat mitzvahed, having grown up in an Orthodox community that didn't allow women to read from the Torah. Her mother had supported this tradition. Now Emily was leading her mother into a new version of how to be Jewish and female—strong, confident, and knowledgeable—a reality symbolized beyond the "standard things" when Emily brought out her sax to lead the congregation in a lusty *niggun* at the end of the service.

An Israeli friend told Yvette that the transliterated syllables of "Emily" in Hebrew (*Ema li*) mean "mother of mine." Yvette remarked, "On one level, Emily was a teacher for me in this process."

Seeing her daughter assert her Jewishness left Yvette calmer and more settled—"Judaism feels less about fear and angst than it once did. We pushed at my fear of *What if my child identifies with organized religion?* and we got through it—I know now that our family can hold that kind of struggle."[9]

Yvette and Tom's relationship to Judaism has been changed by this experience. They love the singing in the synagogue. "There's more joy and contentment in the services than I remember from my childhood," Yvette said. Tom observed that "a lot of what I read in the Jewish prayer book is kind of Buddhist stuff."

He reflected, for example, on the Shema.

"I always get chills when the rabbi and congregation recite the Shema. It begins, 'Listen, Israel.' How Buddhist. It is saying, 'Wake up.'—listen and hear! Then it goes on to claim that 'the Lord is one'—it is speaking of the unity of things. Underneath the apparent disorder and difference in the world is a much deeper connection and unity. What's more Buddhist than that?"

The morning blessings that begin the Shabbat service remind Tom of the Hindu and Buddhist use of repetition of prayer intended to center you and encourage you to go deeper into yourself.

As we talked, Tom stood up to get his Reconstructionist prayer book and read aloud lines that moved him—"Blessed are you, our compassionate God, who protects the humble"—and told me how the attention to compassion is a key idea in Buddhism and the protection of the humble comes right out of the

Catholic Beatitudes. Often during the Amidah section of the service, Tom and Yvette will close their eyes and do *annapana,* the Buddhist attention to the breath and breathing, or as part of the Amidah, Tom may draw on imagery and prayer from his Buddhist practice, such as *metta*—sending thoughts of loving kindness as he experienced during his recent retreat at the Insight Meditation Society in Barre, Massachusetts.

The Challenge and Opportunity of Interfaith Marriage

Who decides about the kids' religious education and who does the work? When a Jewish woman marries a non-Jewish man, she may decide to raise the children Jewish, and he may go along with that, feeling some of the pleasure and relief of a religious tradition different from what he knew as a child, freed from whatever baggage he experienced growing up.

When a Jewish man marries a non-Jewish woman, conversely, he may feel ultimately that he wants the children raised Jewish, and his wife may be fine with that, but he may wish to leave the "spiritual stuff" to his wife, who then tries but struggles as a non-Jew. Wives who are not raised Jewish are often quite happy raising their children Jewish, but a lot depends on whether the Jewish husband is willing to provide that context for his kids. Our kids ask the big questions, and resurface buried religious issues for us.

I still remember how stunned I was by the way my children brought up the religion question almost out of the blue.

"Daddy, which part of me is Jewish and which part of me is Christian?" asked my then six-year-old daughter one day, as we drove home through the lovely New England countryside. It was the day before Rosh Hashanah and I'd been talking with both of my kids in the car about going to temple the next day. She probably had been thinking about how to combine her mother's Protestant heritage and her father's Jewish one.

The kids and I got into a confused dialogue about calendars. It was the year 5753 on the Jewish calendar. Over three thousand five hundred years the Jews had been doing their thing, subtracting a few years for the creation and prehistory. I pointed out this long lineage to my children with some pride. A pride I hadn't been aware of until my kids reminded me.

"But there's only nineteen ninety-two years in the world," replied my then nine-year-old son, a child of the Western calendar.

"No, no—that's only since the birth of Christ."

I tried to explain that Jewish history goes way back, past the birth of Christ. I didn't want to sound possessive about this, as if Judaism was better than Christianity or anything, but I became aware of a deep wish to interest my kids in this part of their religious heritage.

"Well, Daddy, do you mean the Jews lived when there were cavemen and dinosaurs and everything?" my thoughtful son responded.

That dialogue was the beginning of my recognition that my wife was right: we did need to think about our kids' religious and ethical education. How inept I felt at that moment!

People intermarry for many reasons and not simply because they happen to "just fall in love with the right person." Of course we love the people we marry, but there are deeper roots to intermarriage. For some, marrying outside the family's faith and tradition is also an act of rebellion, a rejection of at least part of what our parents stand for.

For some of us, marrying a non-Jew carries with it the hope of getting it right—not repeating aspects of our parents' lives that caused us (and them) distress growing up. One man told me about how marrying a decidedly non-Jewish woman fulfilled his wish to avoid the "suffocating closeness" he felt as a child in his family, where he was the main object of his mother's regard and attention. A Jewish man's relationship with his mother may shape his relationship with Judaism—he may feel angry or dominated by his mother in a way that makes him want to avoid his Jewish heritage, melding mother and tradition into one un- easy package.

Often Jewish men and women may need to move beyond an infantilized stance toward Judaism—like a little boy in the grip of a dominating mother or a daughter defying her clueless fa- ther—and find ways to empower themselves and discover their own authentic adult voice, which may involve a different rela- tionship to Judaism.

Marrying a non-Jew can also express the assimilationist wish of joining American culture through one's spouse and not simply re-creating a "Jewish home." One woman I know, raised in Atlanta in a home in which it was very important to not be "too Jewish" (defined as "like those New York Jews—loud and out there and with that accent!"), married her husband "first of all because he was incredibly attractive to me—there was a lot of attraction between us." Asked to describe what made him so attractive, she replied, "He looked like a perfect WASP!"

Marrying a non-Jew may also express the "Desdemona wish"—the desire for adventure and the exotic through mar- riage. In Paula Vogel's theatrical rendering of the story of Des- demona, daughter of a Venetian noble who marries the great warrior-leader Othello, the Moor of Venice, the playwright ex- plores the wish to marry someone different who will bring ad- venture and change to your life when you are bound by social rules of propriety and obligation.[10] Maybe there is a "Desde- mona Complex" among those of us who marry outside our faith. Many of us who marry non-Jews then become good Jew- ish doctors, lawyers, teachers, therapists, mothers, and fathers. Perhaps on some level we hope the marriage will provide the exoticness to balance the Jewishness we cannot escape in our lives. At some point, though, we may come to wonder whether Judaism itself is really so boring and old hat as we imagine. In nurturing our own authentic Jewish voice, we may find some of the exoticness and magic we so much seek in our lives.

If we intermarry out of a desire to be different from our family of origin, as we age our "Jewish" side returns more fully to consciousness. It may be the arrival of children, the aging of parents, or a sense of having "separated" enough to return. How we handle our own spiritual-religious struggles, then, will say a lot about how our children deal with the Jewish parts of themselves.

In one interfaith couple I met, the man was raised Orthodox Jewish yet hadn't been in a temple for twenty years. He and his Catholic wife have several children under ten years of age. He told me about having felt so pushed around by his parents, forced into becoming devout, that "I didn't want to put my kids through what I struggled with, but now I want to give them something." His wife feels at home within the Jewish community, so they've decided to try and raise the kids Jewish. With a trace of sadness he says, "My father's dead. It's too bad that he'll not be able to see the kids' bar mitzvahs." He wants now to feel more a part of his family's tradition, and he struggles with the question, "What values do I really want for my children? I wish I could avoid this question entirely." Why? Because the old Judaism was too painful and confining; he's rejected his father and remembers only empty stifling ritual in the synagogue, so all he has to go on is empty ritual and rebellion. He hasn't yet formulated the positive values that guide him. Rebelling *from* doesn't answer what you're moving *toward*. A thoughtful fifty-year-old man once said to me, "I want to run from this discussion of faith and values, but where am I going to run to?"

At these moments in family life, couples have the opportunity to look individually and together at what they really want from faith and tradition—what matters about their faith, what childhood memories are truly sweet, what would be wonderful to recapture for your children from your own traditions. Instead of Judaism or Christianity becoming simply Chanukah or Christmas, you can make faith into what you want by finding in the traditional ritual what resonates, or you can make your own. One couple I know created their "Eastover" celebration, an amalgam of Passover and Easter that brought together Christian and Jewish friends to celebrate rebirth, renewal, and freedom in a community celebration that not only embraced both faiths, but also developed family rituals expressing the lives and histories of the participants.

Of course, this is not just an interfaith issue. Not many of us when we first marry actually carefully contemplate with our spouse-to-be the moral education or religious faith of our children-to-be. As we age, we have children and need to begin a dialogue. It may feel very strange and unfamiliar, in either a single-faith or a multifaith marriage. Each partner needs to communicate a basic respect for the traditions of the other spouse's past, making clear that their joint history is safe in the household. When dealing with your own past, no matter how alienated or unsure you may feel about it, having kids makes you want to represent it well. Trying to ignore your heritage is a bit like wishing your mother had never been born—you wipe yourself out in the process.

It may be hard for a father to take an active stance within his family, not knowing how to meld, to experiment, to start a dialogue with his wife and children. So he gets authoritarian (well, you are Jewish!) or withdrawn (whatever you want, kids).

The same may be true for mothers and wives—the pressure to be the moral agent in the family, thinking about religious education, may be burdensome. "I sometimes just want to throw up I get so anxious around the holidays," one Jewish mother in an interfaith marriage commented to me in December, as she juggled Catholic and Jewish crosscurrents in her family. A non-

Jewish wife may feel self-conscious participating in Jewish rituals in front of the in-laws, wondering if she is doing it right. Mary and Noah sang their *aliyah* together at their son's bar mitzvah, and she felt very appreciative and supported by her husband's help beforehand, since she worried about how her devout in-laws would respond.

The extended family can also play an important supportive role. For example, Tom's Catholic mother, in her letter read at Emily's bat mitzvah, normalized and put into context Emily's choice as a part of her father's family's search for, and experimentation with, faith. "Follow your heart," her grandmother advised, and in fact urged her to take Judaism seriously, just as she had taken Catholicism seriously. Tom's mother was able to see beyond differences to the deeper meaning of being a *faithful* person, no matter what form that took. Tom reflected that his mother had always been "very ecumenical" and was interested in other faiths, so that there was a meaning structure available for understanding Emily's choices. In that way, Emily was placed within the context of both her mother's and father's families, without feeling that she must choose or reject one or the other.

The process for husbands and wives may need to start with both acknowledging their uncertainty and vulnerability. Then, both need to reflect on what is truly important in the traditions of their pasts, and they need to listen to each other. Even in families where the children are being raised Jewish, there is room for other spiritual traditions.

This is, of course, the task that all marriages face. We assume that same-faith marriages are just that, yet melding differences in what and how to observe and express one's spirituality (or lack of it) can be as alive in marriages between two Jews as in interfaith marriages. I grew up in a very Jewish home created by two Jewish parents, yet they wrestled mightily about whether to keep a kosher home or not—and within that struggle lay two *very* different versions of Judaism. How often do we attend synagogue? What prayers really matter to each parent? How spiritual are we in our everyday life—on a family trip to Yosemite, do we pause to say a prayer at the miraculous way a moose walks near to our car? Each partner may have a different answer. I know a Jewish couple, both very observant, who fought bitterly because one partner sometimes insisted on having a cigarette on Shabbat. We all to some extent live in interfaith marriages.

As our children explore their spirituality, we have the chance to re-explore our own. "When we took them to Sunday school, it turns out we stayed and got involved, but it would have been easy for me to distance myself," Ada observed.

Don't confuse organized religion with spirituality. Even if you are not into traditional Jewish ritual, there are many ways to nurture your children's spirituality, such as being connected to nature, to the outdoors and camping and canoeing. Many families find in nature and the outdoors a profound way to explore spirituality—their own and their children's.

On the other hand, as Tom and Yvette observed, spirituality alone is not enough for some kids. They need religion. They need the concrete stuff of spiritual life: stories, ritual, institutions, songs—and maybe their parents' participation.

A friend of mine had been raised Unitarian by "closet Jewish parents" who took little interest in their spiritual background. Once he said to me sadly, "When you grow up in a home where all symbols are of equal value, you have none." So it comes down to whether the parents are vitally engaged with their children in the discovery of spirituality. You can raise a child within one religion, but not believe in it yourself; you may hand your child Unitarianism but keep your faith in the closet, out of sight, and the child will feel empty. If we just leave religious education to the rabbi or minister, do the kids feel our absence? And if we engage our children in moments of faith and belief, those memories will be building blocks for their future.

Parents can be age-appropriately up-front about their own questions about faith; questioning is a part of family life. Arthur worried that he was "schooling my children in ambivalence," yet when parents are clear about their own questioning, such matters can become part of a dialogue with children.

Besides, are the parents in single-faith marriages so clear? There's plenty of room for ambiguity and sidestepping even if you go to temple faithfully every weekend. All parents struggle with basic questions of faith, belief, tradition, and observance, no matter how they were raised. We might not worry so much about interfaith marriages if we consider the difficulties of two Jews struggling to combine Conservative and Reform backgrounds to find consistent messages to give their children.

We should not underestimate the loneliness of being an interfaith couple. We live in a culture that likes things clear and simple, for people to be "either" Christian or Jewish. Holidays can be times of stress, but they can also be times of reaching out and getting support from other interfaith couples. Sandra went to a Chanukah party that was attended mainly by intermarried couples, and she remarked how relieved she was to be among her "own kind"—those who wrestle with matters of belief and faith, couples in which one of the parents is not Jewish. A ten-year-old adopted daughter of one family was Asian. Sandra's daughter walked right up to the girl and asked, "Where are you from?" Without missing a beat, the girl replied, "I'm from Korea." She was being raised Jewish. Sandra felt pleasure and relief in her daughter's exposure to such matter-of-fact realities of modern life. She laughed because there were so many non-Jews there, and I asked her what she meant. "Well, I guess it means being among people who struggle with questions of faith and meaning. I sometimes feel I'm around people who are just 'too Jewish,' which really means people who think they know it all, have it all solved. You can be 'too Christian' as well. At the Chanukah party, I felt welcomed by these people who have similar struggles. Diversity as well as faith was welcomed."

A Wider Lens

The important question is not whether our children are Jewish. More important is whether our children—and we ourselves—have a respectful, reverent attitude toward life and toward different beliefs. We might all be married to Jews, but if our children were narrow or bigoted, comfortable only within the narrow bounds of their own faith, would we have done right by them? What we need is to raise children who are comfortable with ambiguity and who can welcome living amid differences.

Interfaith families that are able to bring a vital sense of different religious traditions into their homes may be pointing the way for many Jews as they show us how to live in the modern world. Jewish educator Joseph Reimer, for example, believes it is crucial for Hebrew schools today to understand how children deal with seeing many religions practiced in their extended families. In one Hebrew school he observed, the teachers "seemed to wish that we still lived in a world in which Jewish and Christian religious practices were clearly distinct and separate! But in our actual world many children see both religions being practiced within their extended families. Jewish educators face an increasing burden of explaining what it means to become a Jew when not all the members of your family are Jewish."[11] To answer such questions, Jewish educators would do well to listen more to what is happening in the homes of many members of their congregations.

Many of us raised in "Jewish only" families seem to assume that we grew up with a continuous and straight and profound identification with Judaism. Yet that's not the case. We may go through long periods of being disconnected or alienated from our Jewishness, only to find it beginning to flower as we—and our lives—change. So, too, with children of interfaith marriages— when the seeds are there, they may blossom unexpectedly.

The attitude of the Jewish community toward the "intermarried" is crucial. Intermarried couples become a Rorschach test on which we project our fears, wishes, guilt, and shame about assimilation. At one point even Paul and Rachel Cowan embody this uncertainty. In *Mixed Blessings,* they observe that the larger Jewish community hasn't figured out yet whether to treat the intermarried as "problems or people." They go on to say, "As pariahs or as men and women *who are not yet committed Jews* [emphasis mine]."[12] Why should we assume the intermarried are uncommitted? The Cowans are among the most sensitive observers on this topic, so their choice of words reveals how easy it is to fall into stereotypes.

Language has a sort of imperialism to it, capturing subjects for the user's bias. For example, we have the word "outmarriage" replacing "intermarriage" among Jewish scholars. What a phrase! "Outmarriage" carries with it the implication of "out," "exit," "leaving." This may not be the conscious intent of a scholarly phrase referring to households containing one Jewish and one non-Jewish spouse, but it reveals the bias that such Jews are "outsourcing" their faith. In many such households, this may not be the case.

Such negative expectations can become a self-fulfilling prophecy. Judah Girardi's mother was Jewish and his stepfather, Italian Catholic. Judah's father died when he was nine years old, but his stepfather was very accepting of Judaism. Judah and his brothers were bar mitzvahed and remain Jewish-identified. Throughout his life, though, Judah has struggled to fit different pieces of himself together. When he was quite young there were some painful anti-Semitic incidents, including swastikas painted on his house when they lived in a very conservative Catholic community on Long Island. As a teenager, Judah also experienced some of the loving, welcoming aspects of Catholicism, particularly in his stepfather's family.

In graduate school Judah met Lily, raised Christian but not affiliated with a particular church. They decided to marry. Judah had become part of a Jewish group; several professors, for example, would pick him up for Friday night services and they'd all go back to someone's house for dinner afterward. So Judah felt quite Jewish and Lily felt attracted to, and welcomed within, Judaism.

When Judah approached his local rabbi about marrying them, though, the man expressed scorn about Judah's plans. He wouldn't participate in such services because they were a "blanding of religion." (He did inform Judah, though, that for an honorarium he was willing to say a blessing afterward at the reception.)[13]

The next rabbi they asked was warm and accepting and told the couple he would be delighted to marry them. Such marriages were a wonderful "blending" of faiths, the rabbi encouraged them, and he was happy to officiate.

Judah started to cry when recounting this story of search. He explained that he finally had felt accepted upon hearing the second rabbi's words. Judah has struggled with belonging at many points in his life—as a Jew in a prejudiced Catholic community, as a Jew in a Catholic father's family (he refers to his stepfather as "my father"), as a boy and man with Catholic allegiances among Jews, and now as a Jew marrying a non-Jew. The rabbi's words meant a lot to Judah because they communicated the welcome he so much wanted to feel and to knit into his life. Today, Judah and his wife belong to a synagogue.

Listening to Judah, I was reminded of a story a rabbi told me. He had officiated at an interfaith wedding and then one day, out of the blue, fourteen years later he received a phone call from the woman he had married. He had not seen her since the ceremony. She was calling long-distance to tell him that her son was about to be bar mitzvahed and to thank him. She told the rabbi that it was because of his acceptance that she was able to marry and to now have her son bar mitzvahed.

Those worrying about "the survival of Judaism" might do better worrying less about the attitudes of the intermarried and devoting more attention to those attitudes of their own that drive Jews in interfaith marriages away from Judaism.

Part Three

*Finding the Joy
in Judaism*

CHAPTER SEVEN

The Psychology of
a Vibrant Judaism

Welcoming the Internal Pharaoh

The first step toward a more vibrant, personal Judaism needn't be going to synagogue, learning Hebrew, or reading a book on Jewish history. It involves becoming more attentive to our own creativity and attitudes toward authority. We need look inward, as well as outward. There is a psychology to the way people create new connections to Judaism and honor traditional ones, and it involves finding "play spaces" in our lives: moments when we can find a balance between holding on to the past and changing the way it's always been.

It can be advantageous to be mindful of the part of ourselves that believes we must be obedient, that doesn't feel truly empowered to make Judaism our own. As adults we often approach Judaism from a childlike place, rooted in experiences that we have never outgrown. Competent professionals, committed spouses, and parents ourselves, we become like children in relation to our conception of Judaism.

We are often split internally: There's a judgmental, self-critical part, which I call the Internal Pharaoh, demanding obedience. And there's a more playful and rebellious part, seeking to express what is most heartfelt within us. In wrestling with Judaism, we are really exploring our own attitudes toward authority and personal autonomy.

The tension between creativity and authority is captured movingly in the story of the shepherd boy who played his flute during synagogue services, told to me by a fifty-year-old man who felt quite at home in his Conservative synagogue. It was a moment of real spirituality for him. "My spiritual moment occurred at a High Holiday service with my parents forty years ago." During the rabbi's sermon he had been admonished for the fourth time to stop fighting with his younger brother for elbow space on the armrest "and to LISTEN!" To everyone's surprise, he did. "The sermon was about a little shepherd boy who also did not feel connected with ritual observance and pulled out his flute and began to play at temple as his way of showing his love for God. The congregation objected and wanted him to stop playing, but the rabbi said that the beautiful melody lifted the heavy prayers of the congregation up to heaven."

The man concluded, "It was the first time I actually understood a sermon, and the point that there are many different ways of observance and of reaching for God from the heart has remained with me."

The story is compelling because it directs our attention to the tension between established ritual and personal creativity. The boy is breaking precedent—he is ecstatic, worshiping in a novel way. The community wants to pray using the forms and experiences they have always done and understood. The rabbi accepts and enjoys a different way of worshiping.

This story goes to the heart of the question of how different people go about being Jewish in all different ways. What is the role of breaking structure in the synagogue and outside of it? How do we create new forms of Judaism even while we acknowledge traditional ones?

The tensions between creativity and structure exist for us all on many levels. Our own creativity can be at odds with the institutionalized rituals of Judaism, and the two parts of ourselves, the playful, creative part and the dutiful, rule-following part, often conflict with each other. Mercifully, this tension between the revolutionary and the status quo is a part of Judaism and its great history. It is within all of us, within every person and every culture, and Judaism over the millennia has survived despite—or because of—this struggle.

Adults play, just as children do, although we are often more private about it. But play is not frivolous. It is an important way in which we can find a more authentic personal voice within Judaism. Play helps us resolve the tension between personal creativity and structure.

Donald Winnicott, an influential British pediatrician and child psychoanalyst, believed that the "play space of mother's lap" is a significant force in the development of the individual. For the young child, mother's lap—and explorations of the world from it—is the place where the crucial internal psychological work of processing and digesting experience goes on. As we grow older, mother's lap becomes a metaphor, and we find other safe places where we can suspend our rational, logical mind long enough to allow parts and potentialities of self to emerge. Journals, diaries, relationships with trusted friends, and therapy are examples of potential play spaces.[1]

So, too, are the prayers, rituals, and communities of Judaism. A play space is not a physical place so much as the psychological one created by individuals or groups, in which they feel safe enough to experiment, risk, and take a fresh look at themselves and life's challenges.

Judaism can become a play space in which men and women work out their ambivalent relationships with authority, achieve a deeper integration of masculine and feminine parts of themselves, and even find ways to reconcile more fully with parents.

Different people find different kinds of play spaces, in family activities, prayers, and specific rituals, both within the synagogue and outside it.

We begin by becoming mindful of our internal roadblock to change, the Pharaoh within.

What better place, then, to explore the individual struggle with authority and creativity than the play space of the Passover seder?

Freedom and Oppression at the Seder: Being Creative about Authority

The Passover story has more than historical and religious dimensions: it is also a metaphor for the internal journey that starts with being enslaved by persistent childhood images of authority and religion and culminates in a freer and more autonomous sense of self.[2]

Jeremy grew up in a home where there was considerable emphasis on doing it right, perhaps most strongly at the Passover seder, where the children were distractions and the premium was on knowing the answers to the many different elements of the celebration. Jeremy's parents and relatives weren't sure how to engage the children in spiritual play and there was a tension between the adults' worship and the children's play. "We were shushed and told to sit still a lot." On the other hand, Jeremy also has many wonderful sensory memories of the seder, of the shiny crystal place settings and colorful, distinctive-smelling foods on the table.

For years after he married, Jeremy and his wife, Dara, had a lethargic relationship to Judaism. He didn't understand much of what happened during synagogue service and he went once a year "because it was important to my parents."

After they had children, Jeremy and his wife wanted a more evocative seder for their children, but he wasn't sure how to make that happen. When his children were about five years old, Passover occurred in the middle of the week and because of business commitments and scheduling difficulties, Jeremy and his wife realized that they would be home, instead of at either of their parents' houses. It would be the first seder held in Jeremy's home as well as the first at which his parents were not present.

Jeremy found himself the oldest one present and had the opportunity to create his own seder. What to do? He felt unequal to the task and missed having older adults around to rely on, even though he knew he felt resentful of their authority. Looking through his bookshelves the week before Passover, though, he found an older Haggadah and was "determined to put something together that made some sense for me and for my family." He invited some neighbors who were equally unversed in what happens at a seder.

In reading through the Haggadah a few days beforehand, Jeremy found a section that really moved him. He felt both admonished and inspired by the Haggadah's instruction that "according to tradition, it is our responsibility to tell the story of the Exodus to our children, making sure that it is understood. . . . For this story must become their story. They must understand its message so that they too, will pass it on . . . from generation to generation."[3] Jeremy began to realize that he was part of a generational link, standing between his parents and his children, not simply an isolated individual. However, how could he make that link meaningful to him, at Passover? He was embarrassed even by that question. "At age forty-eight, I'm too old to be wrestling with Judaism, feeling like an ignorant little kid."

He decided to take the day of the first seder off from work and devoted himself to planning it. The Haggadah indicated that it is traditional to clean the house before Passover, a sort of spring cleaning, to do a *bedikat chametz,* a "farewell to *chametz,*" a thorough search and sweep-up to clean the house of food containing leavening agents. To Jeremy's surprise he did clean the kitchen. He scrubbed the large kitchen table, washed the wooden backs of the bunk seats around the table, swept and mopped the kitchen floor. He found he liked doing what had always been in his family "women's work."

While working, he turned on the radio and found a PBS Passover broadcast, and heard several pieces he had never heard before, including a modern "Passover Cantata." Jeremy loves classical music, and this was the first Passover music he heard that had a modern ring.

As he thought and worked, he found himself recasting the meaning of Passover. He had always been disturbed by the "Jewish-centeredness" of the seder, how little reflection on anyone else's sufferings had been present. He began to see the Passover story as applying to many other peoples as well. He thought about the Armenian genocide, what had happened in Vietnam, the killing fields of Cambodia, and the warfare in Bosnia and Kosovo, which was headline news at that time.

As he cleaned that day, reflecting and listening to music, Jeremy was in a play space in which he was recasting the meaning of the seder (and his sense of himself) as an adult with the power to make it a meaningful event by his own lights, not just as a droning repetition of what would please his parents.

At the seder later that day, he also struggled with his authority as a father, confronting his own Internal Pharaoh.

"I had wanted to follow the Haggadah pretty much the way it set out the seder. I didn't really know what else to do." In the past, of course, there had also been the "leader," usually Jeremy's father or perhaps another older relative, who would tell everyone where to go and selected people to read particular sections from the Haggadah. That night, though, it wasn't clear who the leader was.

"I started out telling people to read this part or that, but as we went along people started to want to skip to this part or that, let's not read that prayer, let's skip to the prayers over the wine, and then someone else wanted to do this and that. I began to compete with them, I felt angry that they weren't letting me read, and I got more and more determined to do the whole Haggadah!"

Jeremy smiled ironically at how trapped he felt in a hierarchical image of authority. He was going to lead the seder by imposing his will on everyone!

There is a reason why the Pharaonic image is so powerful more than 2,500 years after the collapse of the Egyptian dynasties—the image of the all-powerful Pharaoh captures a way we learn to construe the all-powerful leader with his childlike followers. The Pharaoh and Moses—the battle between obedience and rebellion—speaks to a drama alive inside many of us today.

Jeremy's family had always gone through the whole Haggadah before eating dinner. As the leader, he took on his father's role. "I'm supposed to lead and no one was letting me do that as we all lurched through the Haggadah sampling what seemed interesting."

But the kids were hungry and complained. They were losing interest in the seder. Then Jeremy had a moment of inspiration. He remembered some of the games that the kids used to play when they were sent away from the main table so the adults could finish the Haggadah. "Some of us would sit together and pretend we were Moses, or the Pharaoh, and we'd act out what was happening at the table."

So, to close the seder before dinner, Jeremy suggested a game: a TV interview in which one of the kids was the interviewer and each member of the group was a participant in the Exodus drama.

"You mean like on MTV or CNN?" asked his son.

The kids and adults got very engaged in this new version of the Haggadah. One of the kids left the room for a few minutes and returned with sunglasses, a fedora, and an adult overcoat reaching to the floor, all ready to face the "You Are There" cameras in the Egyptian desert. The kids took turns being interviewed, while the adults watched. One of the kids was the Pharaoh, another Moses, one of the girls was Miriam, Moses' sister, another wanted to be a cat in the Exodus. In his interview the "Pharaoh" talked about his Pyramids, and why he wanted the Jews to build them: "I want to be remembered, I coulda been somebody," intoned the child-Pharaoh. "Moses" talked about standing up to authority and his conversations with God. The interviewer had a great question: "Listen, Moses, you actually talked with God, so I have to ask you—Is God male or female?" Everyone wanted to become "Moses" to answer that question.

In allowing himself to draw on his childhood memories of pleasure at the seder and to relax some of his rigid stereotypes about being "a leader," Jeremy created a memorable seder experience. He did this by "playing," by allowing himself to bring new elements into the situation and taking a different view of himself. His ideas of authority shifted from strict obedience to a more flexible ability to be present and available.

The struggle with the Internal Pharaoh goes on in the synagogue as well as in the home. For those of us connected with a synagogue, the rabbi often becomes a representative of the critical, judgmental parts of ourselves.

In thinking about how to find "play spaces" in the synagogue, it is particularly important to pay attention to our attitudes toward authority. Too often we often approach Judaism from a passive place; we want to be given to, and we feel we have little power. We look to our rabbi, to our elders. While, of course, there is merit to the esteem in which a rabbi is held, it is also important to consider two features of modern Judaism (and of religion today, in general) that contribute to the tendency of many of us—who already feel that we "don't know" well enough—to become passive and disconnected from our own passion in the synagogue.

First, in the modern American practice of much of Judaism, there is a tendency toward passive worship in which the congregation is led through the service by the rabbi. Many of us do not expect to link what happens in the service to our own experiences and deepest feelings. Scholars point out that the very assimilation of American Jewry has led to the splitting off of the synagogue from the everyday experiences of American Jews.[4] Since a lot of us don't know a lot about Judaism on a ritual or nuts-and-bolts level, we then turn to "the expert." On a psychological level this can mean that we come to see the rabbi as the one who knows, the one we go to for the Judaism in our lives, the way we go to a doctor for health, a teacher for knowledge, the supermarket for groceries. This role of the rabbi as organizing and leading worship is relatively new and contrasts with the traditional role of the rabbi as the resource rather than the focus.[5]

Second, change is often instituted from the top down—rabbis, synagogue boards, or a small group of committed members (the insiders) start by creating new rituals or prayers. They may include meditation, movement, chanting, and alternative prayer books in the service. All these are fine. Yet it's important to remember that these top-down changes come *from* the leadership *to* the congregation. Equally important are "bottom-up" innovations—ones that originate with the congregation itself. But that requires getting past our infantilized attitude toward Judaism.

How ironic that the Internal Pharaoh is often experienced in the person of the rabbi. Ronnie, for example, around the time of her son's bar mitzvah kept feeling oppressed by the rabbi's decisions, culminating in a dramatic moment. Ronnie's husband is Protestant, and they had decided to raise their children Jewish. However, his family was still devoutly Christian, even though quite accepting of their son's decisions in this matter. The bar mitzvah invitation became a flash point for tensions within Ronnie. She had put on the invitation the date of the bar mitzvah according to the Western calendar but the rabbi wanted the Hebrew calendar used as well and said that the Jewish year should be printed not just in English but also in Hebrew. This felt like too much for Ronnie. "I'm worried about how my husband's family will react, and just don't feel comfortable myself with so much Hebrew on the invitation."

She was angry but wouldn't talk to the rabbi about it. One Sunday afternoon, Ronnie and several Jewish friends got together over coffee and bagels, as they often did. One of the women had recently bar mitzvahed her own son and found the rabbi to be quite helpful and willing to compromise. Were they talking about the same man? Ronnie shared her concerns about the invitation and several other prescriptions he had offered for the celebration. "Talk to him" was the advice. Still, Ronnie hesitated, and a week went by. At their next Sunday coffee and bagels gathering, she mused, "I feel like my father would want that Hebrew on the card, but I'm worried that my husband's family will be put off." Ronnie had been very close to her father, who died years before she was married, at a time when she was distant from Judaism. He was strongly Jewish-identified. Now she imagined her father as critical and judgmental and demanding of an observant bar mitzvah. Since he was gone, and she felt his absence, there was no room in her mind for compromise. The rabbi became critical and judgmental to her. Some of Ronnie's fear of, and anger at, the rabbi was pumped up by her feelings about her father. In fact, she didn't want to go along with every detail the rabbi suggested and had good reasons for wanting to compromise on the wording of the invitation.

In order to move closer to Judaism, Ronnie also had to make some room for herself and not simply follow all the rules, especially when they didn't make sense for her or her family. Sitting in the coffee shop on those Sundays, Ronnie was confronted with her own Internal Pharaoh, the part of herself that constricted her playfulness and creativity. She was "playing" in that very coffee shop, by talking and relaxing and looking anew at her struggles in the relative safety of friends. She began to see that her father loved her very deeply right up until his death and that she loved him. She saw that she was doing right by him and her family in having the bar mitzvah. She also thought about her own son's determination to do it, and she realized that these details were not the heart of the matter. What truly mattered in the end was that all involved felt reasonably good about the bar mitzvah. She played with the possibilities of the bar mitzvah, imagining different ways to do the invitation, no one way being the only right one. She decided that she did need to talk to the rabbi about the invitation and other details of the service that did not feel right to her. When she did so, she found the rabbi willing to listen and change and suggest compromises.

Thoughtful rabbis are aware of how they can become containers for projection of congregants' struggles. A major change in perception comes when we can see the rabbi not as a patriarchal authority but as an ally, a fellow seeker, who teaches by example rather than by pronouncement. Rabbis also struggle to combine leadership and compassion, without turning themselves into Pharaohs. They also struggle to find teachers and mentors who do not demand blind obedience and are too self-important. One thoughtful rabbi, Sheila Weinberg, reflected that her own attraction to Buddhism came in part from the very human nature of Buddhist teachers compared to some of those in the rabbinate: "Many of us have had our fill of preachers who don't practice, of brilliant intellectuals who are not aware, sensitive or respectful of boundaries in their personal lives." Writing of her Buddhist teachers in contrast, she said, "It is incredibly compelling to be in the presence of someone who radiates love through patience and the offering of full attention..."[6]

For many women, rabbis play a pivotal role in helping them play with and welcome and eventually put to rest the Internal

Pharaoh. Many Jewish women have grown up feeling, and continue to feel, excluded from the Torah and the sanctuary, the center of Jewish worship. The tradition in Judaism was that the sanctuary is "men's place" and that the home is women's place. While the movement of women into Judaism—in the rabbinate, on synagogue boards—changes these divisions, old stereotypes live on for generations. It conveys a powerful devaluing message to the women when a son is bar mitzvahed while a daughter is not bat mitzvahed, or when the bar mitzvah becomes a major event while the bat mitzvah takes a lower priority. "My parents would drive over an hour twice a week to take my older brother to *shul* for his bar mitzvah lessons, but it was 'too far' to drive when it came time for my bat mitzvah," recalled one rabbi, who is now very sensitive to gender issues in her congregation, "so I didn't have one until I was twenty-seven years old."

Often, the sense of difference between brothers and sisters is communicated more subtly. Deborah, for example, remembered an argumentative childhood home where Judaism was the ability to argue and debate. That didn't interest her as much as it did her parents and brothers. "My family came from a radical tradition, and dinnertime was basically a time for argument and disputation. We weren't into the religious aspects—that was superstition to my parents. Judaism was about argument and assertiveness. To be heard in my family I had to be logical and verbal."

Deborah learned how to do that well, becoming a successful labor lawyer. However, as she grew older she found her "spiritual, reverent side" pressing for expression. She wrestled with the profound issues of identity that shape midlife for many adults: what does it mean to be "male" versus "female," being "aggressive" versus "receptive," being a busy lawyer versus a reverent Jew. She wanted to find a way back into the synagogue to explore some of the mysteries that had been left behind in childhood.

Even in the midst of a powerfully playful, reverent experience, she heard the restrictive voice of her Internal Pharaoh:
"When I was in law school, a boyfriend took me to a Hasidic
Shabbat service, which was wonderfully passionate, with dancing and singing. At one point they passed the Torah around the
room, from one person to another, some dancing with it. It was
clear they all felt so at home with the Torah, but when it got to
me, I took it and just passed it on. I had never held one, and it
was as if a voice inside me said, 'You shouldn't be holding this!'
so I got rid of it as fast as I could."

Deborah's rabbi was very important to her at this point.
"He came across as a real person. He told me that he wrestled
a lot with whether there was a God and what form God took
in our lives. He told me about his own struggles, he reassured
me that I didn't have to believe everything entirely, he encouraged me." The rabbi's willingness to enter into a dialogue as a
real person, to "play" with Deborah by validating her uncer-
tainties and revealing some of his, helped her continue her explorations. Though still unsure about what her place is in the
synagogue, Deborah has not given up on her playful search for
her own Jewish voice.

Being able to have access to the Torah is very important for
many women and a source of great joy in pushing against internal prohibitions and social ones. Consider the awe and playfulness wedded together in this woman's description of her first
reading from the Torah in her thirties: "A spiritual moment I
hold dear was getting ready to read from the Torah for the first
time. It was summer and I was thirty-something, and it seemed
to make sense to have my bat mitzvah before my wedding. I'd
been preparing some six to eight lines of Hebrew from the
Tikkun, a book that shows the script of the Torah scroll side by
side with the Hebrew print, but I was encouraged by the rabbi
to look at the Torah scroll itself beforehand. After Friday night
services the evening before I was to read the next morning, I

took the Torah scroll from the ark when the *shul* was quiet and carried it to another room, maybe the rabbi's study. I opened the scroll, which I had seen close up beforehand, but this was different. I felt a power come toward me, almost like a strong wind, which made me jump back. I was glad I'd practiced from the scroll that night beforehand, because I thought that in front of the small summer congregation, I'd have been too overcome, too overwhelmed to read. It's a power that I felt only that once." It's no wonder that many mothers find the bat mitzvahs of their daughters a powerful experience, seeing their daughters participate in ways that many of them were denied.

Often when we feel marginalized, we internalize a powerful voice that we don't belong in the larger group and how dare we try to enter? This is very true for Jewish men and women who are gay and lesbian. For all Judaism's history of being oppressed, even with the powerful Jewish awareness of the pain of being marginalized, many Jewish communities still act as if the only Jews in their congregation are those who would fit into a Norman Rockwell painting. This silence on the part of the larger community colludes with the self-questioning, self-devaluing part of individuals in the minority within the synagogue.

For a Jew who is gay or lesbian, the Internal Pharaoh may demand that they be mainstream to be good enough. Such a voice says that if only they were straight they'd be acceptable; what is wrong with them for being different? Rabbis play an important role in helping minority groups feel welcome enough to "play" with Judaism. For example, Marilyn, a Jew who is also lesbian, remembered a rabbi who came to talk to her congregation yet in his presentation on "contemporary Judaism" mentioned nothing about the experiences of gay and lesbian Jews despite the fact that "we were a large component of the congregation." Marilyn's Internal Pharaoh squawked at her for weeks after that event, telling her she was not "really" a good Jew, given her sexual orientation.

Marilyn contrasted that experience with the joy she felt at a chance meeting at a local amusement park with a different rabbi who was wearing a T-shirt that said, *There's one in every minyan.* "His own daughter was lesbian and he was willing to say in public that gays and lesbians are a part of Judaism, too." This man's playfulness, openness, and willingness to give some visibility to Marilyn's identity helped her feel more welcome and willing to face the judgmental part of herself that kept her from more actively engaging with the synagogue. That serendipitous encounter led directly to Marilyn's greater Jewish involvement.

Judaism and the Midlife Years

The years between thirty-five and fifty-five are a time of profound change in our understanding of ourselves and the world, and these psychological transformations have implications for our Judaism. For many Jews I have talked with, the middle years are a time of particular ferment and creativity. If we are fortunate, Judaism can offer avenues for the resolution of some of the most challenging tasks of the middle years, particularly those having to do with our need for reconciliation with our parents and coming to terms with our own mortality.

Lette is a forty-five-year-old mother of twin ten-year-old daughters, who is married and works as a financial planner. She has spent a lot of time exploring Eastern spirituality and stopped going to synagogue many years ago. She's a quiet, thoughtful, friendly woman who lives in Newton, Massachusetts. She came to an open meeting at a friend's house on a Saturday evening to talk about Judaism. When she walked in, we were surprised. We simply hadn't expected her to be interested in where Judaism fits in her life. That seemed to be settled—it didn't have a place.

We talked for a while, all of us spread around the comfortable living room, about Judaism: our disappointments and hopes. As the evening wore on, we became more personal and began talking about ourselves: our lives, the parts settled and unquiet, our aging, our parents' aging.

One of us asked Lette about her mother's health. We all knew that her eighty-year-old mother had breast cancer. Lette sighed and told us that she was working on finding the right treatment protocols for her mother, spending a lot of time talking to doctors and researching breast cancer therapies. To help her mother, Lette had become an "informed consumer" of medical treatments for cancer.

The talk in our group then turned to aging parents and health care, our efforts to calm aging parents' health anxieties, calming our own anxieties about our aging and theirs, and learning to live without our parents.

Then Lette started to cry. The sheer burden of her efforts broke through. She had been spending so much time taking care of her mother, who took care of her? And a new theme appeared: Lette had been going to synagogue services more often now, in fact for the first time in years, with her mother and without her. She expressed a different sense of Judaism than she had earlier. She told us she was deeply moved by the synagogue, by hearing prayers she remembered from childhood, by the community of it all—"people all gathered together"—and she enjoyed going there with her mother, seeing her mother's pleasure in being together with her daughter in synagogue, just like the old days. Lette told us about her mother's hope that the girls will be bat mitzvahed, and her own puzzling wish—"I can't believe I'm saying this"—to do just that; a desire that complicated her life, since she was in an interfaith marriage.

And so when we began to talk about grief and loss at midlife in our group that night, we started to talk about the deeper reasons that had drawn us together to (re-)explore the meaning of Judaism in our lives.

What leads us back toward Judaism as we age? At the deepest level it has to do with a shifting identity and sense of self in the world. Much of the current debate within Judaism is about how *it* can change to become more welcoming, yet equally important is to understand the changes within *ourselves* that lead us to reassess the role of faith in our lives, to develop a "second" (or "third" or "fourth") faith construction as we reach the middle years. The key internal identity shifts have to do with our understanding of ourselves, our sense of power or powerlessness in our lives, and changing relationships to our parents as we all age.

Lette, for example, wants to feel some way of being "held," and one of the most profound ways she felt held as a child was in temple, before the disappointment and betrayal of her childhood that led her to turn away from Judaism. Lette's father had died suddenly and tragically—in the hospital a few days after a car accident—despite Lette's fervent prayers to God. After that loss, Lette "gave up" on Judaism.

Perhaps Lette is hoping that this time around faith will save her mother; or is she hoping to find in Judaism a comforting "mother" to lean against while she is so bravely taking care of her own mother? Listening to Lette talk about all the medical treatments her mother faces, I could see one reason why we turn back to faith as adults. We need to find a comforting, sheltering "home" to weather the storms brought by the decades at ages forty, fifty, and sixty.

In these midlife years, we truly begin to understand and *feel* the limits of time, the finiteness of our own lives and of our parents'. The world may seem, paradoxically, much colder and much warmer. It's warmer in the sense that we may feel less driven and less scared because we understand more about what really matters, but also much colder because we feel our aloneness, having given up the youthful illusion that our parents will be around forever, that they'll protect us from life, that ultimately we are immortal. You can name your own youthful illusions, there are so many of them, but deep down the normal weaning from them must involve some recognition of "the tragic perspective" in human life.

The search for shelter within Judaism from the coldness of life is not simply a regression back to childhood. We're not talking about nostalgia for the "old days." Over the next months and years, I had the privilege of watching Lette redefine her faith and express it in positive ways. She enrolled her children in Hebrew school, joined a temple, and negotiated with her husband a way to bat mitzvah the twins that felt comfortable to him as well.

Most important, Lette felt more empowered and autonomous. She was making a free choice, rather than being driven by childhood fears and conflicts. She was taking the risk of approaching an area of her life (Judaism) that had felt frightening and scary, rather than staying rigidly separate from a conflictual area while trying to appear "independent-minded." She was seeking support and help from our group and elsewhere, rather than remaining isolated in her struggle, thus getting new information about the world. And she felt pleasure (as well as trepidation) and felt good about *herself* as she reconnected with Judaism.

Lette's story illustrates a deeper point: as we age, our relationships to Judaism may change, and how we re-define our experiences of Judaism often has to do with our changing senses of self and the key relationships in our lives. Over and over I've heard and seen how Judaism is both a vehicle to express new parts of ourselves even as it changes us.

Coming to Terms with the Fragility of Life— and of Ourselves

Over the years we have become familiar with the idea of the midlife crisis. Yet one of the most seminal articles on this topic is already over thirty-five years old: "Death and the Midlife Crisis" by British psychoanalyst Elliot Jaques, first published in 1965.[7]

Jaques argues that the middle years bring a profound change in our orientation to the world, both in terms of *how* we work and the *content* of our work. (By "work," Jaques really means our way of interacting with the world.) He notes a pattern in the lives of many creative people in which midlife brings with it a psychological crisis such that one of four things may happen: their work dries up, there is an actual death, their true creativity begins to express itself for the first time, or there is a "decisive change in the quality and content of creativeness."

Jaques sees a difference between the mode of working pre- and post-midlife. He characterizes the creativity of the twenties and early thirties in terms of its rapid, impulsive nature: "a hot-from-the-fire creativity. It is intense and spontaneous, and comes out ready-made. . . . Mozart, Keats, Shelley, Rimbaud are the prototype."[8]

In contrast, Jaques sees the creative activity of the late thirties and after as far more volitional, patterned, and thoughtful, although not necessarily less "hot and intense." He refers to this kind of activity as "sculpted creativity." "There is a big step between the first effusion of inspiration and the finished product."[9] As we form and re-form the creative product, as we work it and rework it, an interplay takes place between intuition and inspiration, between what we make and our response to it.

In the difference between the "precipitate creativity" of our twenties and the "sculpted creativity" of mature adulthood, Jaques sees a profound psychological journey. We move from the idealism and optimism of late adolescence and early adulthood, in which we believe in the boundless power of change, in the importance of external achievement, and in our own invulnerability, to the more "contemplative pessimism" of midlife, in which we truly recognize that all of us have both good and evil within ourselves, which contributes to our difficulties in life. It is the recognition of the reality of personal death that truly drives us toward "the depressive position at midlife" and the necessity of working that through. We've reached some of our youthful goals, others will never be met, parents are elderly or gone, and children are growing up.

There are many "deaths" and losses that we face as we age. Once you begin to understand how brief the individual life is, you become aware of many deaths that need to be mourned—the loss of versions of the self that you hoped to make real in the world, of the vision of what your children might become, of roads and possibilities not taken or no longer possible.

Jaques concludes that "it is this fact of the entry upon the psychological scene of the reality and inevitability of one's own eventual death that is the central and crucial feature of the midlife phase."[10]

One of Jaques's insights is that our midlife experience does not just arise for us fully born at that time—rather, the way that we experience the sense of mortality and powerlessness as we age is connected to our earliest sense of safety and danger in the world. As grown adults confronting the reality of death, we go back into our earliest identifications with mother and father and what it meant to be a helpless infant and baby; these early experiences form the backdrop for what it means for each of us to confront our limits and losses as adults.

What is the mourning to be done? We need to find a way to reconcile the love and hate within us (largely based on our identifications with the "good parents" and "bad parents" of our childhood) and to restore hope and a sense of internal safety—the feeling that the world is OK enough for us to go on and feel generative and productive. Out of this internal struggle comes the "tragic perspective" that is part of healthy midlife development.

A renewed interest in Judaism as we age reflects what I call "the recognition," a fundamental shift in how we experience ourselves in the world. We face our limits, our vulnerability. As the father of a spirited boy and girl, both approaching their teens, it began to dawn on me how much hope and faith are involved in watching your children grow up. Similarly, as my parents lived into their eighties, I felt drawn back to Judaism not because things hadn't been worked out between us, but because they *had*: I became aware of all that can't be said between the generations, what goes beyond words even when you've "done things right." We want to find familiar rituals, reassuring and expressive, that give voice to sentiments that we lack the words to convey.

Judaism, among all the great world religions, is particularly centered on continuity between generations. Thomas Cahill was particularly insightful when he wrote in *The Gifts of the Jews,* "That accomplishment is intergenerational may be the deepest of all Hebrew insights."[11] Judaism's emphasis on the family, relationships, and the connection between young and old offers a way to manage the crucial tasks of adult life.

If aging and experience bring greater familiarity with the tragic perspective on life then we need a ritualized, timeless container that allows us to express what can't always be understood by our rationality or expressed in words. Jewish rituals and observances—traditional and reconstructed—offer us a way to express gratitude, to show loyalty, to find our "place" in time and space. We may feel that when we stand during the Amidah (perhaps bending a knee), or when we construct a meaningful ritual with our families or in the woods on Yom Kippur, we are engaged in a timeless act, feeling part of a tradition and a people, speaking (without saying so directly) of gratitude passed from older to young and back again.[12] I use the word "may" consciously—not all behaviors have the same meaning. What is crucial is the person's experience underlying the ritual. For many of us who come back to Judaism, there is a search for a safe "container" that will shelter and support us as we confront life's mysteries and dilemmas.

Sarah, for example, is a single mother, divorced for ten years, whose son Adam has chosen to be bar mitzvahed. Their story illustrates how Judaism can offer an adaptive return to the lost childhood and family shelter we need to confront life's challenges.

Adam has little relationship with his father, and Sarah herself was raised as a "casual" Jew. Talking over coffee, Sarah finds herself "shocked" at the fact that her son is having a bar mitzvah. "I've sort of been thrown into this whole thing."

Adam is being tutored in order to catch up since he hadn't gone to Hebrew school before. They've found a synagogue, and several afternoons a week Sarah sits in her living room and listens to her son practice his Torah portion in the next room with his tutor.

In her account of being "thrown into" all "this," it's as if an *outside* force has led her to reconnect with Judaism. Yet it's clear that powerful feelings within her have been aroused; she tells me about listening to her son practice Hebrew and his Torah portion—"you hear this incredibly gorgeous Hebrew being sung, but I have no idea what it means in my house." There *is* a sort of psychic homelessness conveyed by Sarah's use of the voice of *you,* as if indeed she is feeling displaced, in a new situation, with this Hebrew and Judaism in her home.

For Sarah, growing up Jewish was a mixed bag. She would celebrate the Jewish holidays with her extended family, but she remembers her mother's nervousness and unpredictability. Being with her mother's mother was nice—her Passover dishes were lovely old-world china—but "my mother was very nervous about those dishes and almost 'killed' my sister when she broke one." Sarah's mother was unstable and prone to violent rages, saying, "You know what I want, you know what I want." Her father would try to help during those times but wasn't able to calm Sarah's mother very effectively. The family as a whole rarely went to synagogue.

Now Sarah finds herself a fifty-year-old single mother with a son who is about to be bar mitzvahed, with aging parents, facing a whole new life stage. She describes the bar mitzvah as emerging from the hope of "feeling like you belong to a larger group." That was one of the basic reasons Sarah wanted Adam to have a bar mitzvah: "to realize that family is so small, that he belongs to something larger." Sarah's hope is to give her son a larger context than just her own "messed-up family" as he transits to manhood. Sarah had originally hoped to have the bar mitzvah take place as part of a visit to Israel by just the two of them— "maybe wishing my family would not at all be involved."

With these words, Sarah gives voice to the hope of escaping some of her family's chaos, and maybe her own internal chaos, as she reconnects with Judaism. We all carry around within us distorted images of our parents. Some of Sarah's mother's rage and unpredictability came from her own sense of growing old, and as Sarah confronts that same life stage as a single parent, her own mix of despair, rage, hope, and love comes to the fore. Jewish rituals of transition and change such as the bar mitzvah offer ways of wrestling with this common human dilemma. We are reminded of our place within the larger group, of the generational continuities in our lives.

(Re-)connecting with Judaism carries with it the hope of avoiding old family patterns. For Sarah, that means the hope of being *different* from her mother, a hope first expressed in a rigid, artificial way ("I'll have the bar mitzvah in Israel and my son won't be tainted by the family legacy of anger and abandonment"). Yet it also carries with it the hope of integrating hopeful, healthy parts of her family upbringing, of being a different kind of mother—rooted in her family, perhaps with some of her father's calm.

Sipping her coffee, Sarah goes on to explain why she decided to keep the event in this country. "The bar mitzvah is a celebration of family, friends, rituals." She becomes tearful. "I'm very emotional about all this. I'm sure I'll be crying and having a hard time."

Sarah wants to bring her family together, to root herself and her son and her parents in a sense of continuity. In that sense Sarah is doing very generative work, trying to use Judaism as a way of knitting together painfully split parts of herself.

Sarah explains, "My son has never had a relationship with his father and so this is another time I really wanted *my* father to be involved in this."

There have been many times she has looked to her father, trying to involve him in the family to help her manage the painful experiences surrounding her difficult mother. Sarah wants a different journey for herself, so she is turning again to a male presence as she did when younger. Her son's tutor is a man, and Sarah finds that listening to the two of them practicing Hebrew brings to mind memories of sitting snuggled up with her grandfather in *shul* and of her father bringing home fresh bread on a Sunday—experiences that express the hope of a grateful, nourishing male presence in her life (and, most important, by recognizing such hope and memory, finding such calm within herself).

In the course of the bar mitzvah preparation, Sarah's father disappointed her. She wanted him to say an *aliyah* and he balked. "I'm not going to get up there. I don't remember Hebrew. I'm not going to embarrass myself." Sarah once again felt abandoned by him ("whenever I really count on my father, he disappears") and the two had a big fight. Sarah also got angry at her rabbi for his remoteness, and he became a lightning rod for her disappointment at the unpredictability of the men she counts on.

As the bar mitzvah approached, though, Sarah and her father worked things out, largely through her efforts. She recognized his limits, and came to see that she has much more control in what happens these days than she did as a young child. She began to understand his fears of not looking good in the temple, a place he has not spent much time, in front of the whole family, and to recognize *her* quickness to anger. He agreed to read a poem, in English. Sarah needed to "forgive" her father his imperfections in order to feel OK about being back in the *shul*. She even wound up forgiving the rabbi his remoteness!

So, too, for some of us: the hope in our experience of Judaism as we age is that it will evoke the power of the father, the one who can help and protect and reassure us through difficult transitions in our lives.

Integrating Our Masculine and Feminine Sides in Judaism

Sometimes at midlife we look to Judaism to find within ourselves the "heart" that we lost or misplaced growing up. Betsy, at age forty, is a convert to Judaism. The movement toward Judaism helped her integrate aspects of her father and mother that were lost when she was young.

Betsy's father was "the warmth in my family. He was the heart. He could cry, had access to his emotions. He was the nurturer. My mother was more cold and distant." He died suddenly of a heart attack. Betsy had come home from college to find him dying and was unable to resuscitate him, and so blamed herself for not saving him. After that, "my whole family changed; it didn't have a heart anymore."

Isolated in her grief, Betsy found her faith community quite distant. "The pastor would visit and just talk and pray with my mother, but there was no mention of 'How are you doing? Are you getting through?' Nothing about how thin you look—are you eating, sleeping? Nothing pastoral."

Betsy went through a decade of grieving and religious experimentation, trying to find in various churches some of the community she lost when her father died. In graduate school in New York City, she found herself making friends with several Jewish people, whom she found very warm and caring. "They were not very religious Jews—initially I didn't even *see* the religion." She remembers instead "the getting together and the family connections" that had so much durability. Even within troubled families, Betsy found the strong bond that was affirmed around the Jewish holidays. "At every Passover, for example, they'd gather with their families, everyone together. One of my friends flew home for the day at Passover, the first night seder. Even though she hated her family, she'd be there! One day a year she'd give to them."

Soon Betsy moved into a large apartment in Brooklyn in which her roommates were Jewish—"dear, warm friends" who described themselves as cultural, secular Jews, and whom she found "very intellectual." One day Betsy made an important connection with one of her male roommates, Ted. "I'm kind of a hyperactive person, always have had my share of accidents. One hot day I had another—trying to move a floor fan, I caught my toe in the blade and it was bleeding a lot. I was very scared and Ted held me while I was crying. My toe looked mangled and bloody and Ted was very kind and warm. I thought I needed stitches and to go to the hospital, but Ted had been trained as a paramedic in the army and he cleaned off my battered toe and said that I just needed it to be kept clean and bandaged it with some medicine."

The experience of caring from this trustworthy man had a profound effect on Betsy. "He calmed me down *and* he respected my boundaries, and did it in a concerned, loving way." Betsy portrays in this story the way Judaism represented a caring presence, perhaps even a caring *male, fatherly* presence.

Finally, after having given up on faith entirely, Betsy decided that—a decade after the death of her father and several failed efforts to find solace in different Christian communities—it was time to take a closer look at Judaism. "I felt no need for faith or spiritual community until my late thirties," she told me. "When I felt myself looking for community rather than for faith, I felt if I was going to be a part of a community, why not a Jewish one?"

Pascal's wager is often invoked to explain why people become more connected to religion as they age. Pascal argued, in essence, that you might as well bet on there being a god because if you bet on there *not* being one and are wrong, the consequences are far worse than betting wrong the other way. That is, facing mortality and the possibility of heaven and hell, you might as well bet on heaven. There are no atheists in foxholes.

Betsy's story reminds us that the search for faith may have less to do with God as traditionally conceived and more to do with the desire for generational connection, with community, continuity, and honoring of the generations.[13]

Then Betsy had an experience that truly symbolized the internal sense of stability and wholeness that she sought, and that intimates the development of a different love for her parents:

"It was the first time I really knew I was Jewish, preconversion. One day I was home in my apartment, in the bedroom, when I heard a noise in the other room and thought there was a robber in the house. I heard doors opening and closing, sounded like the place being ransacked. I thought he would kill me. I had been studying with my sponsoring rabbi and I started to say the Shema to myself. Wow! When I reached for help, I reached for Judaism, I didn't reach for Jesus. It's odd but I felt very Jewish and was reminded of who I was. There I was, hiding behind the waterbed, trying to be as small as possible. The noises went on for forty-five minutes, which seemed like a long time for a robbery. Then the person started to talk to herself and I realized it was the cleaning lady! Still, I learned something very important in that experience: how Jewish I felt, huddled behind the waterbed reciting the Shema."

For Betsy, who experienced very clearly the dangerous possibilities of the world, Judaism became a sort of containing presence, a warm, reassuring, calming experience. As she speaks about Judaism, she conveys her evolving feminine experience of it, as if she is working her way back from the warm, lost "heartfelt" father to the warm, lost "heartfelt" mother she may once have known. As a matter of fact, Betsy's rabbi is a woman, and when Betsy told her about her experience of the robber and the Shema, the rabbi's warm, affirming reply meant a lot to her: "I told my sponsoring rabbi about how Jewish I felt at that moment and she said, 'It's in your bones.'"

Judaism, for Betsy, as for many of us, is a way of affirming a version of herself as male and female. Judaism can allow us to feel the connection to both our mothers and our fathers, and it helps us honor and give voice to the masculine and feminine parts of ourselves, to feel more whole and integrated than we can feel in everyday life. We may struggle to combine both sides of ourselves, but a common theme for Jews is the way that Jewish prayer and ritual speaks to our gendered selves.

For example, when I asked Betsy about some of the rituals and beliefs that underlie her Judaism, she offered me very female images, beginning with "the pagan moments in Judaism, the way in which the religion is based on many pagan beliefs including the lunar cycle. It's so earthy. The holidays follow the earth's changes and seasons, not some arbitrary dates based on Jesus' life."

As she explored Judaism, Betsy realized that she had a lot of freedom, including finding ways of exploring and asserting her femininity beyond the cold, patriarchal, masculine Judaism. "I realized that I could do what I wanted. I surely didn't believe in God, Adonai-the-father kind of notion. I liked being connected with Jewish stories and the Psalmist part of the old Testament. A favorite part is the Twenty-third Psalm—the Lord is my shepherd, protector."

So when I asked Betsy for a moment in her life when spirituality and Judaism came together, Betsy thought for a moment and told me about the *mikvah* ceremony (ritual bath) finalizing her conversion, an experience that drew both on her deep identification with the warmth of her dad and the recognition of herself as a vital, empowered woman. She began by invoking both her mother, no longer so cold, and the *Shechinah*, or feminine vitality of the divine. "It was in my home, my mother flew in, a friend played the guitar. Very *Shechinah*-ish. I had already been to the *mikvah*, which looked like a laundromat, a big closet with a tiny swimming pool, painted blue. There I was, naked, nervous, in front of all my friends, the pregnant rabbi, witnesses. After the *mikvah* we had a service back at my home, and the rabbi's hand was on my head. That's one thing I remember most—when the rabbi put her hands on my head, they felt very warm. A friend played 'Ailee, Ailee,' which is a song by Hannah Senish, the poet and fighter, and my Hebrew name which I was given that day is in honor of her. At the naming service after the *mikvah*, when I got all the papers signed, and I was named and seen as a Jew, my mother gave me an heirloom, a brooch with an ivory face that my dad had given to my grandmother after he came back from World War II and she gave it to my mother, her daughter-in-law. My grandmother is a very heart person, and it meant a lot to me that I was given that brooch."

I've heard this theme so often in different ways—varying stories, common struggle—and seen it in myself: the way that Judaism allows us to wrestle again with our attachments to our parents, to put a struggle *out there,* in the rituals and prayers, and maybe reconnect better with our parents as a result, either directly through our actions or by re-evaluating our feelings about them.

Not everyone has the same experiences; we do not all walk back to Judaism along a single avenue. Under the different ways of reconnecting with Judaism, though, lies that deeper struggle to honor self and parents and find a play space to reconnect with the deepest stirrings of awe and meaning against the seeming emptiness of the universe.

As I talked with Betsy over the years and followed her connection with her local synagogue in New York, where she became an involved, busy, and valued member, it became clear that Judaism was both the assertion of who she hoped to be and one way of making that identity real in the world, through ritual, prayer, and the community.

Sculpted and Foreclosed Judaism

Jaques considers "religious renewal," along with other grandiose strivings, as an attempt to avoid one's own internal divisions and anxieties about aging through the search for an omnipotent god, and "obsessional attempts at perfection."[14] However, religion may also be an avenue to a more whole sense of self, the "sculpted resolution" of the midlife crisis that Jaques writes of, in which there is a real give-and-take with reality and some restructuring of our deepest anxieties and fears. In fact, any choice may reflect a more sculpted or defensive (closed-off) orientation to life.

Maybe things are not so either-or. As we age we want to come to terms with aging, our mortality, family changes, and parents' aging, *and* we don't want to face those issues. Not only do we want to find in prayer and ritual the deeper aspects of ourselves, but we also want to lose our anxiety in obsessive ritual and davening, and maybe we want to give over the hard work of being an adult to the omnipotent god of our childhood. Religious and spiritual impulses can be part of a new maturity at midlife or a sedative to our troubled minds.

So the question is, What *kind* of Judaism do we create in our lives, a "sculpted" or "foreclosed"? Is it exploratory and playful, deeply connected to our struggles around hope and love and meaning, or is it rigid and rule-bound, serving more to contain our despair than to find a way to explore it, understand it, and move beyond it in an authentic way? In our experience of faith and Judaism we can become more playful, we can make a fuller connection between the internal world of passion and feeling and the external world of ritual, prayer, and observance. As we age we may be able to accept more ambiguity in the world, more uncertainty, and we may demand less perfection, placing fewer all-or-nothing demands on ourselves and those we love.

I'm not characterizing any specific observance or prayer as either sculpted or foreclosed; it's the *process* not the *content,* the question of whether there is some relatively free connection between who you are and the Judaism out there. You can be Orthodox, Conservative, Reconstructionist, Reform, Humanistic, or none of the above and still be sculpted. Or foreclosed.

There are many paths leading back to a vibrant Judaism. Once we give up guilt and shame and childhood battles, and the need to observe very traditionally, many options open up for us, all of which are indeed "Jewish." The possibilities of the seder, of Shabbat, of Purim, of our everyday work lives, and of the synagogue experience expand dramatically when not constrained by expectations of only one narrow "right way."

The next chapters explore the many shapes of a joyous, creative Judaism—at work, in the home, and in synagogue.

CHAPTER EIGHT

Creative Solutions to Careers: The Real *Tikkun Olam*

The real meaning of the biblical phrase *Tikkun Olam*—to heal, repair, transform the world—is a reaching out to the world beyond a narrow sense of "the Jews" or "the chosen people." For the men and women you'll meet in this chapter, their work in the world is a continuous part of their Jewish identity. Some are not particularly observant yet are vitally engaged with Jewish themes through their careers: social activism, music, economic reform, the arts, gay and lesbian advocacy. These are not overtly "Jewish careers," yet through such work each of these people is working on his or her Jewish identity. Here is a conception of what it means to be Jewish that moves beyond ritual observance in synagogue.

The old historical "givens" are not the center of the universe for the Jewish men and women in this chapter. They feel a changed relationship to Israel and a shifting relationship to the Holocaust, and they are more open to thinking about what it means to live within the Diaspora. Cindy Greenberg, for example, is the project director of the Jewish Social Justice Network, located at the Jewish Fund for Justice in New York City.

A mutual friend described her as "an old-time social activist, union type; she's at the center of the Jewish social justice scene." Cindy told me, "My generation, those of us in their thirties—some of our ideas have resonance to our parents and grandparents but others don't, and many of us struggle with how to relate to that." She feels that "people in our mid-thirties relate differently to Judaism, more experientially, rather than in terms of big-ticket items like Israel." For people like Cindy, Judaism is expressed when walking down the street in one's community and seeing what needs to be done—community organizing, poverty work, police-community relations, decent housing.

Even the phrase "Jewish values" becomes problematic within this perspective. Many Jews are uncomfortable with the way "Jewish values" are invoked when referring to such matters as social justice, social action, educating others, and feeding the homeless. At a board meeting of our synagogue, the rabbi was talking about the "Jewish values" of education and empowering the poor, and a very Jewish-identified woman said to me, "Why is that a Jewish value? It's a *human* value." She meant that the phrase smacked too much of Jewish sanctimony, of separating us from "others" who have no values—the chosen people notion in its exclusionary, oppressive form.

"I remember appeals for money to plant trees in Israel when across town from the synagogue people were homeless—it felt to me as a kid that the community had its priorities wrong," another man remembered.[1]

The artists and social activists in this chapter connect their work to the ongoing struggle to understand what it means to be Jewish and to help "heal the world." One uses concert music as a way of expanding the possibilities of Judaism, another uses his work as a playwright and actor, while a third uses creative writing. Several use traditional community organizing to express what it means to them to be Jewish. None, given who they are, would see "healing the world" as the work of only Jews, yet each finds a way through work and creativity to both explore what Judaism means and to reach out to others, lowering the barriers that divide Jews from each other and from non-Jews. Each of them has been able to transform the meaning of Judaism into a larger, inclusive vehicle that allows others to connect and feel at home.

Eric Stumacher and the
Apple Hill Chamber Players

Eric Stumacher is the executive and artistic director of the Apple Hill Chamber Players, a nationally and internationally known chamber music group. He is also a pianist with the Players, and a piano soloist who performs worldwide. It's a long way from their concerts at Lincoln Center in New York City, but Apple Hill is located on a former farm in Nelson, New Hampshire, where old wooden buildings dot the one-hundred-acre landscape and the annual free "concerts in the barn" are a high point of the summer for many residents and visitors. Apple Hill is also the location of a school for students of chamber music.

The Apple Hill Chamber Players perform nationwide and worldwide year-round. One of their activities is of special interest: the Playing for Peace Project in the Middle East. For over a decade, the Apple Hill Chamber Players have been touring the Middle East, visiting not only Israel but also Lebanon, Syria, Egypt, and Jordan at times when this was not easy, as well as bringing Israeli and Arab students together to Apple Hill to study chamber music. As the originator of these efforts, Eric has wrestled with what Judaism means to him and how to be a decent human being in this world.

When I told Eric over the phone that I was interested in learning more about the kinds of nourishment he finds in Judaism, he immediately recognized what I was interested in and he said that "the spiritual core of Judaism at its best holds up beautifully and profoundly." But he told me that he was very disturbed by the "filters" within Judaism that separate it from other people, ideas like "the chosen people" and the "special-ness" of the Jews.

"Having visited so many sides in the Arab-Israeli conflict, I can see that there are many points of view. If I say that I am cho-sen, what does that say about you who are not Jewish?" Eric is passionate in his belief that all religions today struggle with the issue of "living in a world that calls for not one right way, but simultaneous right ways, multiple right ways. I'm interested in ways of finding ways of saying that you're right *and* I'm right." Eric is particularly proud of Judaism's willingness to question things, to create room for development and creativity.

He uses music to that end. Music carries with it an inclusive impulse, a transcendent urge to bind people together beyond the superficiality of our differences, calling us toward the more pro-found inclusiveness in our human situation. Mozart recognized this, as did Beethoven.

At Apple Hill, Eric says, "the mission here is not only to cre-ate the most beautiful music possible, but to also use the music to bind people together, create community, across different reli-gions, different generations, the young and the old."

After performing as a chamber music group for fifteen years, in 1988 the Apple Hill Players had the chance to do a tour of Is-rael. While the initial invitation was to simply tour Israel, Eric devised the idea of including Arab audiences in Israel and reach-ing out to Arab and Israeli students, providing scholarships to bring them together to study at Apple Hill itself in the United States. This tour was so successful and so popular that it has been repeated every year since. In 1992 the Apple Hill Players' tour included Israel, Jordan, and Syria and was the basis for the feature-length documentary *Playing for Peace*. In 1995 their tour included areas of the West Bank and other Palestinian sites. In 2000, with help from the U.S. State Department, the Apple

Hill Players went for the first time to Lebanon. They were the first American group to perform in Lebanon since the civil war of the 1980s. They gave a sold-out performance at the American University of Beirut, a performance attended by the American ambassador to Lebanon and other foreign and local dignitaries, plus hundreds of Lebanese, while outside the performance hall the event was picketed by Hezbollah, protesting the U.S. support for the recent Israeli retaliatory bombing of a number of Lebanese electrical plants.[2]

Eric's time in Lebanon left him with few illusions about the human capacity for violence. "We traveled around and heard a lot. No one was free of horrible behavior. We hear a lot about the Israelis and the Syrians in Lebanon, but during the civil war period the Christian, Muslim, and Druze Lebanese went house-to-house slaughtering each other. The Beirut Academy of Music was burned to the ground, all the pianos destroyed. The Syrians and Israelis became odd bedfellows, working to separate the slaughterers and restore some order."

Eric's experience with the human capacity for hatred and misunderstanding leaves him at times contemplating the Middle Eastern saying "Instead of resting on the seventh day, God should have called a consultant."

Still, Eric is committed to inclusivity and understanding, to "making the global world happen, even if it is tough sledding ideologically." And a piece of that effort comes out of his being Jewish. He was very moved recently by Kathryn Watterson's *Not by the Sword*, a book about Cantor Michael Weisser of Lincoln, Nebraska, who befriended Larry Trapp, the grand dragon of the state Ku Klux Klan, after receiving death threats from him.[3] Weisser understood that much of Trapp's behavior might be due to his background as a juvenile delinquent (shared also by Weisser himself) and the effects of his diabetes, which ultimately was to kill him. Eric described how Weisser and his family—

targets for Trapp when they arrived in Lincoln—reached out to Trapp, creating a connection through which Trapp was able to renounce his bigotry; he actually died in Weisser's arms. One aspect of the story that particularly moved Eric was Jewish spirituality as a transcending force in the community: virtually all the Christian clergy members of Lincoln wound up attending Weisser's Friday night services, finding in the synagogue a place where they were able to explore their own spirituality, free of the constraints of the clergy role in their own churches. "That's what I hope for," Eric said, "Judaism as an open, inclusive place for everyone."

For Eric, the search for such an inclusive place is part of his own journey to make a meaningful Judaism in his life. For him, the key task is getting past the "chosen people" notion that so dominates some Jews' version of their religion. "If Jews are chosen, what does that mean for other people on Earth who are not chosen? How do we get past an insular Judaism and break the victim cycle, in which we are also seeking retribution for past injuries, such as with land for peace in Israel?"

His daughters are now adults, but a defining moment happened for Eric when his oldest daughter was five years old. The family had gone to see *Fiddler on the Roof,* and the play ends with the Jews being thrown out of their village. On the way home, his daughter asked why the Jews had to leave their homes. Thinking about her question, Eric also wondered about "the parallel question: why do *other* people in Israel today have to leave their homes?" He didn't answer his daughter right away, in part because "her question led me to think about what it meant to me to be Jewish."

Until then, Eric had been a passive Jew, one who knew he was Jewish but without much active involvement. He was born in Philadelphia, raised in Bucks County in a "consciously integrated, multifaith community with lots of Quakers in which we were the only Jews." Eric's parents were "observant but not religious." Both raised Orthodox, they brought up Eric in a Conservative synagogue in Elkins Park, Pennsylvania, where he went through Hebrew school. "After my bar mitzvah that was pretty much it, until my kids were born. When my first daughter arrived, I went to the phone book and looked up Cohen, eventually finding the president of the synagogue, whom I became close friends with. Our daughter had her naming ceremony in the first service in the new synagogue building, which was being completed that year I called him."

His daughter's question led Eric to think about what it meant to be Jewish in a new, more profound way. Instead of responding in terms of "we-they" (e.g., "being Jewish means protecting yourself against being driven out" or "being Jewish means getting back what was taken from us"), Eric's explanation to me went toward the "us": "We human beings are operating with internal mental hardware that has evolved ten thousand years ago, among territorial people who didn't travel much. Strangers when they appeared incited an impulse to kill and the fear of difference. We have something new in the modern global community—people trying to get along. One antidote to the hardware is to create software to keep the human race going. Religion could be a better software than it is, teaching how to live together, reducing the divisions between people."

For Eric, being a Jew also raises hard questions for him as an American: "What would happen if Native Americans knocked on our doors and said, 'This is my country, now get out, we want our land back'? That is the same thing that many Israelis are saying and many American Jews who support Israel are saying."

For Eric, the answer is to go back into the music, to use the deeper rhythms of music to remind us of our commonalities, to bring together diverse audiences of Jews and non-Jews, Israelis and Arabs, and diverse performers, to nurture the voices of performers of all backgrounds. Music becomes the software to re-program the hardware of our mistrustful genetic inheritance.

When I asked him if he felt that he lived life according to particular Jewish values, Eric replied, "Jewish values? I don't know if they are only Jewish or not. I try to stay away from that. I try to honor the voice in all people and to bring out the best of that voice, in my professional and spiritual pursuits."

So, Eric doesn't think much about "Jewish values," nor is he traditionally observant—"I don't attend services much, although we went to the community Passover seder the other night and enjoyed it immensely." Eric's inclusivity, his way of using music and goodwill to bring together people, is deeply rooted in his experience of being Jewish and offers a vision of Judaism that encourages us to make room for all faiths, to find the deeper connections and bonds that unite us amid our tendency to divide and fight.

Amanda Joseph and
"The Torah of Money"

Amanda Joseph is the director of TZEDEC (the *Tzedek* Economic Development Campaign), a program of The Shefa Fund, located in Philadelphia. The Shefa Fund, founded in 1988 by Jeffrey Dekro, is a public foundation promoting Jewish social responsibility through grantmaking, low-income community investing, and education.

The goal of TZEDEC is to bring Jewish investment to low-income communities traditionally neglected by mainstream financial institutions. TZEDEC enables federations, synagogues, family foundations, and individuals to "invest Jewishly" in community-based banks, loan funds, and credit unions. These local institutions then lend money for affordable housing, small business development, worker retraining, and child care and other community services. TZEDEC has catalyzed more than

$10 million in American Jewish investments since its inception in 1997.[4]

Amanda is in her early thirties and holds a master's degree from the Yale School of Management. She points out that low-income community development is an area that hasn't had a lot of Jewish community and institutional participation. Orders of nuns and church groups are well represented as investors in low-income-community development, but synagogues and Jewish organizations are not. Overall, church groups have invested close to 20 percent of the amount loaned nationally to community development financial institutions.

Amanda wants to change that. And she wants to shift Jewish consciousness from merely "giving" to a *tzedakah* that also emphasizes partnership and investment as the highest form of giving. A TZEDEC brochure quotes Maimonides, from *Laws of Gifts to the Poor*: "The highest degree of *tzedakah* is upholding the hands of people reduced to poverty by making a gift or a loan, or entering into a partnership, or finding work for them, in order to strengthen their hands...."

For Amanda, the phrase *Tikkun Olam* is powerful and resonant. It means partnership, not charity or passive giving. She is committed to the idea of Jews using their many resources—of which money is just one—to help communities in need. "This isn't just about cash, but about Jews using our political and organizational skills to help others." Which is why the word *investment* has a broad meaning to Amanda: "Hopefully, we make emotional and spiritual investments in others—including in our own communities—not just financial ones. We invest smartly in community groups that are doing good work directly, rather than just being traditional Jewish moneylenders. The aim is to invest in people and communities so that they can become self-sufficient. We try to help individuals and groups who have traditionally a hard time getting loans from banks: low-income borrowers, women, minorities, in urban and rural neighborhoods.

"The TZEDEC campaign is about more than getting money into the hands of low-income communities," Amanda notes. "It's also about how effective we can be in engaging the Jewish community in a conversation about the larger good. We hope to get Jews to think and experience the world differently."

Amanda loves what she does. Her voice registers excitement when she tells me that, for example, in Boston the Combined Jewish Philanthropies invested $100,000 in a community development loan fund to stabilize Boston's low-income neighborhoods by renovating abandoned properties and creating affordable housing. In Minneapolis–St. Paul a local synagogue made a $25,000 deposit in a community development credit union. In Washington, D.C., TZEDEC worked with local investors, including the District of Columbia's federation endowment fund, to invest hundreds of thousands of dollars locally, including an $18,000 deposit in a low-income community development credit union that offers affordable loans and financial services to church members. Amanda explains, "The church-based group holds the hands of its members in ways that banks just can't anymore—if a member misses a car loan, someone from the credit union goes and talks to that person, helps them figure out how they will repay it. There is respect and pride and caring in the process."

The idea for TZEDEC is rooted in Hebrew free loan societies of the nineteenth century. When immigrant Jews were not able to get loans from banks, they formed *Landsmeinschaften,* lending money to each other so that they could pay the rent on pushcarts and purchase supplies.[5] "Now we need to extend the idea from Jews lending money to Jews to helping other disenfranchised groups." Amanda points out that particularly in these times, when Jews are relatively affluent, we have a responsibility to use our money to make the world a better place. She observes, "I have a big thing for being responsible and accountable, which is the way I choose to be Jewish, to identify as a Jew." One of the ways Amanda expresses that conviction is by trying to bridge cultures: bringing Jews to help non-Jews through targeted investing, uniting the secular world of community development and the social justice ideals of Judaism.

For Amanda, her graduate degree from Yale is part of consolidating and expressing in the world her Jewish identity. She is, as she says, a person energized in the most positive ways by the challenge of reconciling disparate elements of contemporary Jewish experience.

Bridging disparate experiences is indeed a central part of Amanda's experience and informs her Jewish identity. She begins her own story with the clash between her parents' versions of Judaism. Amanda's father came from an upper-middle-class Brooklyn family that had been in the United States for two generations and was well established in Conservative Jewish circles. Amanda's mother was the daughter of immigrants, raised in the Bronx within a family uncertain about how to fit its Jewish identity into life in this strange American land. Her grandfather distanced himself from traditional Judaism, tried to make it in America, even while holding on to the old ways. The household was kosher but his son did not become a *bar mitzvah.* "For my mother, what was Jewish was all the political activism going on around her—the organizing, the consciousness." Amanda notes, "My mother's connection to Judaism was very strong, but not like my father's, who really had the Jewish knowledge of ritual and observance."

That difference between formal ritual and knowledge and profound love for and engagement with the social world of Jewish activism is the pivot for Amanda's energy. Her memory of childhood is dominated by nurturing, warm memories of the Jewish nursery school and Jewish after-school programs. "I loved all the stories in which the Pharaoh always wound up the 'bad guy,' and I have a vivid memory of a class project, making a menorah out of wood, washers, and glitter."

Amanda's earliest Jewish exposure was in the nursery school

at Rodeph Sholom, an influential Reform synagogue on the Upper West Side of Manhattan. When she was five, the family moved from Manhattan to Long Island, and Amanda enjoyed her time at a Modern Orthodox Hebrew school. "Our teachers came from Borough Park and were very involved and passionate. We didn't always agree with them because they seemed so different from us. The women wore wigs! But I enjoyed their energy, commitment, and patience."

Yet the suburban life felt like a blatant culture clash, exemplified by her mother's struggle with her own Jewish heritage. Amanda's mother loathed the separation of the sexes in the Modern Orthodox synagogue and felt alienated from institutionalized Judaism. She would generally attend High Holiday services, but to Amanda it seemed "always a struggle; uncertainty was in the air."

Amanda's mother's family never attended synagogue, and so she had no background in observant Judaism. "The whole experience was foreign to her." Moreover, Judaism was in part defined across the chasm of a class divide within the family— Amanda's mother, from an immigrant family, struggling to survive, had married into a prosperous American Jewish family with established Jewish commitments. "My father's family knew summer camps and country clubs, my mother's family had to make very little money go a long way." Among the extended family there were understandable tensions around these differences.

Amanda's childhood then was marked by mixed allegiances to Judaism: her mother's profound engagement with being Jewish alongside bitterness about institutionalized Judaism; the reality of class differences in her family mingled with her father's less conflicted, easygoing engagement with Judaism; and Amanda's enjoyment of the warm Hebrew school and summer camp environment. The socialist-Zionist Hashomer Hatzair camp influenced her very deeply, as did the commitment to Jewish ritual and practice of the teachers and rabbi at her Modern Orthodox

Hebrew school. "What I carried away was the knowledge that there are many ways to express Judaism and to have a relationship to Israel beyond suburban clichés."

The impact continues: "I have such mixed feelings—I still have to write G-D without spelling it out because of what I learned in Hebrew school. That's how we did it." Yet Amanda doesn't attend synagogue regularly and has not made studying Judaism a priority. "There are many people who see me as a 'super Jew,' and I'm often shocked, because I don't really know all that much."

When Amanda went to college at Bryn Mawr she was not involved with Jewish life on campus. "I felt Jewish, but didn't want to have much to do with Hillel or services." Even today, Amanda observes, "most of my close friends are not Jews." She remembers as a kid fantasizing about "how great it would be to be a white Christian in America, eating white bread, being part of a large family, not as burdened by what felt to me back then as the heaviness of being Jewish." Just to be homogenized and not to stand out.

After college Amanda worked in an entry-level job at the Metropolitan Museum of Art in New York City but didn't find a meaning and purpose that engaged her. She went to Israel. "I had a very negative image of Israel based on all the neighbors growing up who went and seemed to picture it just as a tourist attraction—'look at this cute soldier,' 'even the garbagemen are Jewish' kind of thing." In contrast, though, were the positive memories Amanda still carried from her socialist-Zionist camp. "The songs, the laughter, the fun, the politics (as much as a kid could absorb), all with Jews who seemed so committed and engaged—without the summer camp experience I never would have set foot there."

Amanda spent a year and a half in Israel, reconnecting with relatives and learning about the many ways of being Jewish, expanding her vision of Judaism beyond the suburban blandness and entitlement she perceived growing up. She worked on a magazine published by the World Union of Jewish Students, an international student political organization that focused on many causes. "We worked with Jews from all over, every country, all types, Orthodox, Conservative, the secular, left wing and right. While the man who ran the organization was a settler and he commuted to work in Jerusalem with a gun on his car seat, he was very supportive of the diversity in our community, of the students and different brands of Judaism."

Amanda began to feel the diversity of Jewish experience: those active in the Women in Black organization, who stood on street corners around Israel on Friday afternoons, before Shabbat, holding placards urging passersby to "End the Occupation," contrasting with angry right-wing Jews who excoriated her for visiting a Palestinian home one Saturday afternoon during a visit organized by peace activists ("that's like sitting in Hitler's living room," one settler colleague admonished her).

Amanda was encouraged to stay when she talked of going home: "You *are* home," she was told, and she realized that was not true. "I needed to go home and digest these eighteen months—it was a life-changing experience. I began to deal with Judaism as an adult."

That meant exploring the world of social action and social justice. Amanda became involved with a support group in New York City for the Women in Black movement and with the New Israel Fund, and that work led to Americans for Peace Now, doing community organizing and program administration. Amanda began to realize that "my extracurricular pursuits seemed so Jewish since arriving back from Israel," and she found herself thinking about how being Jewish might be a larger part of her life and work. The way this question formed itself in Amanda's mind was, "Could I be a full-time Jew?"

As she reached her late twenties, she entered a period of soul-searching about work. "I wanted graduate training, but something practical, that would change my work and was part of my Jewish identity."

Amanda chose business school and went to the Yale School of Management, recognizing that she needed organizational and financial skills to build on her experiences in different organizations. The decision surprised her. "I wouldn't have predicted it a year earlier, but I realized that business school offered the practical skills that I needed."

On the application form many of her essays were on Jewish themes, including her experience in leadership in the Women in Black movement and the role models she found in the activists she met. Amanda realized that it is in the very nature of the Jewish community to create its own institutions; it is the historical legacy of being part of the Jewish community. "We've had to re-create and organize ourselves over and over in Jewish life, and these skills are ones that we can offer to others in need." To her surprise, Amanda found that "I had a great experience in graduate school, felt I encountered a whole new world, and I welcomed the fact that I was Jewish in it."

Amanda graduated in 1996 and became interested in community economic development. She did not seek work in "anything *specifically* Jewish," instead wanting to get experience in the area of community development. She became a loan officer with the Self-Help Credit Union in Greensboro, North Carolina, "the Lehman Brothers of community development financial institutions."

Amanda found that when living in the small Jewish community of Greensboro, "choosing to be involved really made a difference. In New York City, you could fade out of the community in terms of participation and still feel like a Jew; that's harder when you live in a small town. I was pretty naïve, didn't know much about Jewish life outside the New York metropolitan area."

As we talked, Amanda observed, "for people of our generation, it's so easy to walk away from Judaism because of bad experiences in Hebrew school, or conflicts with parents, so easy to toss it away and be American, but I feel a real visceral sense of tribal obligation—I may not practice as many Jews do but..." She paused, then went on. "I think of all the people who have lived before me, lived and died for being Jewish. How can I walk away from that? It's a source of obligation that is not oppressive." She concluded, shyly, "I discovered in Israel this Jewish place within myself, that Jewishness is the pillow I put my head on at night."

When The Shefa Fund called, she wrestled with the opportunity to work on progressive issues in a Jewish context. The fund uses the phrase "The Torah of Money" to refer to the moral-ethical implications of how we as Jews in this time of wealth use our money, power, and privilege. We may be used to giving charity, to being the leaders, but how do we learn to be good allies, to use our resources to support others and empower them? For Amanda, being Jewish means reaching out to all people, including non-Jews, not with charity but with *tzedakah*. "Righteous giving means not just charity, but a real engagement in changing the world, aspiring to create a just society, as we are taught in our texts."

Yet, for Amanda, what it means to be Jewish is also an open question. Though she lives in a progressive Jewish community in greater Philadelphia, initially its homogeneity made her uncomfortable. She grapples with a more sophisticated version of her mother's struggle—what is my place, particularly vis-à-vis an established Jewish community? She has her mother's sense of nudging the comfortable American Jewish community, calling us all to task, to not be complacent in our suburban comforts.

Amanda confesses to consciously taking her time about assimilating herself into the Jewish community she lives in, seemingly the "world capital" of a progressive and learned Judaism, with a "rabbi on every corner." She moved into that part of Philadelphia for her job at Shefa with the TZEDEC program, and found herself at first missing the more religiously diverse communities she had lived within. "I've learned the challenges and joys of *shtetl* living," she said. She has, though, come to feel more at home where she lives, to feel less of an outsider in her consciously Jewish community. Still, more observant friends spot her periodically in *shul;* she knows they wonder, *What are you doing here?* Amanda recognizes insight in this surprise; she is not observant traditionally.

"Internally, I know I'm Jewish, I have my own relationship with God, even though many Jews may not feel that's enough," Amanda says. Yet Amanda's voice shifts, deepens, when she talks of Heschel's concept of the awesomeness of existence, felt every day in the mundane details of our life. When asked for an example, Amanda spoke of seeing faded morning glories in the side yard while living in Jerusalem—when she first wakes up—and then told me that upon awakening she recites to herself the two-line Orthodox prayer *Modeh Ani,* which she knows only in Hebrew. "I learned it as a kid and got into the habit of saying it every morning. It's my daily meditation."

She apologized for not knowing the exact translation ("I give thanks") but then said that "the Judaism I grew up with was more flexible, not a bunch of 'shoulds' or 'this or thats' or 'good and bad.'" Her mother decided to have Shabbat dinners at one point during Amanda's childhood, "and for years we did, but never said the full kiddush. For years I didn't know there was a paragraph before and after *boray pre hagofen.*" Her voice had a hint of sadness, despite the laughter of that moment. "If I grew up in a family where there were more rituals, I would have the language and the prayers," but the culture clash within her family made that hard. Yet however imperfect, there was something important in those childhood experiences. "I didn't understand the fullness and depth of those rituals until I was older and saw, particularly in Israel, a 'complete' Shabbat. But it was good my family did it; I got the cultural fluency later, after the basic training."

Even today, Amanda notes that "my mother is the first to send me newspaper clippings about things Jews are doing wrong, to each other or to others. I tell her 'Mom, you have such a strong Jewish identity, you're always there talking about, arguing about, kvetching about and with Jews.'"

"Your mother has a lover's quarrel with Judaism," I noted, and Amanda responded, "I exemplify that conflict. I'm comfortable in a world of Christians, I'm not threatened by fundamentalists, I love Christmas carols and respect those traditions. I ate bacon as a child and shrimp for many years, before I returned from Israel with a heightened sense of Jewish consciousness and gave all that up."

However, Amanda went on, "I still live with the daily reality, fear that 'it can happen again.'" For Amanda, Jewish security in an ambiguous world does not lie with a "Fortress Israel" approach—in which Jews arm themselves against all threat—but rather with remembering that "our affluence brings responsibility." She wants to embrace a multicultural world without fear while also paying attention to the responsibilities and awareness that will ensure our survival. "Some Jews become insular because they're afraid. I have that fear of it happening again, too, but there are different ways we as Jews can deal with it—the path I see is not to cut ourselves off but to really be in the world with integrity and value and be open to it. My fear is we close ourselves off and then we become vulnerable." She stopped. "Bringing these worlds together, the secular, community development, social justice, rich and poor, Jews and Christians, that's the kind of Judaism I want to bring to the community. Responsive. Just. A Judaism that recognizes our obligation to ourselves and the community in which we live and participate.

"We all make a choice—it's so easy for American Jews to walk away from suffering that is not perceived as our own. We can isolate ourselves and live off the fat of the land, but then we forget how recently we were *not* in that place in this country. *Tzedek* work engages us all in a challenging conversation about how to be true to our values as Jews. This is where we have to resolve it, to do work in the world, make it better. That is Jewish tradition."

That commitment to remember the world, to bridge the gap between rich and poor, is Amanda's continuation of her own, and her mother's, desire to be a part of Judaism without also feeling demeaned by it.

Jeff Raz: Theater as Jewish Practice

Jeff Raz is a playwright, actor, and drama teacher, living in San Francisco with his wife and young son. He is trained as a clown, and juggling and mime skills find their way into his performances. Jeff teaches drama in high schools and colleges, using theater to explore the tensions of differences and bonds of connection between people.

One of the defining mysteries in Jeff's life, and in his relationship to Judaism, was the suicide of his father in 1966 when Jeff was eight years old. His father had joined the army in 1944 when he was underage (and 6' 4" tall) to "save my race." His own father got him a commission in the Pacific as an officer but he chose to go to Europe to fight Hitler as an infantryman. "He carried a gun and a camera. He may or may not have actually photographed the camps—there are pictures in the only album I have from him of piles of bodies that probably came from one of the camps." For Jeff, there has always been a connection between his father's suicide and the concentration camps—a connection Jeff explores in his work in the theater.

His father returned to the United States profoundly haunted by what he saw in Europe, and he struggled with depression throughout his adult life, which eventually led to his suicide. Jeff and his brother were raised by their mother, who sought connection to a Jewish community that only minimally reached out to the struggling family. Jeff remembers the "cluelessness" he felt about Judaism in his family and the clumsy efforts to join other families for holiday celebrations, no one really comfortable in the shadow of a father's suicide.

Jeff's solo play *Father-Land* is set during the first visit to Europe of a character named Jeff, a struggling actor in his early twenties.[6] In the play, while performing street theater to earn a few shillings at Covent Gardens, the character "Jeff" blurts out to an attractive young German woman, Helga, who steps forward out of the crowd to volunteer to participate in a crowd-pleasing balancing act, "Where you from? Germany, Germany. You know, some of my family members went to summer camp at Dachau."

The street audience is shocked, as is Jeff, who as the narrator confesses: "I don't know where that came from. That's the wildest thing I ever said onstage."

In fact, Jeff as narrator acknowledges onstage that no one in his immediate family was ever in Dachau. The play goes on to explore how it is that an American Jew with only a distant relationship to Judaism (and to the Holocaust) had such a profound reaction to a German woman, and her to him. Helga confesses to "Jeff" that she grew up in a house confiscated from a prosperous Jewish family, most of whom died in the camps, a fact denied by her mother and her grandfather, a Nazi collaborator.

As the play evolves, "Jeff" confronts his own denial about the impact of the Holocaust on his father, as well as his father's denial. He remembers his father as simply a soldier in Europe during World War II: "He wasn't in much danger, really, he was just a photographer. I don't know anything else about him."

The ghost of "Jeff's" father appears at one point, wearing his familiar glasses, and testifies in a bland way about his own suicide. "I grew up in Rochester, New York, a nice Jewish family. I joined the army in 1944, didn't see much action in the war, I was a photographer. When I got home, I went to college, met my wife, and became a physicist. Unfortunately, I had a chemical imbalance that made it impossible for me to work after a few years, so I considered what it would be like to live in an institution and I decided to take my own life." Father and son are bound together in similar denial, a family taboo about looking at the impact of the war on Jewish men.

A visit to Dachau with Helga—Jew and Christian together, each on a shadowy, guilty pilgrimage to see and understand—cracks open "Jeff's" numb, frozen stance about his father and Judaism. He begins to learn more about his father's suicide and the impact of photographing the camps. It is a raw, cold day and by chance they take refuge in the camp museum. "I wondered what it would be like in the pajamas the prisoners wore. I was wearing a coat and a sweater, and I was freezing." In one room of the museum, "Jeff" comes upon several of his father's photographs and has a transformative confrontation with his father's ghost.

As the play concludes, "Jeff" begins to understand more of the imbalance in his father's life. What was out of balance was not just his father's physiology and his mood swings, but also his privileged life in the United States and the fate of the people he had seen in the camps. The mental boundaries blurred. He was unable to forget those smelly, dirty Jews who were his people, partly him, and unable to fit that experience into the scientific life of a successful academic. Both father and son struggle to make sense and meaning out of their connection to Judaism while living as "big, healthy Jewish boys" in America.

"Jeff" and Helga, too, are joined together, both struggling with the weight of their fathers' wartime experiences and denial of them. The Jew and the German are neatly balanced by the need to understand and come to terms with the older generation's denial, shock, sorrow, and guilt.[7]

Father-Land is a demanding play for Jewish and non-Jewish audiences. It invites us to think about how knowledge of the Holocaust shaped our parents' lives in hidden ways ("does the smoke bother you?" Helga inquires at one point, lighting up a cigarette). It explores how the children of the World War II generation ("the greatest generation," in Tom Brokaw's idealized perspective) suffered from what their parents couldn't talk about, even as they profited from the successes and courage of the "greatest generation." The play also reminds us that we are only slowly coming out of the denial of the Holocaust in our own lives. In doing so, Jeff invites Jews to consider how they are inextricably joined to Germans now, in the way that after human catastrophe, succeeding generations on different sides of the experience are nevertheless joined.

As a former street performer, Jeff Raz strives to use his solo theater performances (of which *Father-Land* is only one) to get people involved and talking to each other. He does this, in large part, through humor, a vehicle not usually associated with the Holocaust. Since he was trained in part as a clown, physical comedy runs throughout Jeff's performances. The street theater balancing act early in the play, for instance, involves a volunteer from the audience, who winds up perched, standing on Jeff's strong shoulders, representing Helga. The sight is awkward, touching, and very amusing. The line about "summer camp at Dachau" usually plays funny: people laugh, and that's all right with Jeff. He reflects, "A great acting teacher of mine, a sophisticated European, once said that 'great comedy is 51 percent comedy and 49 percent tragedy.'" Like many Jewish writers and performers (Philip Roth is one example of the former) Jeff uses humorous scenes to help people think about tragic, hard-to-face matters. "My dad killed himself. When I say that, people hold their breath. When we can laugh in the face of death, then the breath comes out of us and we are less frozen."

Jeff was particularly pleased with one comment from the audience after a performance of *Father-Land*—an older man came up to tell him that he had been reluctant to come to the show but was glad he did, saying that "it was a relief, the play was so different. I thought I was going to get another one of those Holocaust shows." Instead, the humor and physicality allowed this man to see the tragic themes in a different light.

Jeff's purpose is quite serious. He performs *Father-Land* in his university and high school classes as a way to get students talking about how we misjudge each other, fail to look beyond stereotypical labels. "'Are you Jewish?' students will sometimes ask me, and I'll point to my nose and ask, 'What do you think?' as a way of defusing the intensity of diversity discussions. They'll laugh, then I'll say, 'Well, no, actually I'm really Italian...no, really, I'm Greek...No, really, I'm Jewish.' My purpose in being provocative like that is to get us into the visceral nature of ethnic attributes and attributions. I'll ask them, 'If I'm not Jewish, would it make a difference in seeing *Father-Land*? How about if I was Italian?'"

Jeff believes that we can become aware of differences and diversity between people much more effectively through the arts than by use of traditional diversity lecturing and "diversity training." The arts are specific and personal and they use narrative, which avoids over-generalizing: "things get nasty when we start talking in generalities like 'you people do this or that.' It is much easier to hear and see when we speak of 'Jeff,' and 'Helga,' and 'my mother or father.'" Art gives a human face to the tragedy and possibilities of divisions between people.

Writing and performing his solo plays has allowed Jeff to explore his changing sense of his own Jewish identity. As someone

who grew up without a strong connection, he has used the theater to sort out what kind and how much of a Jew he really is.
At these audience discussions, for example, someone would
bring up a point of theology or Jewish history, and for a long
time Jeff responded, "I'm not really a practicing Jew." He remembers "trying to slip away from Judaism that way" until one
evening a woman said to him, "Your play *is* practicing Judaism." That affected Jeff very deeply, since "she meant that the
practice of the Jewish religion is about questioning and bringing
up issues, grappling and wrestling."

One way in which Jeff feels his Judaism is as one who
wrestles with difficult issues. The mystery of really "knowing"
you are Jewish, and the meaning of that, runs throughout several of his plays. When I asked him his definition of a "good
Jew," Jeff replied, "Could you ask a more loaded question? In
my play *Birth Mark,* I have a play within a play of Oedipus
where he is a Jew but doesn't know it. His accuser, speaking
from the rack, asks him, 'Do you always answer a question with
a question?' The reply: 'Who's asking? I mean yes ... no ... aah,
I am a Jew!'" Then Jeff reminded me of the woman who told
him after a show that "I should never say that I'm not a practicing Jew since my play was Jewish practice." He commented,
"I half agree."

Jeff offered Howard Gardner's definition of an expert as one
that "might work for good Jews": (1) deep knowledge of the
craft, (2) creative, innovative, and/or beautiful use of the craft
(making it art), and (3) knowledge of the history and present
practice of the craft. "As a Jew," Jeff rated himself, "I only have
a small piece of each of those."

Jeff and his wife, Sherry, have adopted a baby boy, not born
Jewish. Jeff wrote the play *Birth Mark* to explore the experience
of adoption and the Jewish issue of whether a child born of a
non-Jewish mother can be Jewish.[8] The subtext of the play,
though, is the question of what it means to be Jewish and to

consider yourself a Jew. Does it come from matrilineal descent alone? From what your parents teach you, how you are raised? From what you believe and how you act as an adult?

Esther is Jeff's most recent play, a hip version of the Purim story, and it contains a graphic, straightforward acknowledgment of Jewish aggression, as well as the more traditionally celebrated themes of Jewish heroism and survival. Jeff uses this story "to highlight the cycle of revenge in a modern context—Kosovo, Ireland, Jerusalem—and to talk about the need to look at what isn't being said in stories." It is the rejoicing in the death and destruction at the core of the Purim story, without looking at the moral and ethical implications, which Jeff brings to central focus with humor and chutzpah. As he says, "This grappling with the old stories, as a writer, performer, and teacher, feels both spiritual and very Jewish in style and content."

Jeff is also transforming personal loss and puzzlement—the fate of his father, the relative absence of Judaism in his past, the role of denial and "not seeing" in his life—into universal themes that connect to the experiences of Jews and non-Jews alike. And he is using points of his own vulnerability to create safe, provocative spaces in the classroom and theater where people can examine their own hateful and loving impulses and the places where they meet.

Felice Yeskel:
Being "Jewish, Lesbian, and Working Class"

Felice Yeskel was momentarily puzzled when I asked what she does. "What I *do*? There are many things I used to do, many I do now." She is a social activist, organizer, and educator. She helped found and is currently co-director of United for a Fair Economy, a Boston-based nonpartisan, nonprofit organization devoted to increasing public awareness of and action about the growing economic divide between the rich and the rest of us.[9]

She is also the director of the Stonewall Center at the University of Massachusetts, Amherst, a lesbian, gay, bisexual, and transgender educational resource center that has served as a model for many colleges and universities nationwide.

For Felice, Judaism has always been intertwined with being lesbian and being working class. "Luckily, I have never been plagued with confusion about my Jewish identity. I learned Jewish pride at home," she wrote in a chapter for a book on being gay, lesbian, and Jewish.[10] Her lesbian and working-class roots have provided her with a profound understanding of what it means to weave together diverse aspects of the self within a Jewish identity.

In Felice's home there was tension around assimilation and achievement. Growing up in New York City, she was admitted to an elementary school for academically gifted students, an opportunity her mother saw for Felice to become upwardly mobile and work her way out of their working-class environment.

Felice's father emigrated from Poland and came from an Orthodox background. As a child Felice went to an Orthodox Sunday school, which she remembers as "old and scary." Then the family also joined a Reform temple. "On the High Holidays, my father went to daven at the Orthodox synagogue, and I went to the Reform temple with friends, while my mother stayed home and watched TV."

Felice's father worked as a "bagman—he collected the sacks that flour came in, in his truck from bakeries for recycling, making about half a cent a bag. It's amazing that he made a living."

At age five, Felice found herself in an uptown elementary school for intellectually gifted children, surrounded by children from privileged homes. She recalled, "I felt shame when I had to tell kids what my father did. He was a bagman, and I thought he was the only one in the world. *Well, have you ever heard of a bagman?* When I asked him what I should put on the forms in the space for father's occupation, he said, 'Peddler.' I wasn't sure which was worse: being a bagman or a peddler. Why couldn't he do something 'normal'?"[11]

Felice's sense of difference was also entwined with her recognition at age eleven that she was lesbian. While reading a dictionary she came across the word *lesbian* and found a name that defined the urges and desires that she had been wrestling with. It was not a happy recognition: "I felt a wave of nausea in my stomach. I felt *that's me* and it was the worst thing in the world." Every day she would say to herself, "I'm a lesbian and I guess I have to kill myself." Being a lesbian felt like a betrayal of her mother's dreams of advancement for her. "My mother was so wrapped up in my getting married and having babies because Jews are going to disappear from the world. Heterosexuality was an obligation and more than that—being lesbian felt that I'd be disappointing my mother who did so much for me.

"As an only child, all my parents' hopes and dreams centered on me. My mother wanted me to have an easier and better life than she had. To her that meant living a comfortable upper-middle-class life in suburbia with a professional man, raising children..."[12] Her sexual identity and social class struggles mixed together with Jewish identity: "Realizing I was lesbian made me feel as if I was throwing a huge wrench into the parental plan.... If the Jewish family was the primary agent of Jewish survival, where did I, as a lesbian, fit in?"[13] The painful feeling of being an anomaly defined her adolescence.

Going to synagogue was not a happy experience. "Although I stayed through my confirmation, I remember sitting in synagogue one Friday night when I was in high school and being struck with the hypocrisy of the whole thing. Everyone gossiping about other people, no one paying attention. I had a real crisis—I didn't believe in God anymore."

The issue of course was not only theological, as Felice struggled to fit the reality of her lesbian identity and working-class experiences into her Jewish identity.

"Then an important thing happened: one of my teachers in Hebrew school was a graduate student at Columbia University and was quite radical. He told me that you can be Jewish without believing in God, without even going to synagogue. Being Jewish meant doing good in the world. He introduced me to the concept of *tikkun olam.*"

This was the late 1960s, and Felice became politically active, helping to shut down her public high school in protest against the war in Vietnam. Her political activities caused some tension in the family: "My father in particular was upset by the black armbands we wore to protest the war, in memory of the dead; he felt I was flaunting Jewish mourning customs."

Basic questions about authority and identity defined her late adolescent experience: "What is the source of authority? Who gets to decide how good a Jew I am? What's right?" Felice's father's accepting attitude toward her early religious choices in fact became a backdrop for her empowered answers to these questions. During the antiwar protests in 1969, Felice found herself very moved by Arthur Waskow's *Freedom Hagadah,* which he performed on the steps of the U.S. Capitol. "From then on, I have rewritten the Haggadah every year to reflect the themes of slavery and freedom in my life. Before I heard about Reconstructionism, I knew Judaism was a living tradition, and that we make choices." She recalls her own family's acceptance of different life choices: "My father liked davening in his Orthodox tradition; I didn't and went to a Reform temple; my mother didn't like any form of traditional observance at all."

Social action became an important way for Felice to give voice to her Jewish identity, the means of expressing her spiritual connection. The particular social change work has changed over time, including lesbian and gay organizing, anti–nuclear weapons work, anti-intervention in Central America, Middle East peace work, and—for the last six years—economic justice work.

United for a Fair Economy (UFE), which Felice founded and co-directs with Chuck Collins, is a national nonpartisan organization devoted to education and organizing efforts directed at a fairer distribution of income and wealth. The group believes that the growing gap between the rich and everyone else in the United States is potentially disastrous for our democracy, economy, culture, and quality of life. It is not a specifically Jewish organization, and it works with a wide variety of religious institutions, unions, community groups, schools and colleges, and grass-roots organizations. UFE sponsors educational workshops on the growing divide around the country. In the summer of 2000, when a Republican-led Congress voted to repeal the progressive estate tax, President Clinton decided to veto the measure. Several members of UFE's Responsible Wealth project joined President Clinton at the White House when he vetoed the bill, including Martin Rothenberg, who spoke in support of the president's veto.[14] When the Republican-led Congress attempted to override the veto, UFE identified the swing votes in the House and conducted an educational, organizing, and media campaign in those districts. The override failed. During the 2000 elections, another UFE program, Art for a Fair Economy, sponsored a group called Billionaires for Bush (or Gore), which demonstrated at campaign stops, the debates, and both conventions, using satire and humor to point out the role of corporate money in the electoral process.

Not long ago, Felice returned from a speaking tour for her newest book, *Economic Apartheid in America: A Primer on Economic Inequality and Insecurity* (co-authored with Chuck Collins). It is a hands-on, accessible guidebook to the problem of economic inequality, its consequences, and a range of actions people can take to build a fairer economy for all. At many stops on the tour Felice had the opportunity to meet with local organizers, students, and educators.

In addition to her political work, Felice has worked to transform institutional Judaism. After Felice organized an event for one of the editors of *Twice Blessed* and over three hundred lesbians came to the Amherst synagogue, the vice president of the synagogue said to Felice, "I had no idea there are so many lesbian Jews!" She asked Felice to be on the planning committee and join the synagogue board, which brought Felice into contact with the "institutionalized homophobia" within synagogues. As an example, she told me about the board's rewriting of the mission statement of the synagogue. "The board wanted it to be diverse and welcoming, but it took three or four meetings to get across that we needed more than just to say that— we needed to *name* the groups we welcomed. We had to say openly that 'we welcome gays and lesbians, single parents, intermarried folks, the divorced.' Instead of just a broad statement about 'diversity.' It took a while for the board to accept that."

Felice and her partner have worked to build a shared Jewish practice for their family, one that—like Felice's family of origin— allows space for their differences. When they met, her partner was very observant, having been a bat mitzvah in her twenties. She strictly observed Shabbat, while Felice enjoyed lighting the candles but in general was "nowhere near the level of observance of my partner." Over the years together, they have come closer to a shared practice, particularly as they had a child and wanted a more consistent Jewish observance in the home. "We compromised on Shabbat—she does more activity outside the home, driving, etcetera, and I do *less*."

One of Felice's favorite quotations is from the book of Isaiah, where the fierce prophet redefines the nature of fast and our notion of atonement on Yom Kippur. His words capture Felice's passion to push traditional Judaism to make a more inclusive place for the diversity of Jewish experience. It is not, Isaiah writes, a self-preoccupied fast of starving our bodies and "lying in sackcloth and ashes" that is called for, but rather social action. Isaiah says,

> No this is the fast I desire:
> To unlock the fetters of wickedness
> To untie the bands of perverseness
> To let the oppressed go free;
> To break every yoke.[15]

Genie Zeiger:
"Writing Is a Form of Prayer"

Genie Zeiger is a writer and writing teacher who leads writing workshops entitled "Exploring Your Judaism."[16] She lives in western Massachusetts. Genie's workshops attract Jews of many different stripes, from those who feel very alienated to those who are involved in their synagogues. In these workshops she creates a space where participants listen to themselves and others and begin to sort out the meaning of life experiences as a Jew.

"If you knew how I grew up, it's no surprise that I chose a profession that invites people to put the truth of their experience into words," Genie observes wryly.

She grew up in Brooklyn, New York, in the 1950s and "everyone in my community seemed scared after the war, after the Holocaust. I found the reality of what people spoke about and didn't speak about to be very hard." From an early age Genie turned to books to understand the world and people. "As a child, I was very lonely. I think I was born with a very active soul. In the fifth grade I wrote an essay about wanting to be a poet. I was also obsessed with the Holocaust. From age twelve or thirteen, I read everything I could find about it."

No one in Genie's immediate family was a Holocaust survivor, but Genie remembers as a young adolescent becoming very "scared of God." Her mother was an observant Orthodox Jew, and her father agnostic—"at least until he was seventy-five, when he called me up one day to tell me that he was an atheist." Genie wonders if that was her father's way of distinguishing himself from a Jewish community in which he saw himself as a failure. "He was a failed Jewish businessman" who struggled as a middle manager in several companies. This struggle was part of the silence in her family that so shaped Genie's childhood. "When I was quite young, my father was fired, unemployed for six weeks. And he didn't tell anyone, not even my mother. He got up every morning, dressed, and left as if he was going to the office, until he found a new job. His silence and his loneliness, wrestling with all that on his own, not telling anyone, stays with me."

As a teenager, Genie herself wrestled with silence and what could and couldn't be spoken about. In the late 1940s and early 1950s, relatives of hers came over to this country—from Russia, Czechoslovakia. "I liked them very much; several had gold teeth and they seemed very exotic." Yet no one in the family talked about the war and Jewish experience, nor where these exotic people came from or what brought them to this country.

So Genie began reading as much as she could about the war and the Holocaust, searching for answers: The diary of Anne Frank, *The Last of the Just, Exodus, The Wall.* Genie's mother cautioned her, "Stop reading so much; your eyes will fall out."

Genie's own relationship to Judaism was very troubled. "When I was young, I read the Book of Job, and so much of Judaism seemed about beating your breast and God's punishment. I never have understood that. On Yom Kippur we repent for the sin of this and the sin of that. That really bothered me. In the Old Testament, God comes across as really mean and narrow-minded. I remember one Passover walking to temple, over a mile to get there, and I bought some peas, and realized I didn't know if they were kosher or not and worried the whole time that I had done something wrong."

The one figure in her childhood who connected her to Judaism was Mr. Danziger, the affable temple assistant. In her memory of him, we get a glimpse of how children explore their world, often resisting their parents' attempts to "protect" them: "He had a thick accent, wore a dark coat, and I loved him more than the rabbi." The young Genie knew little about him except that "there was no Mrs. Danziger, nor had I ever met a Danziger boy or girl. Where did he come from? I never dared think about this: it could easily have been the moon, or the inside of a box of chocolates."

Given the silence and the loneliness, both within her family and within Judaism as a whole, it's not surprising that Genie became a writing teacher who emphasizes the importance of "finding your own truth in your own words."

Genie, trained as a social worker, left her therapy practice over twelve years ago to concentrate on her writing and on teaching writing. "There is something different about writing something down, rather than just talking about it. There is an honoring of the experience in writing, taking the time in writing that allows us to go deeper and to connect more fully with our imagination."

Genie believes there is more truth in imagination than in what "really happened." We need to explore the deeper meanings of images and sensory awareness that occupy our attention. Writing is a special entrance into yourself and a way of sorting out what you feel and believe. "If I look outside the window as I speak to you and I notice a tree that I really like a lot, I believe that there is a soul in that tree that awakens something inside me, which is why my attention has gone to it. Paying attention to sensory detail lets our souls awaken more fully. I often tell people in my writing groups to notice their preoccupations more fully, if they're on the street and there is a particular slant of light, the way our sense gets caught on something." Genie told me about a woman in her writing workshops who was distracted by the fact that her old farmhouse was increasingly becoming a haven for wildlife—mice, chipmunks, snakes, and frogs. "She was upset and angry but I asked her to write more about her obsession with wild animals entering her living space. Of course, she was concerned because it affects her daily life, trying to avoid mouse poop and all, but I also felt there was something deeper. As she wrote, the wildlife in her house became a metaphor for her life—for her desire for and fear of a closeness to life, her closeness to the earth, her desire for a more grounded life and yet, as she aged, her fear that such groundedness ultimately ends in death."

Genie offers writing workshops for many kinds of people—from adolescents to the elderly and the infirm—but the Jewish workshops are her favorite. "Jews have a long history of intellectual activity and pondering the world. For Jews who are confused about their Jewish identity, writing is an excellent way of entering into your own language for understanding your experience." In the story of Jacob wrestling with the angel, after a night of soul struggle, the angel names Jacob "Israel," which means "one who wrestles with God." Genie finds a connection to her work here: "Writing is a great way to wrestle with God—to get to the truth of your experience."

Genie's workshops do for a divided inner self, the war within each of us, what Eric Stumacher's Playing for Peace concerts do for divided regions and the wars between peoples. They encourage unity and connection rather than division. Genie uses writing prompts and poetry to stimulate people to write together, using freewriting as the methodology. Often she'll read a poem to begin, perhaps Gerald Stern's "Behaving Like a Jew" or one by Yehuda Amichai, in order to invite a look at ourselves from a more lyrical perspective.[17] Then she will invite the group to do some "freewriting," where you write for five minutes, on a specified prompt, without worrying about how well you're doing or whether it makes sense. Just keep the pencil moving.

Writing prompts include *I first realized I was Jewish when...*, *Because of the Holocaust...*, *I behaved like a Jew when...*, and *If the whole world were Jewish...*

Sometimes Genie asks people to write a dialogue about the Jewish and non-Jewish parts of themselves. The proud and self-hating parts of each person emerge from this exercise. The Jew will often be described as always asking difficult questions, not comfortable anywhere, too loud, dark skinned, embarrassing. The non-Jewish parts of our selves are quiet, contained, and not intrusive. On the evidence of her workshops, many people feel that the Jewish part of themselves is different from the mainstream; it clunks slightly as they try to fit it easily or smoothly into their identities. Often the internalized shame comes out in the writing: "people will write about the Jewish parts of themselves as too hairy, too sexual, too noisy, materialistic, too much—too much jewelry, possession—too human."

Genie believes that discovering the truth of one's experience is related to connecting to the untold stories in one's life—writing about what throughout one's life could not be said is in itself healing. In one group a woman wrote in response to the prompt *I knew I was Jewish when...* about the moment when her mother suggested she have her nose "corrected," informing the fourteen-year-old girl who had thought until then of her nose as just fine that this was a gift from the family to her. The surgery meant to the teenager that something was wrong with her, that her Jewishness was defective and shameful, "corrected" by having it removed. The woman had indeed tried to "remove" her very connection to Judaism for years, until she recently, at age forty, felt an urge to find her way back, an urge she was exploring through Genie's writing workshop.

When you sit through an evening class, the careful writing and thoughtfulness evoke the long tradition of Jewish study and inquiry through the ages. After five minutes, or longer, of writing, Genie invites the group to go around the table, and each person, if willing, reads aloud what he or she has written. There is something important both about writing in groups and the witnessing that comes when a story is read. Genie has clear rules about what kind of response makes for safety in a writing group. It's a different kind of witnessing. "People respond only about the writing itself, not about the nature of the experience, good or bad. No one says, for example, 'That must have been hard for you.' We refer not to 'you' but to the narrator, so as to create some safety and distance on what was written. So someone might say, 'I loved how you described the person coming home with such and such detail.'"

There is also a condition of safety in writing in groups. "There are other warm bodies with you; you are not alone as you grapple with your imagination. The silence is very important, but you are not alone, you are with others. I think of the silence as sacred, like prayer—we're all together in the same house, if not the same room. I encourage people to spread out, but they know they're not alone."

For Genie, the link between writing and prayer is very real. "I don't necessarily have to know to whom I'm praying. We may think of praying as to God, where we ask for thanks or help or whatever, but prayer can also be just a sense of talking to forces larger than us, prayer can simply be to try to understand what we don't understand, and writing puts into words that impulse."

Genie certainly doesn't see writing and finding one's own authentic language as simply a Jewish value or activity. But she does see a Jewish twist—to find your language as a Jew does mean coming to terms with your Jewishness. "Being Jewish is so much a part of our body, soul, and mind, one we often can't see, regardless of how religious or not you are." Her daughter recently went to her acupuncturist for various complaints. The acupuncturist took hold of her wrist and said, "You have a Jewish pulse—it's very active, very nervous after having been chased for centuries." For Genie, the image of the "Jewish pulse" captures both an awareness of the dangers of the world as a Jew and the delights of Talmudic thought, reborn now through Genie in creative writing.

In a way, Genie has re-birthed her own Judaism, so different from the closed, frightened, lonely experience she knew as a child. She is not traditionally observant. Although a close friend of hers recently became the rabbi of the local synagogue, "I still can't get myself there." However, Genie wanted me to know that "I love being Jewish." And what is the essence of being Jewish? "Expressiveness—hugging people, loving them, enjoying life through our senses."

"Here's My Judaism"

At the Selma march in 1965, Abraham Joshua Heschel is reported to have exclaimed to Martin Luther King, as the leaders up front were about to set off on the march that would help birth the Civil Rights movement, "Martin, *here* is my Judaism!" For Heschel at that moment, Judaism was expressed through his feet, his brave presence at this crucial, dangerous moment. Not through words alone but through actions. Judaism is often identified with a particular set of beliefs or with specific religious observances or with ethnic identities ("bagels and lox, *here's* my Judaism"). Yet our Jewish identities are often expressed by what we do and the choices we make; identity is truly provisional to our choices and behaviors in the world. "To nudge is to be Jewish," remarked Dara Silverman of United for a Fair Economy, who is not particularly observant in a traditional fashion. She went on, "Work has been my Judaism; it's a form of prayer."

We continue to grow and change and redefine our personal versions of Judaism through what we do in the world.

How do we each create a vibrant, personally meaningful Judaism in the home and in the synagogue? That is the focus of the next chapters.

CHAPTER NINE

Making Judaism Your Own at Home and on the Holidays

How do we capture tradition and make it personally meaningful? By linking what is most real and alive inside us with the opportunities for expression outside us. This is the fundamental psychological challenge we all face in our relationships to Judaism. It's a back-and-forth process: we change the rituals and observances and they in turn change us.

What does this mean, though, in a practical, nuts-and-bolts way? Taking ownership of a ritual, celebration, or prayer can be *more* demanding. It's harder to do *Pesach* when you take the time to consider what is really important to you rather than simply following the Haggadah in a rote manner—and the rewards and joy are greater, too.

Observances of Judaism at home are a wonderful opportunity to create psychological "play spaces" and to find the joy in Judaism. There are a variety of ways—on the Sabbath and during the Jewish holidays throughout the year—in which Jewish men and women have discovered meaningful, joyous ritual and observance that is truly theirs. In what follows you'll likely read about experiences different from your own, some choices you do not agree with and some opinions you do not share. Yet the underlying questions unite us all: how to infuse our observance, practice, faith, and worship with playfulness, reverence, vitality, joy, and honesty.

Joy and Liberation:
Engaging Ourselves and Our Families

Many ways of making Judaism your own can also involve a great deal of joy and release. While at root we may feel we are going against the flow, taking a risk, creating discomfort for ourselves or those we love, the outcome of experimenting can also leave us breathing life into old ritual in a very joyous, full way.

Sidney's Three-D Haggadah. Sidney is a forty-year-old father of an eight-year-old girl, Beth. Both he and his wife remember the seders of their childhood as being "dutiful." Sidney's daughter, though, was hardly dutiful and was very interested in nature, drawing, sculpture. Sidney found himself charmed by his daughter's artistic flair. He also found himself more and more impatient with "the same old rush through the Haggadah every Passover."

Sidney and his wife and daughter made the Passover celebration their own as a family event, drawing on his own sensory-tactile memories and his rebellious desire to get away from the printed page of the Haggadah.

The key was that Sidney turned to his daughter as an ally, building on her concrete experiences. "Last Passover I decided to do it differently. I enlisted young Beth as my consultant and we used the dinner table to create a 'Passover game.' I told my daughter I wanted to make the seder more interactive and artistic and that I wanted to use materials from outside, in the woods near our house.

"She really got involved! We went out and collected stones, leaves, branches of different shapes and colors. We decorated the living room with beautiful long branches that had fallen off the trees, making what Beth called a 'special space' all around the dinner table. I had earlier xeroxed all the relevant parts of the seder and from them we made little scrolls decorated with colorful ribbons. Beth and I put out a white tablecloth and then made a 'seder path' on the table constructed out of the colorful rocks and stones that we had found in the woods. It looked just like a garden path. We used some glitter and leaves and small drawings to decorate the path. We spread out along the length of the path the paper scrolls, containing the four questions, prayers, etcetera. We also put out pieces of clay, along with fabrics of many colors and textures.

"To begin the seder we asked everyone—the kids, parents, and guests—to take a piece of clay and make a figure decorated as they'd like. The figures represented ourselves (plus ones for anyone they wished was here but was not), and the group of figures moved along the seder path for this Passover celebration. The figures stopped at each scroll as we opened them in their turn to read the prayer, or story or instruction. The food was on the table, plenty of snacks so no one was starving. It was just a beautiful sight!

"My parents said that it was the best seder that they had ever been at—the beauty of the colors and the game of moving from one scroll to another, the surprise of it all, kept us involved and eager. Beth was in charge of moving us along, of opening the little paper scrolls and of explaining what was going to happen. She felt really involved and good about what we had created, and interested in the Passover story. I'm very proud of what we did: it was a moment when I felt that I wasn't sitting back and waiting for 'the adults' to do it—I was an adult and had taken the risk to make something that reflected how I felt spiritually and wasn't just doing it the same old way."

Creating new rituals need not mean leaving a familiar Jewish religious or spiritual base. It can simply involve shaping familiar rituals to more fully express who you are and have become. Sidney's story provides us a recipe: be playful, involve the young, draw on what you know.

Each day we face the struggle with freedom and slavery that Sidney portrays: Do our actions come from our own voices? Do we behave in a way that, for better or worse, is reflective of how we are? Or are we acting in a way that is driven by values and beliefs and behavior patterns not really ours, that come from the Pharaoh within us?[1]

Seders are places where it is often very possible to experiment—they're held in the home and often there are children present who can be enlisted to help. Educator David Sobol has explored the importance of "special places" in the world of children, where fantasy and reality intermingle playfully, and certainly the seder offers a special opportunity to create such a place.[2]

Sherry's Rosh Hashanah on the Beach. Sherry and her husband, Jeff, live in a suburb of San Francisco with their four-year-old son, Micah. A few years ago they moved from the city to their new home and were dismayed by the high cost of tickets for High Holiday services in their new community. For years, Sherry and her family had gone to a local synagogue, where they paid $35 per ticket. In their new community the cost was $250 per ticket. What loomed on the horizon was not going to synagogue on the High Holidays for the first time in years. This seemed hard, particularly since both Sherry and Jeff wanted young Micah to celebrate the High Holidays.

In addition, the year had been a very hard one. There had been four deaths in their circle of friends and family: a close friend died of an aggressive form of breast cancer, a brother after sudden illness, one cousin from a heart attack and another from a stroke. The opportunity to let go of the past year and welcome in a new one meant a lot to both of them.

One day, a few weeks before the holidays, Sherry was talking to her friend Connie, a Christian married to a non-observant Jew. Connie very much wanted to teach her son about both religions but was unsure what to do. So the two women decided to celebrate an "alternative Rosh Hashanah," one that they would construct themselves and that would be home-based rather than involving a synagogue.

They mentioned the idea to friends and soon the guest list grew to seventeen people. The guiding principles for the event were (1) that it bring together Jews and non-Jews and (2) that it be loyal to the meaning of the holiday. Sherry observed that inviting non-Jews to Passover increases the Jewish intensity of the event: "At seders the non-Jews want to do the whole thing; they want to go through the whole Haggadah, from beginning to end; they don't skip over things as Jews often do because it is so familiar. We wind up taking a new look at things, seeing the holiday from a new perspective."

Sherry's experience is an example of the surprising way that diversity really does increase learning and empathy: we learn more about ourselves when we look at our familiar experiences through the eyes of others raised in different traditions.

So, Sherry and Connie wrestled with what they would do for their alternative Rosh Hashanah. Sherry remembers, "Sitting around one day at home, I found on a bookshelf *The First Jewish Catalog*, written and edited by Richard Siegel in 1980. The book is a do-it-yourself kit, showing how to do a service, the history of various celebrations." Looking through the book, Sherry recalled reading once about a High Holiday ritual of going to a body of water and tossing in crumbs of bread to cast away the sins of the past year. She called her rabbi from her old synagogue and asked him, and he said, sure, of course, that is a very appropriate and ancient tradition. She looked it up in the

Jewish Catalog and found it. So Sherry and her friends decided to go to the beach and say prayers, cast the bread into the water, and then come back to Sherry and Jeff's house for a celebratory meal. She still remembers the intensity and beauty of what they did that day:

"Luckily, it turned out to be a gorgeous day. The kids went swimming, they laughed and played in the water. It was an amazing experience for them, and for the adults. We had six kids with us, ranging in age from three to ten. What wonderful memories each of them will have—the water sparkled and the sky was so blue and it was warm enough for them to go into the water.

"We brought bags of bread crumbs. One of the women who had converted to Judaism led us. She really knew the most. Her ex-husband didn't want to practice Judaism at all, but Sarah became increasingly Jewish and actually belongs to a Conservative synagogue.

"As we arrived, I said, 'Sarah, what do we do?!'

"She led us through a lighthearted, intelligent talk about Rosh Hashanah, saying it was a time to reflect and to let go of the hard parts of the past year. She spoke in a way the kids could get as well. She didn't use the word *sin*.

"The seagulls were overhead and were wonderful; they got right into it. It was as if they were taking our sins away as we threw the bread into the water. We tossed some to the seagulls and they flew away and wheeled up into the sky."

At this point Sherry's husband, Jeff, added, "As we walked up to the water I was telling a friend how much I just wanted to cast the year away, the whole year. We both felt that way, given all the deaths and losses. Just at that moment, a large glop of seagull poop landed on my shoulder. We all started laughing—there I was with my shoulder covered in this white goop. That felt like the whole year there. Talk about vulgarizing the sacred! We laughed and laughed at that."

He explained, "What mattered most to me is that the day was simple and out-of-doors. So many ceremonies in Judaism are indoors. The kids playing in the water made it a little better: they're in the immediate time, not the past or future."

Sherry recalled, "Then we went home and lit candles and said the blessings over the candles, wine, and bread. We intentionally kept that simple. Two friends and my husband, Jeff, had practiced the Avinu Malkenu and sang it together, in the backyard under the sun. It was gorgeous, their voices and Jeff's guitar. In this Christian neighborhood. The kids playing, the weather, the honey cake. Jews and non-Jews.

"One important tradition on all holidays for me is that we eat chocolate, so we had some chocolate cake as well. Chocolate is for celebration and good luck. To me, chocolate is fabulously rich and comforting. I always have it on birthdays and other celebrations."

Why chocolate? Sherry's answer provided a powerful example of the way that welding our experience to our celebrations provides a richness to what we do. Sherry is a psychologist in the Bay Area and has had asthma since childhood; her Ph.D. dissertation examined the psychological experience of asthma in childhood. She explained about the chocolate: "Well, it turns out that because chocolate has caffeine in it, it can have some bronchodilator effects. From an early age, whenever I ate chocolate I could breathe easier—or at least I thought I could, because I now know that you have to eat *a lot* of chocolate to have a bronchodilator effect. So for me, of course, it's a source of good luck and comfort and needs to be included in any observance of mine!"

An Alternative Kol Nidrei at Home. Not all ritual making is as easy or as harmonious as Sidney's seder or Sherry's Rosh Hashanah. Sometimes things fall flat or you have to back off because an idea you thought was great turns out to be oppressive or stifling to others. Still, though, an unexpected playful impulse may save the day. Recently, before Yom Kippur, my friend Jerry decided on a different sort of Kol Nidrei. He has two children, both in their twenties. "Instead of paying all that money and going to the synagogue as we always do, I asked my kids and my wife if we could all have dinner together and have an open discussion of what Judaism means to us at this point in our lives." Talking beforehand, Jerry told me excitedly, "My daughter was a little resistant because she had wanted to go to dinner with friends, but she agreed to do it." He asked if I had any advice, and I suggested that he not expect everyone to just launch into a discussion. He was asking his family to alter how they did things and talk about personal matters. "Anticipate that this may feel uncomfortable or different for everyone, and keep your expectations in check," I suggested. It's a first step, but only that, and we shouldn't expect our first (or second or third) attempts to be perfect. When we experiment we are powerful, but not omnipotent.

After the holidays, I called Jerry to find out how things had gone. He hadn't mentioned what had happened at the Kol Nidrei family supper and discussion when I had e-mailed him about some other things and inquired, and it didn't come up at first in our phone conversation, as we were catching up on family stuff. So I asked him directly. He hesitated and then said, "Well, I began as you had suggested, saying that this might be uncomfortable but I thought it might be good for us all to talk a little about what Judaism means to each of us these days. For a while it was pretty stilted.

"My daughter Jane said that she was being asked to talk about something that felt 'too personal' and forced to talk about things she didn't want to talk about. We persevered and talked for about thirty minutes, but it felt pretty forced. Later that evening, though, Jane's boyfriend, Michael, started to play the piano and we were singing and making up tunes and all of a sudden he started improvising this funny song, with each lyric beginning 'We are Jewish and we...,' and it had a funny, sardonic air. He was making fun of what we had tried to do but it was also funny and everybody started making up lyrics, humorous and ironic." Jerry concluded, "It was a nice way of keeping it from becoming awkward."

Was Michael helping duck the issue or was he elaborating on it? What is the role of humor and spoof in helping us express who we arc? While the "sardonic air" of the lyrics might imply disrespect or alienation, Jerry's tone as he related the event said otherwise. The sardonic playfulness around the piano was a way for this family to come together and acknowledge their Jewishness in a new way, the humor expressing feeling and defusing the situation at the same time. What could not be said directly, in a "heavy" way, could be expressed in the lighter, more indirect vehicle of sardonic lyrics.

A Feminist Purim. Imagine a hip, feminist version of the megillah, without the celebration of Jewish violence. That's what Jeff Raz has created with his version of the megillah, commissioned by a Bay Area JCC for a Purim party. Jeff is the playwright, actor, and clown whom we met in the last chapter. A few years ago he was commissioned to write his Purim play, *Esther,* for a local JCC, to "expand its demographic" by appealing to its twenty- and thirty-something members. It turned out that members of all ages liked what he created.

What he wrote was a feminist version of the megillah that offers us a different, nontraditional way to celebrate Purim—at home, with friends, or in synagogue—that does not gloss over or hide some of the distressing elements of this holiday that are often invisible in traditional observances.

Esther is a jazz-tinged version of the Book of Esther, delivered in monologue. It begins: "Now it came to pass in the days of the Persian King Achashverosh, yes, that Achashverosh, the Achashverosh who ruled from India to Ethiopia, Babylonia to

Brooklyn (listen, if there had been a Brooklyn, he would have ruled it). Now the Jews, who hadn't moved to Brooklyn yet and still lived in Babylonia, they had a pet name for Achashverosh— Chas Rosh. Isn't that sweet, Chas Rosh? Means 'headache' and believe me he was."

Not your usual megillah. We meet imperious, doomed Vashti ("Get a clue, boy—I'm a Queen, Queen Vashti, daughter of King Belshazzar, granddaughter of the mighty Nebuchadnezzar. I don't do naked for any man, not even him!"), scheming Haman ("Haman was a schmuck but he was a smart schmuck. A smart, politically savvy schmuck. Jerry Falwell, John McCain, Joerg Haider. He laid his scheme on the king: 'We have aliens among us....'"), loyal Mordecai who "rattles off the whole megillah" to his cousin Esther "about how he didn't bow to Haman's hoosegow and now they're all gonna die unless Esther puts on her crown, and nothing else, and goes up to the king and wiggles her thing 'til his ding-a-ling sings and he takes his ring and makes this bad thing go away." And, of course "Beautiful, mysterious Esther":

> She was cool. The King said:
> "Baby, what's your name?"
> "Esther."
> "And where are you from?"
> "I can't tell you."
> "C'mon, baby, where do you live?"
> "I can't tell you."
> "Whoa, a woman of mystery."
> Esther was queen before dinner, before drinks, before
>   they'd even picked a movie, the crown was on her head.

When writing the play, Jeff was very concerned about the bloody, unreflective cycle of revenge and retribution that is at the core of the Purim story. "I found the end of the story, when the Jews kill 75,000 people who would have killed them, very disturbing. I also found it equally disturbing that most people don't know that's in part what they are celebrating when they wave those noisemakers or pray during the service."

After celebrating Esther's clever ability to have the king ally himself with the Jews, Jeff goes on to consider matters usually left out of the sanitized Hebrew school or synagogue accounts: "There you have it, the story of beautiful, brave, brilliant Esther, the queen who saved the Jews. And if the story ended here, we could all drink to her. . . . And laugh at how Haman got better than he gave. But that second decree that the king sent out was no Oslo accord. It didn't say 'We share this world together; princesses and paupers and peasants and Persians and even Palestinians; so get a clue, pound the swords into plowshares, learn 'peace' in twelve languages, slip two straws into your Frappuccino.' No, that second decree didn't say 'Killing a Jew is the wrong thing to do,' it said 'Jews, you can kill, too.' And they did, like some Hamas-hatched nightmare only in reverse, the Jews of the world killed 75,000 of their closest enemies, 75,000 people who would have killed them first."

So, the story doesn't end with Esther's triumph, but rather it includes acknowledgment of Jewish excess as well. At the end of *Esther,* Jeff makes clear that there is both evil and good within the Jews, as in all people—that we have a Haman within ourselves:

> Haman was hanged but he still hangs around us, my dears.
> He's our overblown pride, our anger so righteous, our fears.
> But brave, beautiful Esther can lay down a lesson or two,
> She's proud to come out, proud to shout: "I'm a queen, I'm a Jew."
> Haman ties up intestines and shakes up snake veins
> But Esther's our heart, our beauty, our brains.

At the JCC performance, Jeff recalls, "many people came up to me afterwards, including the director of the JCC. As he approached I got worried—what would he say about the ending, that last paragraph criticizing the Jews? Well, he loved it! He said, 'I liked *everything* about it.' That felt a code word for the last paragraph. Another prominent member of the congregation came up later and remarked, 'I've never even thought about Jews killing all those who would have killed them.'"

Imagine using this reading as part of a family celebration of Purim (or in the synagogue). So often we don't even realize what we are reading in the Hebrew text or, in the case of Purim, that we are celebrating the slaughter of thousands of innocent people. "So many people don't get it," says Jeff. "I've yet to talk to anyone who has gotten what they are reading in the traditional megillah. Mostly people have said, 'I've never noticed the ending. I thought it ended when Esther won.'" Jeff observed that "traditional commentary on the megillah thins at that point. Little is said about all the slaughter. One commentator points out that first the Jews killed their enemies in the cities, then into the country, suggesting that's why it is a two-day festival. Very factual, rather than including some reflection on how come they did this in the first place?"[3]

Jeff provides us an entertaining, passionate, feminist, and honest way of celebrating Purim. It *is* possible to celebrate Purim without it becoming an unwitting ode to violence and human suffering.

Alternative Jewish Weddings and Anniversaries. Marginalized groups often offer us wonderful lessons in adapting traditional rituals. Being female and lesbian within a patriarchal religion, for example, often means creating and re-creating traditional ritual. In doing so, each moment that tradition takes for granted becomes a moment of decision and choice. Felice Yeskel, whom we met in the last chapter, and her partner recently celebrated the anniversary of their commitment ceremony, which they called *Kiddush Arigat Chayenu*, or "Sanctification of the Interweaving of Our Lives." In creating the ceremony, Felice and her partner had read about *kiddushim* ceremonies and decided on the blessings they wanted to include. They identified songs for a choir of their friends. They included a *chuppah* made out of two tie-dyed tallitot each had made, the *tzitzit* tied together to form a single covering for the couple.

The traditional wedding contract seemed quite sexist—"only the man signs it and he hands it to the woman"—so they did an egalitarian contract, written together, decorated by a lesbian artist, and signed by everyone at the ceremony. Felice and her partner wanted it to be a community document. During the ceremony "our mothers each came up and wrapped us in our tallit. We tried to create roles for each of our families as we rewrote the seven blessings." There is a traditional covering-uncovering ceremony in weddings, the sense of which appealed to Felice and her partner, if they could free it from its patriarchal overtones. "Typically the groom uncovers the bride. It harkens back to the biblical story of one of the patriarchs being duped when he married a different bride than he thought. After that the men all checked to see who was actually under the veil." Felice and her partner re-created this ceremony to reflect more fully who they were. Now it had to do with seeing *each other* more fully: "We each uncovered the other. So then the first person we saw after we emerged was each other."

Weddings and anniversaries offer opportunities for us to weave together tradition and creativity. The result can be powerful and inspiring. At a recent interfaith wedding of two friends of mine, Marian and Rob (the bride Jewish and the groom Christian), elements of both traditions made a rich mosaic, communicating the interweaving of two lives. Both are in their forties and have been married previously, and the service reflected the reality of many disparate elements coming together. Beneath a *chuppah* there were wonderful poems and songs—"Bridge over Troubled Water," The Beatles's "In My Life," readings from Victor Hugo and Pablo Neruda ("I wanted your hair, all for myself. / From all the graces my homeland / offered / I choose only your savage heart.") and the traditional breaking of the wineglass. Rob and Marian's service included Marian's teenage daughter from her first marriage, their different faiths and different personalities, all brought together under the *chuppah* at this moment.

There are many ways to express the emotional truth of diversity, of old and new brought together, in weddings and anniversaries. At one wedding of an African-American man and a Jewish woman, a line of African drummers stood facing a *klezmer* band, creating a central aisle down which the couple walked toward their marriage ceremony, while the bands played together, their beat synchronized. Different tones and melodies, joined together into one rhythm.

Even for those who want a traditional Jewish ceremony, it is possible to play with and update tradition. For example, in the traditional Jewish wedding ceremony, only the bride received a ring; nowadays, the groom usually does, too.[4]

The Sabbath. The Sabbath is a deeply meaningful part of Judaism, and many of us yearn for a special time for reconnection and renewal separate from the busy workweek.[5] The Sabbath also occupies a special place in Jewish consciousness. "If you do one thing, light the Shabbat candles on Friday nights," many rabbis advise their harried congregants, who are struggling to remain connected to Jewish ritual in some way.

Yet Shabbat is more than just ritual behavior; it is a state of mind and of time, as Rabbi Heschel has pointed out: "It is the dimension of time wherein we meet God, wherein we become aware that every instant is an act of creation, a Beginning, opening up new roads for ultimate realizations. *Time is the presence of God in the world of space . . .*"[6] In our pressured lives, how do we make Shabbat our own, particularly when the idea of devoting a day to its observance seems overwhelming, amid our commitments to our kids' after-school and weekend activities, to our work, and to our friendships?

The answer may lie in first creating a play space in which we can allow ourselves to explore our attractions *and* resistances to the idea of "the Sabbath" and to the possibilities of "real time," with all its powerful meanings for us.

Writing together in a group is one way to do that. If singing sardonic lyrics around a piano is one kind of play space, so, too, is writing together. One chavurah's experiences in writing together about the Sabbath can be instructive.

Reluctant Ritualists: Imagining the Sabbath. They call themselves "The Reluctant Ritualists," since most of the members shy away from their local synagogues and do not consider themselves traditionally observant. The group has talked at length about many aspects of their "push-pull" relationship to Judaism, and at times members have been known to refer to themselves as "The Discussive Neurotics."

The group meets monthly, each time in a member's home, and has been doing so for about five years now. It is composed of ten members, all working professionals, several in interfaith marriages.

Over the years the group members have learned to talk openly with each other about their experiences growing up Jewish and their hesitations and desires to "feel more Jewish." Although there had been some Friday night meals and candle lightings, usually meetings were held on Sunday mornings while the kids were in Hebrew school. After several years of talking without a prearranged agenda, the group decided to try to build in some structure: at the next meeting they would write together on a chosen topic. The idea was to use freewriting techniques to explore their experiences of Judaism. In this group of busy professionals, finding and taking time for oneself was a recurrent topic. Several members had been interested in making the

Sabbath a priority in their lives, but no one had really done anything about that. So they decided next month they would write on the subject "When I finally celebrate the Sabbath."

Yet when the group met a month later they began talking about the usual topics: their kids, spouses, and hectic lives. One member, Jim, a fifty-year-old social worker, noted, "These are all important matters, which we were used to talking about, but nothing came up about the writing exercise we had decided on the month before." It was as if amnesia had set in, the kind of amnesia that comes when you're anxious about a task. Finally, one of the group reminded the rest, who all remembered the assignment, amid laughter.

The group, though, did develop a ritualized way of going about the writing. A candle was put in the middle of the table and they recited the *Shehecheyanu* as they lit it, marking the specialness of the occasion and focusing everyone's attention on the moment.

The group then freewrote for five minutes on the writing prompt "When I finally celebrate the Sabbath." Everyone wrote without stopping, whatever came to mind, just trying to keep their pencils and pens moving, without worrying about grammar or whether what they wrote "made sense."

When the five minutes were up, they went around the table, each reading what they wrote. Jim, a devoted family man and household fix-it buff, wrote, "When I celebrate the Sabbath, I will stop, I will breathe, and my thoughts of butterfly nuts and leaking faucets and lawnmowers and practicing the saxophone and calling my mother . . . and work, that incredibly interesting, challenging job that appears to be grinding me down like an old molar, will all stop and I will breathe and sit and laugh and maybe even fall asleep on the couch."

A married woman with two young children wrote that when she celebrates the Sabbath, "I will be in another place than I am now," and asked herself, "Where am I now?" She went on, "The

Sabbath is a family affair. Whenever that celebration takes place, it doesn't have to be on Friday night or Saturday or even Sunday ... but I'd like it to be a time when we all agree to slow down with the affairs of the world, really *be* with each other, whether that means talking, playing Monopoly, doesn't have to be heavy. My husband and I have talked about it, and worry as the kids get older and the world seduces them more and more that we as parents can't compete—have we lost the opportunity?"

Next to her, her friend Sandra, also a wife and mother with a busy career, described the Sabbath "as though I've entered a foreign territory—this holiday belongs to my ancestors and relatives in Israel. I've never embraced the Sabbath and yet almost every time I've been to Sabbath services I've felt comforted, drawn in to the moment, the gift of repose and thankfulness of the quiet, of the moment, of rest—but the ritual of a Sabbath? I'm stumped. The two parts of me—the part drawn in, the part held back ..."

One man, the father of a teenager, wrote about feeling "very sad here, a deep load of feeling, about controlling too much." He went on to wonder if he could simply spend a day "to communicate my love for my son, so that he could hear it or is that just a fantasy? When I celebrate the Sabbath, could I simply be with him? Would he let me on the Sabbath? Is there a day of rest for my son?"

The writings gave each member a much deeper picture of the struggles with ritual, with the Sabbath, with taking time for oneself, and of the profound ways each member hungered for a deeper connection with those they love and with themselves, and with each other in the chavurah itself. In the discussion that followed, the group explored their pain in the writings, and the "fear of feelings" that underlay their difficulty with taking time for the Sabbath. If they really observed the Sabbath as a time of rest and contemplation with others, then their suppressed hunger for community and connection and quiet might leave them uncomfortable. Taking time for themselves and for each other in our hurried society was in itself threatening. In giving voice to these fears, though, the group was beginning to create "a Sabbath" for itself.

The writing was a ritual activity that allowed deeper aspects of self to emerge, and for each member to really "own" their fear of and experience of the Sabbath. It was a way of creating a deeper frame of meaning, in their own words, about what the Sabbath meant to them. Writing—by giving us a little distance from the experience—can work to help us "own" our deepest hopes and fears about Judaism.[7] As Yeats said, "Give me a mask and I'll tell you the truth."

Funerals: A Mother's Death, a Daughter's Rebellion. Funerals mark losses and are profound moments in which we confront not only our own fears about loss but also social pressure to "do it right." Men and women who have experienced the death of a parent offer us a perspective on the role of rebellion in making Judaism your own. Often at this moment of great loss, people who have had only a distant relationship with Judaism find themselves mobilized and wanting part of the funeral process or memorial service to be different from what the rabbi wants or what Judaism seems to prescribe.

Joan, for instance, was fifty years old when she lost her eighty-five-year-old mother after a long struggle with heart disease. Joan's mother was a very beloved member of her suburban Chicago community, and her dying had been long and hard. Joan and her husband and their grown children had been with her mother in the hospital when she died. Growing up, Joan had felt that Judaism was like "a charade, very distant, in which the rabbi really didn't know our family." When Joan's father had died years earlier, the rabbi's graveside officiating had left her then twenty-two-year-old son lamenting, "When I have a family I'm going to make sure that the rabbi actually knows who we are."

So, after the difficult process of her mother's death, Joan struggled with how to create a meaningful grieving ritual. There was a "wonderful memorial service, just lovely, with Jewish prayers that meant something to us all and many stories and memories celebrating my mother and her life."

The question of the disposal of her mother's body, though, contained a conflict over Joan's determination to be loyal to her mother's wishes while also feeling "Jewish." Her mother had made clear that she wanted her body to be cremated. The cremation decision became a point of self-definition and rebellion. "Since I live in a largely Jewish community, people would ask about where and how my mother was buried. And I would reply, 'No, she chose to be cremated and we have not decided yet how to share her ashes.' I'd get these looks and reactions! Cremation is a real no-no within Jewish law, but that was very much my mother's wish. A relative of mine visiting from Israel asked and I didn't know what to tell him. A Jewish friend advised, 'Lie.'

"I couldn't do that with a relative, but I did realize that I was mourning, feeling very tender about the agony of my mother's last few weeks and losing her, and I didn't want to have to explain it all, or defend it. And know what? I have lied and felt completely comfortable with it. I did it once. Someone said, 'Oh, so she's buried in Chicago,' and I said, 'Yeah.' Who cares? Let them bury her wherever they want! In a beautiful porcelain casket."

In fact, Joan's family held on to the porcelain jar containing her mother's ashes and took several weeks to decide on a private ceremony to spread the ashes, complete with Jewish prayers.

Joan's decision to cremate and to "lie" expresses many meanings. She is in one way not really ready to bury her mother, to let go of her, and ambiguity about where she is buried may express the need to hold on to her longer psychologically, to not yet "bury" her. While for some Jews, the Kaddish ceremony extending over a year, attending synagogue twice a day to recite the prayers for the dead, provides a way to hold on to the deceased and to work out psychologically the debts and obligations past the funeral itself (as Leon Wieseltier explores in his majesterial account, *Kaddish*[8]), for a person not raised within an observant Jewish tradition, a more private and personal extension of the process may be necessary. By not burying her mother quite yet, Joan may be creating a psychological space and a ritual that allow her to hold on to her mother and sort out the loss more fully.

In fact, Joan is connected to her father as well, since he was strongly Jewish-identified but not wedded to the letter of the law in observance. He was a man who organized shipments of relief supplies to the new state of Israel in the late 1940s and early 1950s but was not particularly observant. Joan's desire to follow her mother's wishes, even if they were not particularly "kosher," comes out of the unorthodox tradition exemplified by her father. In the cremation Joan is creating a personally meaningful ritual that weaves together powerful threads of family love in her life.

Most of all, by defying authority (one that was not *so* harsh, since a local rabbi helped her with her decision) she was finding her own voice, one that resists rules that feel oppressive and that even "lies" when necessary. In feeling what it is like to stand apart and make a decision, Joan is finding that she no longer needs to be faceless and anonymous in an overbearing Judaism such as the one she experienced as a child.

Steps in Finding Your Own Jewish Voice

Cultivate a Playful Attitude. It is OK to play with ritual, with celebratory experiences. The piano playing of Jerry's daughter's boyfriend, for example, allowed a solution to emerge from what seemed a forced Kol Nidrei dinner. Sometimes creative solutions emerge spontaneously. The most meaningful moments can be the unexpected ones.

A playful attitude can simply be fun and may lead to a very meaningful experience of Judaism, different from the solemnity we expect. Lynn, for example, is a mother who has come to love the Shabbat candle lighting, the one Jewish ritual her family follows, because of the "silliness" she shares with her young daughter about taking a breath before reciting the prayers. "In my house I try to be playful and creative about it—my daughter definitely does not think of Judaism as humorless. We light candles every Friday evening and the moment before we say the prayer, we say 'Baa,' like in 'Baa-baa-black sheep,' which is a good way to synchronize ourselves. We all laugh each time and feel silly and very good."

One woman at a focus group on "Exploring Our Judaism" struggled most of the evening to see what—if any—meaning Judaism held for her. She reflected at one point on the Jewish holidays, particularly Passover, and then her whole demeanor came alive as she talked:

"The playfulness in creating the seder seems like my own. At one seder we were not doing enough singing. Not everyone was Jewish, and some of us wanted to sing 'Dayenu.' So we made up our own verses. And, oh, I remember! We made up this game during the seder where we came to a part in the story where we'd stop at a word and someone had to think of a word with that song in it and we'd all have to sing that song, and it wasn't necessarily a sad, dirgeful song. It was silly and fun and we did a lot of laughing. Some people felt that there was too much laughing, too silly. I didn't feel that, I loved it." For this woman, it was precisely the playfulness and the breaking of the traditional "sad, dirgeful" structure that allowed her to feel that her own voice was also present in the observance.

Join with Others. Judaism is an interpersonal, relational, generational faith. Personal rebellion alone is not enough. It's hard to make Judaism our own by ourselves; we need the validation of community.[9] Ultimately it is important to move toward other like-minded and supportive individuals. Judaism, after all, is about conduct and shared ritual. Linking to others and feeling the validation of being part of a group is an important part of making Judaism our own. Rabbis can help and can hinder this process; it can happen outside the synagogue and within it.

Creating small groups can help—Sunday discussion groups, chavurot, coffee time with other Jews (and non-Jews) who may struggle with similar matters. Getting together and sharing rituals and experimenting with them can help. Make it clear that you're experimenting; think about consensus.

Judy, a single mom, had experienced the seders of her childhood as a "most patriarchal event"—her elderly grandfather ran the whole show while her grandmother produced prodigious amounts of food, which was merely the backdrop for the men's performance. "The main event was the men's Hebrew and commentary."

So one year Judy, with her young daughter, organized a "nontraditional seder" with another family. They used a short Haggadah and "we did everything by consensus. If someone wanted to skip something, we'd do that. It was fully participatory. My daughter can now read Hebrew, but her young friend couldn't, so we did everything in English." The two families built on what they knew and loved about Passover, in this case the food and the importance of food preparation. "We treated the meal and food and the table as being of equal importance to the Haggadah itself. If the person doing the cooking at that moment had an urgent announcement or something they wanted to say, we didn't treat it as an intrusion. We also made good food the center—we used very healthy, low-fat, low-salt food and free-range chickens, didn't have heavy desserts." For Judy, the seder felt like "our celebration, not acting out other people's scripts. The whole event was possible because of the people. I have a tendency to yield to the most observant, to defer to the people with the most knowledge and seeming commitment, but instead we had made a commitment to be egalitarian and all make decisions together."

Follow Your Kids. They often know better how to do it than we adults do. During the High Holidays one year, Leah and Josh decided not to attend synagogue with their eight-year-old twins, Max and Adele. They were not entirely sure how they wanted to celebrate the Jewish New Year, but felt that they wanted it to involve a walk in the woods with their kids, since the whole family enjoys their time in the outdoors. On their hike, Leah and Josh explained about the meaning of Rosh Hashanah and Yom Kippur, telling Max and Adele that it was a time of "letting go of the hard parts and troubles of the past year and turning toward the new year." The family was standing at a beautiful scenic overlook as they talked and the foliage was in spectacular form that year. Leah asked her children if they could think of an image of letting go of things. Max said, "It's like the leaves, the way that each year they fall off the trees." His sister, Adele, agreed, and that led to a ritual: the family gathered up some leaves and twigs and each person made a "LetGo"—their funny family phrase to describe the collages that they took to the edge and tossed off the overlook while thinking of experiences from the past year that they wanted to cast away. Only later did the parents realize that their family had created their own version of the traditional *Tashlich,* or "casting away," ceremony.[10] "Ever since then, the phrase LetGo is something we remind each other of in our family on every High Holiday."

Be Mindful of Your Attitudes Toward Authority. Does being a leader mean always having the right answer? Or does it mean

being able to take suggestions and get help from others? One father, Mark, wanted to make a more engaging seder for his family but was at a loss about how to do it. "I think I would have
just forced things on people if I hadn't turned to several relatives
and asked them for ideas about what we might do that was new
and different for Passover. Several of them had some new ideas,
including a suggestion for making our own Haggadah that was
really great. We put together a family Haggadah for the seder
that included poems and stories that our kids suggested, including a couple they wrote themselves. If I hadn't asked for input,
it wouldn't have been half as much fun."

Build on What You Know. Use what you know and don't overlook unexpected opportunities. You can build on the images,
sayings, experiences, the mementos and photos and objects that
you most value to create meaningful new rituals. Eric, for example, is an actor who has struggled through his life to make
meaning out of Judaism. The link to Jewish tradition was broken in his parents' generation, and his early experience of Judaism involved a strong feeling of being an "outsider" among
Jews. Eric has a fine sense of humor and an observant eye. His
family struggled with money when he was a young boy. He remembers that one year their temple arranged participation for
poorer families at the seders of wealthier ones. "We were very
poor back then and one invitation was to a family with an estate
up in the hills. There were gold fixtures in the bathroom, which
I found very interesting. It was very bizarre." The feeling of
being different and not "getting it" was captured for Eric by a
different seder a few years later: "That second seder, we wound
up giving money when we shouldn't have. We couldn't afford it.
The family called Russia during the seder to talk to Russian
Jews. They kept referring to Russian *Jewry,* and I kept wondering why they were so interested in Russian *Jewelry.*"

As an adult, despite his career success and a happy marriage, Eric struggles to sort out what is his own true connection to Judaism. While performing in a touring road show of a successful Broadway play, Eric participated in several seders among the cast far from home. "They were the first inkling that there was something about Judaism important to me." Those seders were amalgams and crazy-quilt affairs that in part came out of Eric building on the life he had created around him.

One year Eric found himself performing in Portland, Oregon, during Passover week. "We decided to do a seder right there in the theater, and the whole cast came. One of the actors was very knowledgeable. He was raised Orthodox and he was like a rabbi, and led us all in what we needed to do. We rustled up some Haggadahs and there was another man there who also knew his stuff and so as the seder was going on they started debating over every point, just like you're supposed to. This went on and on. I was sitting next to a well-known Afro-American actress and the food had been catered and was being served buffet style so it was sitting there. She was waiting as the seder went on and on and these two guys were debating and she kept asking me, 'When are we going to eat?'

"Finally she pushed her chair back, stood up, and said, 'I don't know when *you* are going to eat, but *I* am going to eat.' The two guys were still arguing. I thought, 'I can't let this become a racial moment.' So I stood up and got some food, too, with her and the others."

The theater, the cast, the Jews and non-Jews together, the sense of separateness and displacement that characterizes actors together in their theater, all away from their homes, provide a ground on which this seder became an authentic event for Eric. "For me, that's the way that Passover is *supposed* to be—inclusive. All together. That seder was the only thing except for the opening cast party where everyone in the cast came."

One year, a hodgepodge seder without even a Haggadah provided a true sense of connection and meaning for him. It happened a while ago, during a low point in his life. Eric was touring in a play and the company found themselves performing in Cincinnati, "which is like being nowhere right there and they had booked us in over the Easter weekend, so no one was coming, and the show was not doing well, and we had major injuries in our cast, including the fact that one of our members had been diagnosed recently HIV positive. So there we were—a pathetic, sad, understaffed group in a large theater with no one coming. There were three and a half Jews in the company, and we all decided to have a seder at my dressing room table. The person who was the half Jew remembered the Chanukah prayers only and she knew the most of us all so we recited them and said the word Passover instead of Chanukah. We had fanned out all over town to find some matzoh. At the seder the guy who found the afikoman was Native American, and so I got him a book as a present. It was on Judaism—I had looked for something more inclusive about faith and spirituality but this was the one I could find. We did the ceremony without a Haggadah, telling stories instead. There we were looking for matzoh, telling stories, wine in Dixie cups. We were really down, but that seder mattered a lot." In creating this seder, Eric built on what was available and on those who mattered a lot to him—the members of his cast and the stories, objects, and knowledge in the room that night. The ersatz, created ritual served to restore morale, in a deeply felt moment.

Start Small. Don't look for your whole synagogue to join you in a new experiment. Find play spaces—seders, meals, Shabbat. A small group of like-minded friends or congregants you feel relatively at ease with will help you find your voice. One group of men and women I know gets together every month to write "poem-prayers" together. Each person writes a brief, meaningful poem that expresses his or her hopefulness, sorrow, or joy at that moment. Several of the participants bring those "poem-prayers" into services with them during the year, both to recite to themselves and to acknowledge the role of the group in their lives.

Find Ways to Tolerate Some Discomfort. In finding your own voice you are doing something *different*. Of course, you and others may also resist. A friendly keeping at it may help. Often family members will want to respond if they see that new rituals are important to you. In many families, attempts to change or update seders meet with resistance at first, and it can help to take a few deep breaths, listen to people's concerns, and remind yourself that you are not doing something wrong.

Remember, Too, That There Are Few "Perfect" Spiritual Moments. Be grateful and thankful for the connections you can create and feel from your efforts. Even a "failure" at one time can lead to a "success" the next time around.

Explore Your Family History. Sometimes exploring your family history and taboos and silent places can help you become more able to play more with Judaism. Learning more about the silent places in your family history is a way of creating a more authentic story of the role of Judaism in your life and discovering the reasons for resistance and ambivalence. Sometimes the same resistances to talking in the family can be alive in our struggles with Judaism. For one man, Evan, his father's death when he was nine years old left a void in his relationship to Judaism, since after that loss the family rarely went to the synagogue. The interpretation Evan made as a little boy was that his mother hated Judaism and that there was some connection between being Jewish and his father's death. He told me that he and his mother never talked much about his father. "She cried if she mentioned him. So as kids we thought, 'if Mother cries she must have hated Dad.'"

Opening himself up to Judaism—and to connection with his father—was a frightening possibility for Evan, since he risked alienating his mother. Not too long ago, a movie on TV about a family after the father dies led him and his mother to talk, twenty-five years after his father's death. "It was an amazing moment when we realized that we hadn't ever really talked about Dad very much. We did start talking together about him, and I realized she loved him and if I asked, I'd get great stories. Instead of hardness, there is softness." There is also a greater softness in Evan's relationship to his Judaism, as he comes to feel that it is safe to open himself up to that part of his identification with his father. The prickliness and antagonism toward Judaism he feels has softened since he began to talk to his mother.

Be Aware of Your Own Resistances. Be mindful of your own internal prohibitions and try not to see all resistance as "out there." Making Judaism your own means taking possession of your own history in a new way that can sometimes feel awkward. We often tend to automatically defer to the most observant person, believing that he or she knows best or that we can't really take charge of our efforts.

Feeling on the spot, we may turn away from parts of ourselves at times. That's OK; it's an ongoing process. I remember, for instance, the day I walked out of my synagogue wearing a yarmulke. I had put it on because I was reading in the sanctuary while my kids were in Hebrew school. Then I had hurriedly left, planning to meet a friend downtown for coffee while the kids were in school. On the way I stopped for gas, and as I pumped the gas, I reached up and found to my shock that the yarmulke was still on my head. I grabbed it to put it in my pocket—out in the open in the supermarket parking area, everyone going about their business, and there I was, wearing a beanie!

Then my hand stopped. This was at a time when I was struggling with how "Jewish" I felt. What would it be like to leave it on? To really *own* that part of my history and identity. With shyness, trepidation, but also some determination and pride, I let the yarmulke remain. Men and women walked through the parking lot with bags of groceries and I had my beanie on. I felt vigilant and in new territory, driving through the downtown center of the small town in which I live with my yarmulke on, trying to feel my Jewishness. What I felt was that I stood out. And what I was confronting was my own resistance to identifying myself as Jewish. Not just to others, but also to myself. Even though no one seemed to notice, I imagined everyone did. When I got to the bagel store to meet my friend, I took the yarmulke off before getting out of the car. I didn't want him to see me with it on. Would he laugh, wonder, figure I'm losing it? Eventually I got to the point where I could laugh lovingly at myself. The Day I Caught Myself in Public with a Yarmulke On.

Laugh Often. The predicaments we find ourselves in can be amusing. (See above.) We may need to be most forgiving of ourselves. A sense of humor helps.

Keep Studying and Learning About Ritual and About Permission. Often we are locked into "the rules" and don't see how much permission for flexibility and experimentation there is in our ancient religion, which has had to adapt and change so often in the past, knowing many rebels and mavericks in its ranks. Sometimes rabbis and others can help us adapt ritual rather than standing in our way.

Linda was very concerned about the inability of her family to "do the Sabbath right." What did that mean? That given their busy suburban schedules, with sports for the kids and differing commitments, often on Saturdays they were not able to mark the ending of the Sabbath with a Havdalah ceremony. Then she discovered a ritual fact that changed her whole attitude toward the Sabbath. "Something I learned recently is that it's OK to celebrate Havdalah anytime until Tuesday after the Sabbath. So if we forget on Saturday or have a soccer game, we can light the Havdalah candles anytime we want. In our culture it really feels that sometimes it doesn't make sense to end the Sabbath in the middle of the weekend. So in our family Sunday night is often the time for us to end the Sabbath. We do that, light a candle on Sunday night when we are all together and calm and go around and each of us says how we enjoyed the weekend."

In learning more, Linda was able to create a Jewish form that made sense to her and that felt liberating and comforting in her life.

There's No One Right Way. As Eric's seders indicate, there are many ways to express your deepest feelings. They will come out of which Jewish rituals, words, prayers, symbols mean the most to you, and will often feel at first like a crazy quilt of expression, which will become more comfortable and less awkward over time.

There is an internal psychological journey of liberation from Internal Pharaohs to greater ownership of Jewish ritual and belief with family and friends at home. How, though, do we create within the synagogue itself rituals and forms and observances that feel personally meaningful? Can we really talk to each other in the sanctuary? Can we make the sanctuary feel as if it is "our own"? These are the questions that frame the next chapter.

CHAPTER TEN

Fresh Air in the Synagogue

How do those of us whose link with Judaism was broken or narrowed find passion and support and connection in the synagogue? How do we invest the synagogue itself with personal meaning and vitality? The sanctuary? The service?

We live in a time of considerable ferment in Jewish life. Meditation, chanting, and experiments with music in Jewish worship services, bibliodrama and creative midrash, Jewish yoga and body work are all turning up in the synagogue. The catalogs of Jewish Renewal retreat centers such as Elat Chayyim provide a compendium of artistic and therapeutic approaches to Judaism. Yet these efforts remain at the margins; the synagogue can still be a stuffy place.

There are many possible "play spaces" in the synagogue. We can create meaningful ritual and observance by linking the synagogue and what happens there to our deeply held memories and hopes. Individual prayer has always offered such opportunities. Today congregations and their individual members are discovering exciting, joyous, and profound ways to demystify the sanctuary and to create opportunities for writing, focused talking, movement, and interaction in the worship service.

Some of the examples that follow may feel different from your taste or values. However, the underlying impulse—to transform our experience through worship and to find a joyful experience of Judaism—unites us all.

When we free the act of prayer from simply following the text in a rote fashion, many possibilities open up. It is possible on your own to transform your experience of prayer in *shul*.

Playing at Prayer

For many of us, the Internal Pharaoh is very busy when we pray. We imagine that in order to pray we need to pray to a God, and the God we imagine is often rooted in childhood images of an all-powerful patriarchal figure who sits on a throne. Many uncounted and discontented Jews don't feel comfortable with an image of a personal God who has absolute power and is a single gender. So we don't pray, or we go through the motions, being dutiful and feeling resentful or bored or like a good child who swallows the medicine for Mommy or Daddy even if it tastes lousy.

In reality, though, both inside and outside the synagogue, prayer is an activity where a playful, creative attitude can be very important in helping to create a more authentic, meaningful Jewish voice.

The Patchwork Prayer Book. Fred grew up in a household where images of male and female worship were very distinct. His father was a good davener, but his mother rarely did anything in synagogue. As if to make matters more confusing for the son, his mother held much of the power at home, while his father was more passive there. His mother was an excellent cook and a lively spirit, more "exotic" and interesting. He loved his father and was drawn to the man's competencies. Fred became a high school science teacher (his father was an engineer). More important, Fred's closeness with his mother and his love of her femininity found little expression through his young adulthood years as he focused on "making it" as a man, married, and became a father himself.

As he grew older, Fred struggled with a very real developmental challenge: how to make room within himself for his more receptive, contemplative impulses, his desire to acknowledge the limits of what he knows, the sense of awe and mystery in his life. His children were leaving home, his parents were elderly, and Fred felt he "needed to think about my relationships with the important people in my life, make more time for things I didn't focus on very much." He took a long weekend away to go to his college reunion, and began to reconnect with old friends he hadn't seen in many years and to reserve an afternoon a week for a regular golf date with friends. He also turned to Judaism. The traditional prayers in his synagogue's siddur didn't really speak to him, never had. He disliked the patriarchal language, the outdated translations, and "the emphasis on a distant, judgmental God." There were gender-neutral, more contemporary prayers in a new Reform alternative prayer book his synagogue made available, but those seemed "kind of washed out. It was like they didn't want to offend anyone, so the prayers said nothing to me."

Fred began bringing in poetry that he had been reading outside of synagogue and meditating with it during parts of the prayer service. "The rabbi would tell us to turn to page four thirty-seven or some such of the prayer book and rather than read yet another prayer that fogged my mind, I would insert a poem I brought into the service and meditate on that." On photocopied pages Fred slipped into his prayer book were "Yiddishe Kopf" by Allen Ginsberg, poems by Stanley Kunitz, Grace Paley, Robin Becket, and Yehuda Amichai, as well as new versions

274 REKINDLING THE FLAME

of prayers by Marcia Falk and Shefa Gold. He was particularly
drawn to these lines from Marcia Falk's re-creation of the traditional Shema as found in her 1996 book, *The Book of Blessings:*
"And may our actions / be faithful to our words / that our children's children / may live to know: / Truth and kindness / have embraced, / peace and justice have kissed / and are one."[1] So, while
many in the congregation were reciting traditional prayers, Fred
found himself contemplating the sensuous, loving way that truth
and kindness may be joined, that peace and justice are related.

Fred recalls feeling as if he was doing something wrong; his
Internal Pharaoh—a harsh voice within himself—reprimanded
that the service was a time "to be serious, to pay attention to
what the rabbi was saying." The struggle to validate our own
experiences in synagogue is often little different from what happens in schools and elsewhere: often the pressure to do what we
are told threatens to wipe out the way that we find real meaning
in experiences. Yet Fred pushed back against this part of himself. Non-Jewish poets began to appear in Fred's patchwork
prayer book.

W. S. Merwin's poem "Sheep Passing" led Fred to explore
the relationship between the generations and the passage of time
in ways that traditional prayer does not make possible. From
Merwin's poem he read me a passage about a stream of sheep
running at evening time along a shadowy, winding lane: "the
old throats gargling again uphill / along known places once
more..." The dull "wood clonk of the bells / borne by their
predecessors" mixes with the voices of the lambs: "...the walls
of the lane / are older than anyone can understand."[2] Sitting in
silence in service, Fred contemplated his connection to his parents, his responsibilities to and love for them, the bond that
united him, his parents, and his children. He considered the
"old throats" in his congregation, the frailty of the elderly and
the vulnerability of the young. Merwin's image of the sheep captured for Fred the deep faith expressed through repeating tradi-

tional ritual to express what cannot otherwise be said: "one hoof one paw one foot before another / the way they went is all that is still there."

During many services he thought long and hard about the question Mary Oliver poses at the end of her poem "The Summer Day," a question not all that different from one the Torah raises: "Tell me, what is it you plan to do / with your one wild and precious life?"[3]

Oliver's notion of one "wild and precious life" drew him back to his mother's impetuousness, to the parts of him that he put aside in his rush toward manhood. In doing so he was "playing" with new and different aspects of his personality in the synagogue. The feeling of being part of the larger community was very important to Fred. "Even though I was the only one reading a particular poem, silently to myself, the fact that we were all together in the room, all of us in our own way struggling with life and faith and meaning, meant something to me. It was like I was on my journey but everyone else was also on a journey, so I felt less alone, and part of a larger community of Jews. And I had my own voice while I was there."

What Fred was doing with his "hidden" prayer book was to reinvest the synagogue with parts of himself—the love of women, the desire to be more awe-filled and worshipful in a new way—that were pressing for expression. All of us invest the world with meaningful images that represent the parts of ourselves that we are trying to make real in the world—treasured images of the "good parent" that we are trying to hold on to, of esteemed and valued parts of ourselves we want to more fully make real in the world, to be good fathers, good mothers, friends, more caring and humane, less selfish, less predatory.

Healing Harsh Childhood Images. When we play at prayer, what results may be our getting past harsh internal images—to be OK in synagogue I have to be a world-class davener, I have to do it just right, bend the knee at the right moment, know the proper Hebrew. Fred, for example, is finding a way of reconnecting with his parents, finding his place in the flow of generations. He is not doing so by saying that to them, or writing long letters to them or having heart-to-heart, face-to-face talks. Rather he is reshaping and renewing his sense of his parents, his feelings toward them, and his place in the continuity of the generations through his "patchwork prayer book."

By finding new, more resonant images that speak to the newly emergent parts of ourselves, we can allow Judaism to become an opportunity for transformation in our lives.

Prayer and Visualization. It may happen that Fred, in investing the synagogue with these new images, will change the way in which he relates to his parents—that some of the tempering of his rebelliousness and independence, and of the harsh Internal Pharaoh, will be communicated to his parents. Even when parents are no longer alive, playful prayer allows us to continue to work on the relationships. Marsha, a forty-year-old woman, a working professional, married with two children, who misses her father greatly, says, "It's been six years since my father died and what's missing is my spiritual life." She struggles with her anger at his death and sense of loss. She rarely attends synagogue, although she is very committed to Jewish family observances such as Shabbat, Chanukah, and Passover. When asked if she prays, Marsha responds in terms of her ongoing link to her father: "No...Well...I pray to my dad—I talk to him. I remember him as he was when he was younger, my dad. I'll ask him to help me out, tell him like, 'Dad, I really need something here.' Any time of the day or night. Sometimes at night when I can't sleep...I've created a belief system: all the good that's happened to me since his death is because of my father. He'd love my husband...and his grandson whom he'd never met!" Marsha is using prayer to continue a relationship that she felt was severed too early, and she is reworking it as time goes on, imaging different sides of her father—the loving grandfather—that she never knew in real life, and in so doing is also wooing and speaking to parts of herself—such as the proud daughter, and now wife and mother, who feels beloved of her father and able to give to him things there wasn't time for when he was alive. What grown daughter would not want to see the gleam of love and recognition in her father's eyes when she brings her child home for the first time, making him a grandfather? Instead of the sadness Marsha carried from the fact that he never lived to see his grandson or his daughter's adult accomplishments, in prayer Marsha visualizes a happy father, proud of her, and invokes a sense of herself as a daughter who is able to provide that to him, nurturing her own self-esteem and positive regard.

Tactile Prayer. We can play, and pray, without words, even without visual images. Active, tactile prayer can create a play space that is wordless. One man I know, Elliott, doesn't pray in words or images at all. For him, prayer is about music, song, and touch. To express that point he told me about Julius Lester's response to his son's question as to why he touches the mezuzah every time he walks into his house: "It's tactile prayer."

Elliott went on to explain, "When I pray, I move. I don't feel comfortable praying with words. When I listen to Jewish music at home, I'll sway and move, reaching out to someone, making contact with someone, with other Jews whom I'll never meet and don't know personally. I free myself because I don't have to use words."

Elliott's tactile praying extends right into the synagogue. He is a member of a Jewish Renewal congregation and when I asked him if he prays during the service, he replied again in terms of the music: "Yes, but I don't think of it as a direct dialogue or even that a being is listening. I do believe something is happening when I am davening that is not typical of my week.

It's the music of my people, something I hear nowhere else in my life."

Elliott's efforts evolved from a struggle with his own Internal Pharaoh. He had been taught much of his life to "sit still" during services, and it was only as he wrestled with ways of worshiping that felt real and authentic to him that Elliott realized that he needed to move in order to really pray. In finding ways to use movement and music in his worship, Elliott drew on his love of the Jewish songs and melodies from his childhood, as well as his desire to feel more comfortable and alive in his body as an adult.

Elliott reminded me of Abraham Kaplan's observation that for some of us the seemingly nonreligious aspects of Judaism are the places where our deepest religious vitality exists. For Elliott, it is movement, song, and music wherein lie his deepest prayers.

Such stories reveal how little we know of the very individual ways of praying that compose a single synagogue service. There are multiple, individual ways that people pray, both inside and outside the synagogue. Each of these is a potential play space in which imagination and reality meet, kiss, and become one.

Playful possibilities for taking another look at what may have heretofore been a rather rote, reflexive experience of the synagogue abound. What are you doing during the Amidah? For some of us traditional prayers work very well, for others not so well. When we are all in synagogue davening, what's happening for the person next to you? We are not all having the same experience.

Demystifying the Sanctuary

Prayer is fundamentally a solitary enterprise, even when it takes place among other worshipers. Ultimately, it can be helpful to move beyond hiding prayers in your own "patchwork prayer book," toward other like-minded and supportive individuals. Using the group nature of the congregation can also result in vibrant worship opportunities. Rarely do rabbis and congregants utilize the face-to-face, person-to-person possibilities of the worship service. A synagogue is a community of people, and the congregation present at a service functions as a group.[4] Feeling witnessed by and part of a group can help us to take ownership of our participation in Judaism. On the other hand, all groups struggle with basic issues of safety, of insider-outsider status, and of trust. The fundamental psychological task faced by a congregation seeking to become more creative and engaging is how to create conditions of safety such that the community will be willing to take some risks together.

There are at least two ways to encourage more active participation and personal meaning-making in the synagogue. Both have to do with attending to interaction and "process": demystifying the sanctuary and creating opportunity for writing, talk, movement, and interaction as part of the worship service itself.

The Psychology of the Sanctuary. The sanctuary symbolizes tradition and reverence, with its elements of worship and faith—from the yarmulkes to the ark and the Torah, the rabbi on the *bimah*. For many of us it evokes the awe that comes from entering a "special" space, where we come to focus in a different way from that of the secular world. The unintended consequence of so much awe, though, is often to create a "mystique of passivity" in which many of us become disempowered, feeling intimidated by the possibility of making a mistake or doing something inappropriate.

On the other hand, one rabbi—who moved from pulpit work to teaching and research—suggested that "many, many Jews are under-awed—they are bored or not engaged by the service. We need more drama," he suggested, exclaiming, "Good liturgy engages the heart and the soul!" He went on to emphasize the importance of good music, of newer prayers. All are important, but again are coming from the leadership to the congregation.

How can we also ensure that Jewish meaning-making from the congregants themselves emerges in the service? We need to find ways to make the sanctuary into a creative play space for the congregation as a whole.

One way to bring personal meaning into the sanctuary is to encourage writing moments within the sanctuary itself, either during, or separate from, the worship service.

Writing in the Sanctuary. The sanctuary is the central place to worship in our faith. Writing together in the sanctuary at a time when there is no service being conducted can be a way of demystifying it, helping us see the space itself in a new light, as a safe place free of judgment, performance worries, and other expectations, and as a place receptive to who we are, with our individual preoccupations and needs.

I saw this happen in a writing workshop conducted by Genie Zeiger. The workshop offered a clear view of our resistance to making the sanctuary a more human place and of the measures we can actually take to make it better. Genie offered her writing workshop, "Exploring Your Judaism," at the small synagogue in southern New Hampshire to which I belong. A flyer distributed to the congregation invited people to "discover what it means for us to be Jewish through the medium of creative writing" and encouraged, "Writing is a profound and direct way towards gaining understanding of ourselves and others. No experience is required."

The event took place on a Sunday afternoon, when the synagogue was otherwise unused, and attracted a group of seven members who were not regular attendees at services. Such "offbeat" events are a way of attracting people who may be less drawn to the more "traditional" events.

One of the first things we did after arriving and turning on the lights and heat was to go upstairs to look at the sanctuary. Our sanctuary is a lovely space, truly inspired in design: rows of large windows at eye level frame the large room, which tapers up toward the sky, and the vaulted stained glass window at the very top. Native New Hampshire white oak, with its lively, blond finish enhances the large beams that angle from all sides toward the stained glass—which sits like a yarmulke atop the room. Above the *bimah* dance golden Hebrew letters, which we translated into English:

> How goodly are thy tents, O Jacob
> Thy dwelling places, O Israel!

We didn't start in the sanctuary. Instead, we admired its beauty and then trooped downstairs in search of classroom space to write in. We set up a circle of plastic children's desks in one of the classrooms and then went into the kitchen to find coffee and snacks. The event was sponsored by the temple, and refreshments were assumed, but it felt as if we had the run of the house while our parents were away for the weekend. In retrospect, it felt as if we were all caught in the infantilized stance in our own Judaism—we were the kids and the adults were elsewhere.

As we moved the plastic chairs and desks around, Genie asked, "Why don't we write upstairs in the sanctuary? It's such a beautiful space."

We walked upstairs nervously and moved the pews around a large table we'd brought along with us. We pushed the large table from which the Torah is read out of the way. The Torah seemed to be looking down skeptically at us from the ark. We were all a little tentative. You come to believe that the sanctuary is for prayer and worship and that the only kind of prayer that's kosher is led by a rabbi.

It had not yet occurred to us that we were creating a worship service ourselves that day, using writing to create our own prayer. This is the way that many prayers first got started—the first prayer books didn't have a written text as they do today. In early Jewish services the prayer books merely had a prompt that said in effect, "Say a prayer for your ancestors here," and expected people to make up their own. Over time some texts became the accepted versions. These composed prayers were set down and passed down and became what we use today.[5] Thinking about the tension between individual feeling of creativity and intention (*kavanah*) and form and tradition (*kevah*), Rabbi Sally Finestone, the Reform rabbi at Harvard Hillel, commented to me one day, "The history of prayer books is about how one generation's *kavanah* becomes the next generation's *kevah*." Today we were—unknowingly—trying to convert the synagogue's *kevah* back into our own *kavanah*.

Finally, we settled ourselves, the seven of us in the very center of the sanctuary, around our writing table, piled high with poems, writing paper, pens, refreshments, coats, purses.

Genie placed a candle in the middle of the table, tall and narrow with layers of varying color. Of particular Jewish significance? "I think I got it in Puerto Rico," Genie mused, then laughed. Her face took on a serious expression when she suggested we say the traditional *Shehecheyanu* when lighting it, the prayer that marks all special moments in our lives.

In this way Genie reminded us nervous scribblers-to-be that we were doing a form of worship here, too. No reason to feel shy or awkward. Then Genie explained in a quiet, low-key way that writing can be particularly helpful in understanding our spirituality. It's hard for us to see ourselves clearly because we are so wrapped up in our experience, and writing gives us another, slightly distanced perspective on ourselves.

We were all tense. We talked about performance pressure and fears of doing well enough at this "writing thing."

Listening to Genie helped calm us all. She explained that we were going to do some freewriting exercises, informal and without worry about how "good" they are.

"I'll give you some things to write about and we'll take about fifteen minutes for each. Try to write without stopping, without worrying about what comes into your head." She urged us to try to keep our pens moving. If we weren't sure what to write about, write about that or just keep writing out the beginning prompt.

"I'm not used to writing this way," offers Mike, a software engineer at a dot-com company. "I have a software program that takes your speaking voice and converts it into written text. I don't know about holding a pen. I prefer to say it."

"Well, perhaps I can convince you otherwise today, Mike," Genie says encouragingly, and we begin. It was nice to have a woman in charge, encouraging my spiritual growth. I was more used to having men up on the *bimah,* hurrying me through prayers. The softness of Genie's voice, the invitation to just be myself, calmed me. How often do we just relax in the sanctuary, contemplate and feel it, feel ourselves in it, see what comes to mind when we spend some time there without having to "do something"?

Some people like to go and read in the sanctuaries of their synagogues; others like to take their kids and go play there. In that way we connect this place with our own experiences, with ourselves. We learn to play there, be ourselves. So, that day we slowly connected that beautiful room with our own experience, put into writing what mattered to us as Jews.

I know I'm Jewish when . . . was the first writing prompt. All of us wrote together in the quiet sanctuary. Then we were invited to read aloud what we'd each written. No one declined the opportunity. There was not a lot of discussion and comment after each person read. In fact, long discussion was discouraged. Instead, Genie encouraged us to remark on particular images or themes that grabbed us from what we'd just heard and then we went on to the next person.

The first to read was Josh, a college teacher in his mid-forties, tall and thin, with a still detectable New York accent even after years of living in New Hampshire. Before the free-writing, as an icebreaker, Genie had asked us all to jot down a Jewish activity, whatever came to mind first. Josh had written "talking." His story picked up on that theme.

"I knew I was Jewish when I was in our local Chinese restaurant with Uncle Abe from Los Angeles and the rest of my relatives a few weeks ago in town and he wants to know how come the restaurant doesn't have Sub Gum Chopped Suey on the menu.

" 'In Los Angeles all the Chinese restaurants have Sub Gum Chopped Suey!'

"Despite being in a crowded restaurant my 78-year-old uncle doesn't mind yelling at the waiter, raising his voice. The waiter says yes, yes, he will make Sub Gum Chopped Suey for my uncle, not to worry. While we're waiting for our orders, we talk about the family. All the gossip and stories and poking fun in a loving way! Then the food arrives and I feel the warmth and cozy odors of the Chinese food. I feel relief at the food and in the knowledge that with its arrival we'll all stop talking. Which is almost true, except that my Uncle Abe looks at his plate and yells to the waiter across the restaurant, 'waiter! waiter! What, no cashews in the Sub Gum Chopped Suey—in Los Angeles they always put cashews in the Sub Gum Chopped Suey!' "

Josh spoke with pleasure about the warmth of the family all together and the enjoyment of the food, but being Jewish also carries with it a feeling of standing out, of being the only table in this rural town not only with its own sense of how Sub Gum Chopped Suey is made, but also willing to talk loud, to stand out. Josh acknowledged that he felt embarrassed even as he was happy to be amid his extended family.

The stories continued. Sally, a fifty-year-old bank vice president, divorced with several grown children, wrote, "I know I'm Jewish when I go to a movie, such as last weekend, to see *Life*

Is Beautiful, about the Holocaust and I think about all the killing and mistreatment in the world."

She read to us about the Jewish value system she had learned from her family growing up and tried to create in her family as a parent: "treat people like I would myself like to be treated." She writes poignantly about being aware of the capacity for evil in the world, about her grown children living far away, and "constantly thinking about the safety and well-being of my children."

Mike, who grew up in Boston and moved to New Hampshire about ten years ago, showed us that he doesn't need to speak into his computer in order to write movingly. His writing, through his repetition of the beginning phrase, had the feel of a poem:

"I know I'm Jewish when I drive through southern New Hampshire and see celebrations of holidays I know are foreign. I know I'm Jewish when I say the Shema, eat bagels and lox and look through Jewish magazines. I know I'm Jewish when I sit in my local Rotary club meeting and feel like I'm visiting a foreign country. I know I'm Jewish when I read about Secretary of State Madeleine Albright or Secretary of Defense William Cohen and feel proud. I know I'm Jewish when anyone is talking about Jesus. I know I'm Jewish when I'm with non-Jews and someone talks about Israel, Nazis, or God."

He looked up quickly from his paper when he stopped reading, and breathed deeply. Feeling different and being Jewish were united in Mike's experience. There were words of acknowledgment, knowing looks exchanged, from around the table.

Mike's wife, Judy, a convert who was raised Episcopalian, looked at Judaism from both within and without:

"I know I'm Jewish when the pleasant symbols of Christianity no longer attract me, when my aged Christian mother no longer dismisses my explanations about why I converted. I know

I'm Jewish when I pray, and when I make matzoh balls, worrying far more that they come out right than I ever did when making a Yule log. I know I'm Jewish when I feel uncomfortable at a Christian wedding, which sounds so impersonal and distant compared to the warmth and love at a Jewish ceremony."

As if she had written in response to Judy, Laura, married to a non-Jew, read her piece, which also explored the theme of being in and out of Judaism at the same time, feeling pulled in several ways, of the difficulty of feeling quite at home in any place:

"I know I'm Jewish when I am sitting among friends writing like I am doing right now, leaving my atheist husband at home, who is eating a roast beef and mayo sandwich. I feel Jewish when I leave the synagogue on Yom Kippur and go to my office to see patients and feel guilty at not being Jewish enough, or when I eat Chinese food on Friday night as we did last week instead of observing the Sabbath. What does it mean to feel Jewish and not to act Jewish? I know I'm Jewish when I yearn for a rabbi whose inclusiveness and permissiveness leaves me feeling at home in the synagogue. I know that I am Jewish when I watch my thirteen-year-old daughter and love her brashness and forthrightness."

With these words, Laura is giving voice in the sanctuary itself to the ways she feels both comfortable and uncomfortable with traditional worship, with the contradictions in her life. Her words become a brash and forthright sort of prayer.

Genie has written her piece in a worn notebook, in careful penmanship, using black ink. "I know I am Jewish when I am in a room full of Jews and immediately feel at ease. I know I am Jewish when I walk through our little town in Western Massachusetts and I feel the comfort of being known in a goyische community. I know that I am Jewish when I am in my community and make mention of being Jewish in a subtle way so as to avoid being insulted in some way. I know that I am Jewish when my sister from Brooklyn visits with her kids and her Jewish husband and the noise and food starts and it's as if the walls are doing the hora and my goyische husband retreats out of the living room looking for some quiet. I know that I am Jewish during the High Holidays and I'm happy in temple or at home. I spend the time with my son and daughter if I can, and the fall is here and I feel an age-old melancholy, or is it just my hormones? I think of my parents, now dead. My mother asks: should you be writing like this in a sanctuary? Yes, OK? Sure you should!"

In this sanctuary, at this time, we are giving voice to wanting to be a part of Judaism and not wanting to, belonging and not belonging. That tension is part of the very meaning of Judaism for this group and is the flowing current that shapes how we worship and participate in Judaism. A different writing group might have developed different themes—the experience of being a Jewish woman, for example, or what it means to be a Jewish father. The process of writing and reading and witnessing is transferable to many different kinds of synagogues or groups.

There is an important element to doing this in a group, in the sanctuary: by writing and witnessing each other's struggle, we are making it a part of the synagogue experience as well.[6] In writing and reading aloud and to others we are also affirming our very Jewishness in a way many of us have never before had a chance to do as adults. Certainly never before in a sanctuary. We are saying that it is OK to be Jewish and unsure, to be Jewish and ambivalent, to feel Jewish in the ways that we ourselves define.

Similar activities can take place during the service. For example, it's possible to do a five-minute freewrite before or after the Torah service. Suppose you are reading about the sacrifice of Isaac during Rosh Hashanah. Imagine distributing paper throughout the congregation and then inviting everyone to write briefly about how we each sacrifice our children. To what idols and what demands? Then collect the papers and have members

of the congregation read all or a sample of them aloud anonymously. This would give personal meaning to a powerful section
of the Torah. (Some congregants who were raised Conservative
or Orthodox will feel uncomfortable writing in synagogue on a
holiday or the Sabbath—in that case, they could be encouraged,
via word of mouth, phone calls, or the synagogue newsletter, to
write a contribution in the days beforehand to bring with them
to synagogue.) Or, distribute 5″ × 7″ index cards and ask everyone to write down a memory of his or her father's demand on
them, or of a mother's silence, since Sarah is not consulted in
the text. Then read those aloud, anonymously or not, depending
on the comfort level of the congregation.

Encouraging Involvement. The confidence of the leader in this
activity is vital. Often the best leader for such attempts at congregational involvement is not the rabbi, but a lay member of
the community. Genie, for instance, played an important role in
the story-writing group. She quietly created a safe play space for
all to write and read their stories. She did it first with her attitude: her quiet assurance and giving us permission to be ourselves, to trust that we could indeed write and read and that
there were no judgments to be made here. She invited us in a
non-coercive manner to try something new. She did it also with
the way she used ritual to create a special moment. The candle
and the prayer in a modest way told the group that in the sanctuary with our pens and paper and our stories we were doing
something serious and meaningful.

The key is to experience the sanctuary in a new way. The
quiet, receptive space and invitation to do something different is
so unlike the public praying and "debate" style of worship that
is part of our experiences in the sanctuary: the display of Hebrew reading skills, the passing of the Torah, the formalism of
the ritual.

Yom Kippur: "Top Secret" and Atonement. Writing in synagogue can also be an adjunct to the service itself and a way of deepening our understanding of our connection to traditional prayers and rituals. It can help us engage with our friends and with fellow congregants.

Lauren, for example, is a law professor who volunteered in her Humanistic Judaism congregation to lead an afternoon workshop in between services on Yom Kippur to talk more personally about forgiveness and repentance. She planned to use the writing game "Top Secret" to invite people to write about an experience in which they were able to forgive or to be forgiven, and then try to generate some group discussion. "Top Secret" really provides the mask that Yeats found invaluable, since no one reads his or her own writing; each person reads someone else's.

In Lauren's version of "Top Secret," each person in the group gets an index card or piece of paper and writes about a moment of forgiveness and repentance during the past year. It could be an experience that happened today or a while ago, and it may be something the person has never told anyone else about. Each person in the group writes out his or her experience and then the cards are collected and shuffled. Lauren then planned to give everyone someone else's card to read aloud. That way anonymity would be preserved, and Lauren hoped the mask of anonymity would help people feel more comfortable with the writing.

On Yom Kippur during a break in the services, thirty people interested in exploring issues of atonement and repentance through Lauren's writing exercise went into a Hebrew school classroom down the hall from the sanctuary. Lauren offered the group some brief readings on repentance, with a humanistic flavor. "I chose the readings because they showed how traditional Jewish prayers had a humanistic content in the sense that much of the work of repentance and forgiveness is thrown onto persons, rather than coming from God."

Lauren gave out the index cards and had everyone complete the following sentences:

I would say I'm sorry to ＿＿ for ＿＿.

When I don't say I'm sorry to ＿＿ for ＿＿ I get ＿＿.

Participants could choose this format or the same thing using "I forgive ＿＿" since there was not time to do both. People participated actively, and several expressed how moving the experience had been for them. Some people, of course, wrote more personally than others, but there were enough men and women willing to reveal a bit of themselves to make it meaningful. Lauren also recalled, "I was glad that some people brought up societal, or macro, events and got into the question of forgiving evil or whatever we construe as evil. One survivor said he had come to the point many years ago of forgiving the Nazis for the Holocaust. A fourteen-year-old wrote that he would forgive the students in Columbine High School who did the shooting. Of course, there were issues of parents, siblings, children, friends, those dead and alive. So it turned out to be a richer topic than I ever imagined."

The richness came in part because Lauren created a ritualized, formal structure that allowed people to explore more deeply the meaning of forgiveness in their own lives. These writing exercises are so powerful because they invite a person to deepen understanding within a group. This goes beyond individual, private experience and allows the kind of group connection and witnessing that is so central to the Jewish experience.

Reflecting on the day, Lauren wondered where to go with her experiment. "I don't know what to do with this. Some of us would like to incorporate it more into our services. Next year,

I'd like to try my hand at organizing Rosh Hashanah, and after the reading of the Isaac and Abraham story in the service, have a discussion on different ways we all 'sacrifice' our children. But that is a long way away!"

It was a long way away, but did Lauren also feel that it would be a long stretch psychologically for the community? Clearly it is a stretch to ask a synagogue community to break from tradition, seeking some *kavanah* (creative intention) amid the *kevah* (fixed traditions). What is involved in asking people to reveal more and talk together more about who they are?

Can We Talk?

Writing is valuable; so are "patchwork prayer books"; and so is conversation that allows exchange and connection between members of the congregation. Talking used to be a natural part of the synagogue service, small pockets of congregants commenting on and debating aspects of the Torah reading. Many older Jews' most treasured memories of synagogue service involve sitting around the edges of the sanctuary during the service and talking with friends about what was going on in their lives. Networking, advice-giving, fellowship—all took place in the sanctuary.

So much of present-day Judaism involves a real silence (we sit while others intone prayer) or an "emotional silence" (we don't disclose or share what is happening for us during the service) on the part of the congregation. Prayers are recited but not connected to the individual lives of the people in the room. Prayer, too, is conceived as something that happens between the individual and . . . whomever—God, the divine, To Whom It May Concern. We imagine that prayer has to be to "God," however defined.

Yet prayer can involve a communal sharing. For example,

consider this part of a responsive reading from a Conservative prayer book: "Help us to convert our convictions into conduct and commitment."

Instead of simply repeating this prayer responsively, what if there were an opportunity to either briefly write about or say aloud the commitments you are having trouble making real? What if we could speak about what's happening with our kids, our commitments to our sons or daughters or spouses or partners? Or suppose instead of just reading the famous quote from Abraham Heschel—"Prayer is an invitation to God to intervene in our lives, to let His will prevail in our affairs; it is the opening of a window to Him in our will, an effort to make Him the Lord of our soul"—we then each talked about whether we believed in a God and, if so, how do we conceive of that God? Is it a Him? Her? Something else?

It can be intimidating to give voice to such matters in the publicness of the sanctuary. What if the discussion were played as a "Top Secret" game? Index cards could be distributed and everyone is invited to write down a vexing commitment; then the cards are collected and everyone who wrote one gets a different person's card to read aloud. Privacy is protected in that no one reads his or her own card aloud.

Something similar happened at a men's brotherhood meeting that I attended one Friday when the men were invited to write down the dilemmas about commitment most present in their lives. Here's what the group listed:

What to give up and what to hold on to as I age?

What is the cost of the power role that I gravitate toward in my career?

What is the "emotional intelligence" to foster within myself to have a more satisfying relationship with my wife?

What do I want for myself as a father?

What is the role of friendship in my life?

What do I want to say to and hear from my mother and father at this point in my life?

From these questions, posed anonymously, an excellent discussion ensued. Yet whether or not there is discussion is not important. Simply giving voice to the concerns can be extremely helpful. Such activities build community within the congregation by breaking down the facelessness of the group. We come to see other members of the congregation as real people, not as strangers, critics, heroes, demons.

In addition, members of the community come to share our realities and concerns. By opening up ancient prayers to the lived experience of the community we give them new life. Otherwise, the responsive reading may create more silence than openness. We intone together but don't talk together. Without some greater sense of community there is no energy in the supposedly shared words.

Clearly, there's a need for communal sharing of preexisting prayers and a community evocation of old and familiar beliefs, a kind of touchstone of the heart, but isn't there also a need for us to put into words our own experiences, to connect with each other and acknowledge and affirm what is not being said? How much of traditional prayer is a silencing of the self, and how much of it is an opening of the self to others, a way of finding community and connection by revealing oneself?

Get Moving!

Jill Ann Schwartz's Movement Choir. Talk, movement, and prayer can be combined in powerful ways. Jill Ann Schwartz is a dancer, a choreographer, and currently the artist-in-residence at the Woodstock Jewish Congregation in Woodstock, New York, where she works closely with Rabbi Jonathan Kligler to design movement services for the congregation. Their goal is to bring more joy, movement, and personal story into worship.

Jill Ann is in the process of creating a movement choir with people from the synagogue. They are using the art of movement to explore their Jewish identities and to build a sense of community. The movement choir meets on Sunday afternoons twice a month to explore a particular theme related to the week's Torah portion, as well as to develop a broader movement vocabulary. One week the group used the story of Jacob wrestling with the angel ("Israel means 'god wrestler,'" Jill Ann informed me) as a metaphor for their personal wrestling with Judaism. Jill Ann encouraged people to physicalize the act of wrestling, to discover how they might embody this idea. Each person asserts his or her own experience differently, and it is revealed through the movement quality.

Jill Ann's connection to Judaism has always been through music and dance. She is deepening her understanding of this relationship through her work at the Woodstock Jewish Congregation. She has worked with Liz Lerman and the Washington [D.C.] Dance Exchange, as part of her Moving Jewish Communities Dance Institute.[7] Afterward, Liz served as a mentor for Jill Ann as she developed programs in several Jewish communities.

"I learned from Liz to work with people on the big story and the little story. The Torah has the potential to resonate on a very personal level, if we are given ways to access it. I believe in using movement to access personal stories."

What does that mean?

With her movement choir, Jill Ann worked with one of Liz Lerman's choreographic tools, called "I come from...," as a way to explore and share people's histories of their Jewish identities. They explore this idea through an interviewing process and then in movement. Each person develops his or her own movement vocabulary and a journal of ideas and memories to use in creating pieces of choreography.

"Our sessions include a body warm-up, travel through space to greet others, and various exercises designed to heighten our awareness of expressive and dynamic qualities of movement. Each person sits and talks with a partner for about ten minutes. First one person in the dyad shares an idea about the statement, 'I come from...,' then the other person responds with their own ideas, and then back and forth. This can be a very intimate process, as these statements may have some emotional resonance. One person's ideas will trigger ideas for another. For example, 'I come from a family of readers...' or 'I come from a father who went to college when he was fifteen years old.' These are statements about origins and meaning in our lives. People are often surprised at what comes up when they give voice to their memories of where they came from. Next we take these ideas into movement; each person creates an action or gesture that expresses a particular idea they uncovered through talking.

"So, for example, for one person the statement was 'I come from a small town.' The movement this man found started with his arms raised and back behind his head. Then he brought his hands slowly downward, narrowing his hands and sinking down until his hands were cupped on the floor. This movement expressed the narrowness and rootedness he felt living in a small town.

"Each person in the choir finds their gestures, and then we work to create a collaborative dance that combines our separate movements into a coherent whole." The choir is working toward incorporating the entire congregation into a structured movement improvisation during an upcoming Passover service. The choir will serve as catalyst in leading the congregation in a movement service.

Jill Ann's movement process can be applied to many Torah stories—what gestures and actions come to mind about the powerful story of Abraham's sacrifice of Isaac, for example, read on the first day of every Rosh Hashanah, considered from the father's, the mother's, or the son's point of view? Or to a favorite prayer, or to such themes of personal Jewish exploration as "I come from..." or "I first realized I was Jewish when...?"

Jill Ann hopes that the movement choir, through its work and worship performances, embodies the physicality needed to allow the congregation to experience a visceral Judaism and be a catalyst for other members to explore such ways of worship. She observes, "People worry so much in synagogue about doing things right and sometimes feel so insecure. Yet my rabbi and Liz Lerman both know that Jews love to ask questions. We're taught beginning as young children at seders to ask questions; it's such a big part of our tradition."

Encouraging Talk

The Torah as Current Events. It is also possible to create a powerful, heartfelt discussion of the "big story" and the "little story" of the Torah without leaving your seats, by talking directly with each other. Discussing the Torah within the service is a powerful way of making it real and helping people connect to it. Many synagogues try to develop congregational discussions during the service, yet there is often resistance and reluctance. We are not used to talking openly in the service; we are used to being obedient and to remaining isolated within our own individual experience of prayer and faith, or within the absence of a meaningful experience. Yet discussions that involve the group as a whole, not just the rabbi or a few featured presenters, can help build morale and a sense of the congregation.

Three things need to happen, though: (1) the rabbi needs to be able to tolerate silence better than many do, (2) there needs to be an acknowledgment, often by the rabbi, of the difficulty involved and some encouragement by him or her of the congregants' efforts, and (3) there needs to be a willingness to tolerate uncertainty and to encourage broader participation rather than quickly "finding answers."

The experience of one congregation experimenting with group discussion during a High Holiday service is instructive. Over the summer, while planning for the High Holidays, the rabbi—trained as Reform and new to the synagogue—asked three members of the congregation if they would help stimulate a congregation discussion of "suffering" on Rosh Hashanah by sharing their reactions to the haftorah portion from the Book of Samuel, involving the story of Hannah, a woman who felt great sorrow at being unable to conceive a child. The rabbi planned to discuss the story and asked several members of the congregation to bring in some other short texts that would show how each conceived of suffering and some responses to it. Non-Jewish sources were fine, as well as Jewish texts.

In the story, Hannah is married to Elkanah, and she is very distressed at their being unable to conceive a child. Her otherwise kind husband, with a second wife and children, protests and—without empathy—downplays her pain. ("Am I not more devoted to you than ten sons?") When Hannah weeps and laments at the temple one day, Eli the priest chastises her for being drunk. She protests, "Do not take your maidservant for a worthless woman; I have only been speaking all this time out of my great anguish and distress." Eli apologizes and blesses her. "So the woman left, and she ate and was no longer downcast." Later in the year she conceived and bore a son, Samuel, meaning "I asked the Lord for him."[8]

In her remarks, the rabbi emphasized the power of prayer in this story. In addition, though, the story is a powerful reminder of the redemptive power of witnessing and recognition. The priest sees Hannah's sorrow and, after she speaks, affirms it. She is solitary no longer. It's also a story about what rabbis can provide to congregants, about how men can console women, about the despair of feeling "barren" in our lives, no matter what our gender, and the importance of being witnessed. All of these matters are alive in a different way in everyone's life. Most often, however, many congregations merely read this portion and go on.

What would it be like to really discuss the story and try to put it into the context of our lives now?

On this day, several members of the congregation came forward to talk about what suffering meant in their lives. Or rather, they didn't actually talk about how they suffered—how they may feel "barren" in their lives—but they talked about what helped with their own human suffering. One person talked about how he turned to poetry for consolation in the face of suffering. Marsha, a social worker in an oncology ward who facilitated cancer support groups, talked about why someone with cancer would come to a group and be exposed to others also dealing with "the barrenness" of a life-threatening illness. Marsha didn't have easy answers but said, "All I know is that the sharing of each other's journey seems to keep the pain from becoming suffering." She talked of the authentic connection that happens in the group sharing and then she read some lines from Rilke, a poet of the unknowable, urging us to "love the questions themselves" without striving too much for answers: "Live the questions now. You will gradually, without even noticing it perhaps, live along someday into the answers."[9]

After the three talked, the rabbi opened the discussion to the whole congregation. There was silence. Five seconds went by. Ten seconds. From the congregation, one man remarked, "You're a tough act to follow." Nervous laughter, then more silence.

At moments like these, a rabbi may intervene, calling the discussion to a close, or more likely, beginning to discuss the text and trying to "help" the congregation develop an answer. The rabbi may talk about the meaning of the story from different perspectives. These attempts may be useful and are certainly well intended, but they can also be a mistake, short-circuiting people's attempts to understand their own reactions to what they have just heard. Rabbis can have a tough time tolerating silence, as can congregants. The rabbi may be nervous about putting members of the congregation in an uncomfortable situation. He or she may feel responsible for "leading" the congregation, and silence may be perceived as a failure. Also, silence taps deep places within us. "Silence scares me," one rabbi told me. "I'm not good with silences," she said.

One rabbi tried to get a discussion going during a Shabbat service. Out of the blue he asked the congregation, "How many of you believe in God?" Unprepared, everyone sat in silence. The rabbi, apparently not very at ease with silence, waited a minute then snapped, "Well, I guess we've discussed that enough." Several members of the congregation felt ashamed, then as if they had not done well enough, failed at a task, and were being impatiently dismissed. The rabbi, a thoughtful and kind man, did not intend such an effect. He had asked a great question, but he didn't know how to handle the discussion, how to engage the members, perhaps felt anxious and unsure himself in the face of the quiet, and so left his congregation feeling shamed by his words.

The Importance of Silence.   In fact, tolerating silence is particularly important in group discussions about weighty topics. Silence may be the beginning of prayer. You have to allow some silence so that people can really compose their thoughts. If we hear too much talk, too many questions, we may lose our concentration on what is happening within us.

The truth is, of course, that some of our resistance to real connection in the synagogue comes from the fact that we may not really want to know what we are feeling. We often fear our feelings. Have we lost the sense of the synagogue as a place where people laugh and cry together? In many congregations people have become dutiful and hide in the prayers rather than talking to each other about their hearts' yearnings, about the convictions and conduct and commitment that they yearn for and fall short of.

So, talking openly and directly is difficult. In the synagogue discussion of the story of Hannah, one of the presenters picked up on the comment from the audience ("you're a tough act to follow"). He said, "Friends, this is difficult. We're not used to talking to each other during worship in this way. But this is a real opportunity to begin to talk about what's really important in our lives. Where do we suffer? How do we manage it? How do we pray in our different ways?"

Slowly, hesitantly, a discussion got going. An older woman said that this was so important and that she was glad that we were taking the time to do this in her congregation. Another woman wanted to talk about feeling broken and feeling whole. On some days, she said, she felt quite broken by life and then it was hard to have much faith or connect to Judaism at all. She explained her dilemma: how do you open yourself up and feel humble, yet also feel whole enough to be able to receive or connect with God, or the divine? That comment led a man to wonder about false dichotomies: are you *either* broken *or* whole? Instead, are there ways and moments in our lives in which we are both? After fifteen minutes the rabbi brought the discussion to a close. As a final comment, another member of the congregation suggested that the essence of spirituality is accepting and welcoming the unknown, "the not-knowing that is all around us." She observed that the discussion itself, the listening without having quick answers, felt like a spiritual exercise.

That was it. No flashes of lightning, but the first attempt of this congregation to try to talk more directly among each other. Learning how to do that takes time and repeated efforts to talk about what the Torah means to people today, about our own reactions to parts of the service, about the way we are or are not moved by what happens in the sanctuary. Over the coming months, this congregation may continue to experiment.

The Congregation as a Group. As groups, congregations go through stages of learning how to be together and share worship and prayer. Groups begin with high hopes and unspoken distrust. Who, really, is this person next to me? What do we really have in common? It's natural to project onto others a lot of our disowned feelings and anxieties about self-acceptance. As groups stay together over time there is a process of trust building, never completely established and never finished—to which we have to return over and over, almost every time we get together. Members differentiate even as the group develops more cohesion. Healthy differentiation in groups means that members come to see each other more accurately, in terms of their differences as well as their similarities. Out of this process of becoming more real to each other develop cohesion, morale, and the ability to work together. A congregation is obviously not the same as a therapy group or work group, but groups function similarly in all environments.

Different congregations may find different ways and contexts for members to participate. For example, it's also possible to use a "personal presentation" format. In this format, one or two members of the congregation are invited to take fifteen minutes or more before the service to talk about themselves and what Judaism means to them. It's often a person with a particularly interesting story: a man who found out at age thirty-three that his grandfather was Jewish after having been raised as a Southern Baptist and who then found his way back to Judaism; or a woman who converted from Christianity at age forty; or a woman who decides she wants to be bat mitzvahed at age fifty-seven.

Regardless of the format, though, rabbis need to be able to cultivate silences in discussion, to encourage people to talk in the absence of answers, to take risks, and not to be performing or "onstage" quite so much. To do so means that we need to take more responsibility as members of the congregation for doing the hard work of clarifying what we believe and being willing to speak openly in a place where we may have learned to be passive. The payoff to taking such risks can be a renewed sense of the power of Judaism, its relevance for our times, and of the very human potentialities of synagogue service.

CONCLUSION

The Jew in the Mist—
Being Jewish in Changing Times

Many people concerned with alienated or skeptical Jews approach the matter as if it were a rational argument, or one requiring scolding or seductiveness. They offer counter-arguments to many of the reasons people resist Judaism, or they provide warm and inviting introductions to the meaning of Jewish ritual and belief.[1]

I have tried to take a different approach in this book: to honor and respect both the difficulties men and women have in being Jewish and the often hesitant, sometimes confused ways in which people go about making Jewish meaning in their lives.

To really support Judaism in today's world we need to see Jewish people in the context of their life development. This has several implications for understanding the nature of faith and religion.

"Being Jewish" is not a rational choice—it is an affective set, an emotional phenomenon. Many Jewish outreach efforts focus on "better arguments" ("the 'chosen people' thing doesn't mean what you think it means"), guilt ("if you don't come to synagogue, you'll be responsible for the death of the religion of

303

your mother and father"), or friendly persuasion ("come on down to the *shul*—try it, you'll like it").

Jewish outreach would do better addressing the deeper identity struggles of alienated men and women. People who are reassessing the role of Judaism in their lives, or are hesitant, need to know that they are not alone, that many, many other Jewish men and women are in the same spot. People who are frozen in childhood struggles with parents need to know that this is often a feature of spiritual struggle and search and can lead to new resolutions in their lives. Jews who feel "different" for any of a number of reasons—gay, lesbian, single parent, parent of a child with developmental delays—need to feel welcomed.[2]

The individual struggle with holding on to and letting go of the past is at the core of contemporary Jewish struggles. In constructing Judaism in our lives, we all confront the fundamental anxiety of separating from the past, of living our lives differently from our parents (think of parents in the broadest sense: our cultural parents, all the way back to Abraham and Sarah). In finding, or creating, the rituals that matter to us, in finding our own Jewish voices, we *are* different from the past, and there is some loss and sorrow in that. It is a fundamental fact of human life that growing up and maturing also means doing some violence to the past.

British pediatrician and psychoanalyst Donald Winnicott observed that when a child is internalizing a trustworthy version of those he loves, he also unavoidably distorts and changes who they are.[3] When we make something ours, we also reshape it. To truly take inside oneself a beloved tradition and make it one's own is also, in some way, to destroy it, to change it beyond recognition. The modern struggle to find a personally authentic Judaism is also part of the age-old struggle between parents and children to hold on *and* to let go, a dynamic relived in every generation.

The interplay of psychology and faith is often ignored by rabbis. It's as if psychology may sully faith. However, since the experience of Judaism (or any religion) is tied to family dynamics and struggles with our parents, and since spiritual issues in adult life are related to our childhood and adolescent experiences, it may be helpful to provide skeptical Jews more awareness of these life-cycle interconnections. We may have feelings of ambivalence toward Jewish ritual—synagogue services, seders—related to control battles or identity struggles with our parents. For example, we don't want to go to temple because to do so is to lose a battle with our fathers that began when we were children. Or we *have* to go to temple because it meant so much to our parents, and for us not to do so means failing our parents. More direct talk—either individually, or in small groups within the synagogue—about the frustrating wish to be loyal to our parents even at the price of our own identities, or about the guilty wish to be different from them, may reduce some of the aloneness, and the shame, many Jews feel.

Rodger Kamenetz invoked the image of the Jew in the Lotus when he explored the dialogue between Jews and Buddhists, but our situation might be more aptly described as the Jew in the Mist.[4] Certainly from the individual perspective, finding your authentic Jewish voice means starting from a cloudy, only vaguely conceived place.

Given all the ferment in modern Judaism, and the myriad ways that people are creating and re-creating our ancient faith, it's hard to be sure what directions Judaism will take in the twenty-first century. It can be hard to predict what direction it will take in our *individual* lives. Are we Jews like our parents were, or are we different? Do you stay connected after your children are bar mitzvahed? Do you find your own voice outside a synagogue? Within one?

For many, the struggle with what kind of Jew to be is tied into the question of what kind of person to be, which in turn is linked to what it means to be a man or a woman.

Male and female images of Judaism play a powerful role in

spiritual life. In a room filled with people praying, there are many different images of "God" or "the divine," and these images represent very different experiences of maleness and femaleness.

"We are embodied selves, and Judaism acknowledges our embodiment. *This* life, *this* world, *this* moment in time." So Marcia Falk begins her introduction to *The Book of Blessings.*[5] Falk offers "new Jewish prayers" for everyday life, the Sabbath, and the New Moon festival. A poet and scholar, Falk provides an alternative version of many traditional prayers, including a beautiful alternative Shema that speaks of "the divine" that "abounds everywhere" and "dwells within everything," a spiritual vision far different from the paternalistic image of "the Lord" many of us grew up with. To open oneself to Falk's imagery means to also open oneself to a different sense of the "gender of the divine."

To wrestle with Judaism means to confront our personal gender stereotypes. In the course of writing this book, for example, my own feelings of being "a bad boy" disobeying his father surfaced at several points. The experience of being a grown man, in my fifties, questioning tradition and searching for meaning evoked Hebrew school memories of goofing off and not studying my bar mitzvah portion correctly and of being distracted by "frivolous" matters, less important than learning the correct pronunciation of Hebrew words. What was I doing, at age fifty-five fascinated with the prayers and poetry of Marcia Falk, the chanting of Rabbi Shefa Gold? These women whom I had never met felt like warm Jewish mothers urging me toward a richer, more expressive form of Judaism. Along with the joy of that came painful feelings that can be summarized with the question, Why was I not paying attention and davening like the men of my childhood had always done? To explore a more vital version of Judaism in my life, I had to wrestle with the fear of letting my father down, of not being a "good enough" man. (Of course, in reality many men—including my father—were very supportive of my efforts, but internal images have a life of their own.)

The struggle to find my own voice as a Jewish man was part of the struggle with divided loyalties to my parents that I first began charting over twenty years ago.[6] I mention this in order to emphasize the reality that masculine and feminine images of worship play powerful roles in our spiritual lives. It's easy to criticize the stolid nature of synagogue worship and to want to bring more singing, chanting, and music into the service. Judaism can be a joyful road to integrating the male and female aspects of ourselves, but we may also resist because such activities grate against our sense of what it means to be male or female. As Judaism changes, we need to explore further what it means for a man to welcome more feminine parts of himself into his Jewish worship. And for a woman to welcome more masculine parts of herself into Jewish worship.[7]

We may overemphasize the importance of synagogue worship in Judaism. There are many different pathways to a vibrant Jewish identity: within the synagogue, outside it, through ritual observance, through work in the world. There is no one right way to be Jewish. Many Jews are caught in the monochromatic idea that there is one way to be Jewish. After centuries of emphasis on "the group," in a desire to protect and defend ourselves against a hostile world, perhaps now we can also acknowledge differences in style and belief among Jews.

We live amid a Judaism of many patterns. In one study of over 1,500 Jews in the New York metropolitan area, psychologist Bethamie Horowitz identified seven patterns of "Jewish engagement," ranging from several subtypes of considerable assimilation to varieties of moderate interest and involvement to several ways of being intensively engaged with Judaism.[8]

Indeed the emphasis on ritual and getting people back into the synagogue as a primary Jewish pathway may backfire. In his presidential address to the UAHC in 1999, Rabbi Eric Yoffie proposed that we "make synagogue worship our primary concern." Rabbi Yoffie was appropriately concerned with the decline in synagogue attendance and the "tedious, predictable, and dull" nature of the services.[9] Rabbi Yoffie offered creative ways to enliven what happens within the synagogue, including more attention to chanting, music, and the aesthetics of the services. Yet there are many Jews who live their Judaism entirely outside the traditional observances of prayer, or who have devised new prayer outside the *shul,* in small groups, without rabbis, or who find in their work a connection to Judaism through social action, study, music. By focusing so much energy and attention on synagogue worship, we lose focus on many, many Jews for whom such activity is not a priority, and we may create a "we-they" atmosphere among Jews of different stripes. We can, rather, be curious about each other's different versions of Judaism, as siblings in the same family lead very different lives yet know they are all "family" nonetheless.

We need to be aware that Jewish identity is not the same as observable behavior. Many of those concerned with the "survival" of Judaism imagine "identity" as congruent with ritual behavior. "Keep lighting the Shabbat candles. Don't forget the High Holidays," rabbis advise us.

Yet identity is an internal set, an organization of the self that is distinct from actions and behaviors. As so many of the stories in this book indicate, there is often a profound Jewish identity alive in people who do not participate in traditional Jewish ritual behavior. In addition to emphasizing Shabbat, rabbis could also advise, "What leaves *you* feeling the most Jewish? Tell that to and do that with your children." What we truly love and remember, what is embodied in our lives, will best communicate to children what it means to be Jewish.

To use synagogue attendance, knowing the Amidah, and pronunciation of specific prayers as markers of "Jewish identity" is to create a false sense of crisis. There are many individuals who are wrestling with what it means to be Jewish without participating in traditional ritual definitions of Judaism. In fact, in the Horowitz study, fully *one-third* of those surveyed were on a Jewish pathway entitled "Interior Journey," in which there was a strong internal sense of Jewish identity with quite low religious and communal practice. Comparing people's memories of their childhood with their Jewish identification as adults, Horowitz reports an intriguing finding: For the sample as a whole, "there has been an upswing in the respondents' reporting that being Jewish is an important part of their lives, while at the same time there have been decreases in the extent of Jewish practice, as indexed by synagogue attendance and lighting Shabbat candles."[10] Jewish identity is up, ritual behavior is down.

We need more meaningful rituals. Many Jewish organizations and policymakers don't get the distinction between behavior and identity. As a result we miss the opportunity for actually creating rituals and observances that truly speak to our lives. One rabbi, active in Jewish education and policy, spoke to me in a frustrated tone about policy discussions in synagogues and national organizations "where people keep wanting to support acts of traditional ritual behavior—how to get people to keep kosher, lighting the candles, knowing Hebrew, praying in the synagogue." He described how many Jewish leaders miss the opportunity to develop new, experimental, more meaningful rituals because they don't look at the real lives of Jewish men and women today. "We need new prayers and ceremonies," he told me, citing, for example, how to provide Jewish markers for sending a child to college and the many other points of separation and leave-taking in our lives.

The bar and bat mitzvah ceremony is a profound and wonderful event, but it comes too early, it doesn't really do the job, and the ceremony is less the celebration of adulthood than the acknowledgment of the beginning of adolescence. Most children (and their parents) know that they are not truly the adults that they are said to be during the speechmaking. We need rituals near the end of adolescence as well. "How about prayers for the rabbi and family to say when giving car keys to an adolescent for the first time?" suggested the rabbi.

The bias toward seeing Jewish identification as age-old ritual behavior misses emergent forms of Jewish identification. And it may contribute to the "Jewish performance anxiety" that has been a recurring theme in many chapters, the fear of not "doing it right" that inhibits many people from simply enjoying themselves in their worship. "Are we afraid of Judaism?" one rabbi asked me. He felt many of us are over-afraid and under-awed: we get shut down by fear of looking or acting ignorant, then become bored or not engaged by the service. It can be helpful in that regard for rabbis, cantors, and laypeople to do a better job of modeling "not knowing" both in the synagogue and outside it. One of the joys of being Jewish can be the realization that you don't have to know it all or do it just right.

A final implication that stands out from the stories I've heard is the importance of getting past "Jewish myopia." For many Jews, to find a personally meaningful Judaism means to connect to the world, and not just with "the chosen people." After centuries of distrust, pogroms, Hitler, how do we build bridges to other faiths, to other people? When one Jewish social activist mentioned an example of her work investing in public housing in Chicago, she spoke of how the African-American church group her foundation worked with was "a major player in local politics," and then went on to observe that "our issue of being American Jews is to share the concern of the fate of non-Jewish neighbors, all of us responsibly involved in multifaith issues." She said, "A Jewish issue is whether housing is available for all where we live, whether there is decent health care for all kids."

For her, to be Jewish meant to find common ground with non-Jews. It's not necessary to become a social activist to get past the myopia that religion can bring with it; the same sensibility is possible within traditional observance. So, for example, in a recent article discussing the *kashrut* observance, Rabbi Rolando Matalon wondered whether *everything* becomes kosher in *kashrut*. He noted first that some of the more extreme prohibitions in the *kashrut* practice seem rooted in the "fear of being engulfed and the need to create boundaries in order to preserve...religious and social identity." In today's world, Matalon wrote, "Rather than serving to marginalize us, *kashrut* must be transformed into an instrument for sharing food with others and with 'the other' in sacred encounter." He specifically pointed to the aspects of *kashrut* that "foster mistrust and separation of 'the other,'" including, as in one example, the practice of many Jewish schools to forbid their students to share the food they bring from home, a rule intended to allow children from homes with different levels of observance to attend the same school but which has the effect of sending the message "that *kashrut* equals not sharing."[11]

Emergent forms of Jewish identification today may have less to do with being Jewish in the traditionally observant (and observable) sense and more to do with being a good person in the world, interconnected with others. You may (or may not) be wearing a yarmulke when you're doing it, but your attention is on "the other." From that perspective, in Hillel's famous formulation, being "only for myself" means ignoring how entwined our fate is with that of non-Jews.

Jews and Non-Jews Together: A Traditional Shema in Movement

I do know that it is possible for Judaism to be a deeply embodied spiritual practice. I also know that Judaism can move beyond a remote and highly cognitive place toward an emotionally rich experience that is available to non-Jews as well. I know because I've seen it happen.

Every year I spend a week with my family at the Northfield Conference, a family values camp rooted in the process of spiritual search, located on the beautiful campus of the Northfield/ Mount Hermon School in Northfield, Massachusetts. The conference has a long Christian tradition but over the years has evolved into a community of men and women, teenagers and children, with Christian, Jewish, Buddhist, agnostic, and atheistic orientations, people who are interested in exploring their spirituality and in living, laughing, arguing, and dancing together for a week in June—and are willing to live in the NMH dorms, share communal bathrooms, and eat in the school dining hall to do so.

How you name things disguises deep divisions over the meaning of things. Over the years at the conference we've argued about the title of the evening service and it's currently called Evening Reflections, a mushy title that replaced "vespers," which many felt was simply too Christian. The joke is to refer to it as "twilight reflections," which captures the dim feel to the services, which are designed to offend no one. My friend Lauren, a Humanistic Jew, says that the mushiness reminds her of her synagogue back home but I find the services *too* mushy. We have strived in recent years to offend no one by using more references to Native American prayers and poems, blessings, and so forth that do not include literal references to the totems of Christian, Islamic, or Jewish faiths. The result feels like bland oatmeal. I long for sharper, more defined expressions of faith that not only are polite but also show glimpses of real belief and passion.

The Jewish Shabbat, though, is one service that everyone in the community likes, and most years the Evening Reflections Committee meets to try and plan a Friday evening Shabbat service. Recently we decided that we wanted to create a Shabbat service that included traditional elements of the service. I found I had to do battle with my "Jewish paranoia" as well as the conflicting agendas of my fellow Jews. It didn't help that the committee meets, and the services take place, in the school chapel, where a large cross in the very front of the building looms over the gathering.

The chair of the committee, Connie, a devout Catholic, was very supportive. She remembered as a newlywed having Jewish landlords when she lived in Brookline, Massachusetts, and how much she enjoyed the warmth and gentleness of the Sabbath celebrations going on all around her. She asked about reading a story to begin the service, a children's book called *Joseph and the Sabbath.* She passed it around, and several of the Jewish members of the group found the book "too materialistic."

Other issues surfaced as well: Should we use the pews or arrange folding chairs in a circle up front? Some of us wanted to lose the cross—it's on a moveable base, so it could have been moved to the back, out of sight. Someone pointed out that such a move would be a lot of effort and responsibility, and thoughtfully observed, "It's not the place that matters. Jews have used churches, halls, stores through history. Let's go with this space and fill it with Jewish observance."[12]

Jill Ann Schwartz, the dancer and choreographer from Woodstock, New York, offered to lead us in an alternative Shema she developed—choreographing movement from individual members of the congregation along with the traditional words to create a "movement Shema."

So, on Friday night we began with Connie—not reading a story, but talking personally. She told the group of about 150 Jews and non-Jews about how much Shabbat has meant to her as a Catholic. Connie related how "so many of the families on the street where we lived looked so happy walking to synagogue on Friday evening and Saturday." Now she and her husband and teenage son are trying to observe some form of Sabbath, on a Sunday, by not spending money or watching TV. Their experiments with "a special time, different from the rest of the week," originated in their Friday night experiences twenty years ago on the Sabbath. Tonight, Connie told the assembled group, we were going to explore a Friday night family Shabbat service.

Then came the blessings over the bread and the wine. We had wanted it to be intergenerational. It was easier to get several teenage boys to say the *motzi* over the bread than it was to get their grandfathers to join them. Our elders are so important at such moments, yet at times they seem reluctant to take center stage. Is this another form of performance anxiety? One grand-father when asked to participate earlier in the day had protested that "no one will be able to hear me," but he agreed to come forward after we reassured him that the important thing was that the community see an eighty-year-old grandfather and forty-year-old father along with the teenagers united in thank-ing the divine for sustenance.

Two mothers and their daughters said the prayers over the candles. Both were respected members of the community, well versed in Judaism, and each tripped over the translation of *Adonai* after the blessing. Watching the two of them, each with a napkin over her head, "gathering" in the candles in a tradi-tional female gesture of devotion, was very powerful, as was the wonderful fact of their hesitation and uncertainty about English translations. It was a "leveling" and "equalizing" experience, a reminder that error and uncertainty are a part of devotion, that it is possible to be reverent and to not know.

Then the Shema, inside the cavernous school chapel—scene of how many thousands of communions? The cross looked down upon us. Was it curious about what was unfolding before it? I sure was—what did Jill Ann have in mind? How would it fly in this diverse group? Would the Jews just "do their thing" for all to see, to watch, as objects of curiosity and interest—well-meaning curiosity but rooted in *foreignness* nonetheless—or would we be able to forge some new and deeper sense of community from this ancient Jewish prayer? If we opened up the holiest of Jewish prayer and sentiment, could it actually bring this group of seekers and skeptics and believers closer together?

Short, muscular in her dancer's body, with thick close-cropped black hair, Jill Ann walked to the front of the group and explained what the Shema is and then said that we were going to recite the Shema but in an unusual way. She asked each of us to think of a moment that we wished could have gone on forever. Then, we each found someone else in the room to each tell our memory to. Still in our seats, most of us turned to someone nearby, someone we hardly knew. The room buzzed with moments spent with our children, partners, or parents, times spent alone, as children, as adults.

Then Jill Ann asked for six volunteers to raise their hands and tell their stories—one for each of the words in the Shema. As they talked, Jill Ann listened and watched carefully, her gaze intent. She noted the movements they made as they told their stories.

Two mothers, busy sharing a treasured memory, raised their hands, then spoke almost in unison: "The moments our babies were born, seeing their faces." Each held her hands together, palms faceward, in front of her, as if seeing her baby's face for the first time. From this, Jill Ann took the gesture of arm outstretched, reaching up. *Shema.*

A ten-year-old boy remembered seeing his grandmother for the first time and "how many wrinkles there were in her face." Looking at her he realized "this is how I'll be when I'm old." The impact was such that he rubbed his thumb and forefinger together as he talked of looking up at his grandmother. Jill Ann smiled. We had the movement for *Yisrael.*

Another young boy stood up and remembered traveling to Phoenix with his parents and flying over the Grand Canyon for the first time. He said he felt so much joy at that view, traveling with his parents, *actually flying,* and as he spoke to us, standing there, he wiggled his butt with happiness, with the thrill of it all. A joyously wiggling butt. *Adonai.*

An older woman told of vacationing in the Virgin Islands and snorkeling and seeing all the incredible fish, and she moved her arms as if she were swimming underwater. Jill Ann repeated that motion exactly. *Eloheinu.*

A young girl raised her hand to tell us about getting off a plane in Calgary and her excitement at seeing her older cousins for the very first time. As she spoke her body wiggled and she mimed pulling on her dress in anticipation. Again the backside wiggled and she looked up, as we do when confronting something we love that is much bigger than us. *Adonai.*

A young mother told of having her week-old baby on her chest, lying in bed snuggled with her husband, and hearing him say, "This is paradise." She raised her baby toward her chest with both arms supporting the baby. *Echad.*

Now we were ready. We had all six movements for the Shema, as well as a deep sense of the miraculous in the world, all around us, of why we would want to speak of the divine, of our experience of awe and rhapsody in everyday life.

Jill Ann asked the whole congregation to stand. We recited the Shema, repeating the movements slowly, in one fluid, dance-like sequence:

Shema—arms outstretched, reaching up, seeing your new-born for the first time.

Yisrael—rubbing thumb and forefinger together, feeling the creases on your Bubbe's face.

Adonai—butts wiggling with delight at the first sight of the full majesty of the Grand Canyon.

Eloheinu—arms undulating as you see the miraculous colors of the Caribbean, of the world.

Adonai—butts up, eyes raised as you meet an older, beloved relative for the first time.

Echad—arms raised toward chest, the peacefulness and serenity of lying in bed next to your spouse with your newborn asleep on your chest.

The Jews and the non-Jews all together. My religion and faith suddenly understandable for us all. The exercise embodied a faith in the world around us, the magical Hebrew connected to an understandable movement, not just some obscure chant that might seem just so much gobbledygook.

We all left the chapel, exiting into the lovely June evening twilight on the school campus, quietly holding hands, singing "Shabbat Shalom."

We did it without a rabbi, drawing on our own experiences and hopes and desires and loves, a chavurah for that one night. We constructed the service and worked together, Jews and non-Jews. One of the guiding sources of energy was the wonder of the children, many of them non-Jews, who loved the prayers over the wine, over the bread, the lighting of the candles, and the movement of the Shema.

We learned about negotiating in constructing the service and tolerating the fact that it wouldn't be perfect. The service stalled at times, we weren't always sure what to do when, some of us wanted more structure, others less, some wanted certain prayers we didn't include, others wanted more readings. In the end what we constructed was wonderful, and part of that came from the slightly ragged, uncertain nature of what we were doing. We gave up perfection in order to get something real.

Particularly wonderful was the sense of us all together, Jews and non-Jews, amid a nourishing Judaism—not cut off and distant and demanding, lost in the Hebrew, lost in translation, accessible to only those who know it well, but accessible to the whole world. An accepting, reverent, awe-filled Judaism, welcoming to the whole community.

APPENDIX

Starting and Enjoying Your Own Jewish Discussion Group

As Jews, we emphasize "community" and "the congregation." Yet for many of us, a smaller, more intimate group setting can be a gateway back into Judaism or a way to deepen what is already there. In this appendix, I offer some specific guidelines for creating such a group.

Forming a Jewish Discussion Group. There are many different kinds of Jewish discussion groups. The group I participate in includes men and women who were brought together by our shared ambivalent relationship to Judaism. In the first few months, we awkwardly found our way about topics, meeting places, what was safe to talk about. When one person loftily referred to us as the "Jewish Discussion Group," another member half-jokingly suggested a better title would be "The Losers," referring to our embarrassed sense that all the other members of the congregation somehow had this stuff all worked out and were not spending part of one Sunday every month wrestling with Judaism. But the tradition of small groups of individual Jews talking and debating and disagreeing is an honored one within Judaism, and some might even say it *is* Judaism.[1] The "loser" comment brought the relief of shared laughter and in fact *increased* our commitment to each other.

We began talking over bagels while several of us had kids in Hebrew school, then went out to a local coffee shop. Several of the early members dropped out after a few weeks. We put a notice in the synagogue newsletter, and several more people joined us. We persisted with the encouragement of the rabbi, and it soon became apparent that even starting a group that was skeptical was seen as a contribution to synagogue life. *Aliyot* and even an invitation to one of our members for a sermon followed.

Our group formed around a vague sense of unease and alienation from the synagogue. Some groups form with a more definite agenda: men's groups, women's groups, gay and lesbian groups, Torah study and discussion groups.

One forty-year-old man, Jacob, was very clear, for example, that his Jewish Men's Group and its activities led him back to a more vibrant relationship to Judaism—it was the place where he felt real spirituality lay. The group started six years ago and now there are nine members who meet every third Sunday. Jacob reflected that "we like to say the reasons we exist as a group are 'Jewish,' to distinguish us from other men's groups. We are Jewish and men and a group." In the group, the men talk about a variety of topics that connect to what it means to be a Jewish man. "For example, tonight, with Rosh Hashanah coming up, we'll talk of what happened this year, what we want to be different in the coming year. We often have singing and chanting to start off. Some meetings we'll identify a theme for us all to focus on. One time we talked about men in the Bible: Abraham, Isaac, Jacob. We talked about how come these guys are so much in the forefront of our consciousness every year in the service. Why not current Jewish men or David Ben-Gurion or Moshe Dayan? We felt that each of them exemplified some dilemma for Jewish men. What did Abraham represent by experiencing his faith as involving the possible sacrifice of his son or Jacob with his battle internally about not being the chosen son? Another meeting we each talked about what our bar mitzvahs were like. We all had different experiences. Half or more of us had terrible experiences—anxiety over our performance, family pressure to do it, the disconnect of not really knowing why we were doing the bar mitzvah."

As his own son was nearing bar mitzvah age, Jacob turned to his men's group in helping him sort out the painful feelings he had about his own bar mitzvah experience, so as to be more available to his son. David feels that his Jewish men's group is a primary way he connects to Judaism, giving substance to the notion that it's not just being a parent that reconnects us to Judaism but also the presence of some interpersonal support for our efforts.

Guidelines. The precise reason for getting together is less important than what actually happens when you meet. The most important question group members can ask is, How do we create a safe place for ourselves, where we can talk freely? Everyone's answer may not be the same. The first question each potential member needs to think about is, What do I need to feel safe in this group?

I have found that the following guidelines are important to comfortable group functioning:

Don't make quick judgments about what others say. The point is not who is right or wrong, who is politically correct or not, but rather whether people over time feel safe enough to talk about what is really on their minds.

Try to speak from your own experience, and don't (over)-generalize. We have enough "experts" in this world; often what makes the most difference to people is to hear others speak about what they have experienced directly.

Develop an attitude and an atmosphere that welcome "stu-

pid questions." Particularly within a group of Jews, where we all have different knowledge bases, don't assume that everyone knows the Yiddish phrase, the Hebrew prayer, the historical detail that's being talked about. Make room for people to "not know." Jews value talk and opinions and "knowing," but often the most valuable moment in groups comes when we explore our "not knowing." Imagine a poster on the wall: "There are no stupid questions."

Pay attention to time boundaries. Be clear about when you are beginning and ending, and stick to it. That way all members know their responsibilities to each other, and no one becomes a "captive" of group members who want to go on endlessly. With set beginnings and endings, each person can feel that he or she knows more of what is expected.

Be mindful about the issue of leadership. Do you want a leader? If so, do you rotate leadership from meeting to meeting among the members? Leaderless groups are fine—what's important is to be up front about your decisions about leaders. Some of us are more comfortable with a leader to facilitate and mediate; others less so. Leadership can also be rotated among members of the group.

Pay attention to where you meet. Do you meet in the synagogue or in members' homes or in a local deli? The location can make a big difference to some people's comfort levels. Our group decided to meet *outside* the synagogue, and that increased our comfort level and ability to talk freely. Even meeting inside the synagogue offers choices. Do you meet in the sanctuary, for example? At one point our group decided to talk about our attitudes toward traditional Judaism in the sanctuary itself, and the results were very eye-opening!

Having food at meetings can make a difference. "You can't be a Jewish group, meeting on Sunday morning, and not have food," one person observed.

Consider using some writing exercises. Writing can deepen the connection and self-exploration that happens in groups. Writing together can build trust, particularly when it is accompanied by the opportunity to read aloud without criticism from others.

Groups traditionally are heavy on talking. Writing and talking are very different activities. For some people, writing has a special power, greater than that of simply telling a story. Writing is a way of interviewing ourselves and gaining perspective on what has happened to us. In a group, moments of writing can provide a calm, reflective "play space" to deepen our understanding of growing up and being Jewish today. Writing begins more privately than telling a story aloud; we have more opportunities to move between levels of feeling and thought.

At a meeting, you can experiment by taking a few minutes to do some writing, then going around the group, with those willing to read their stories aloud doing so. Let's say you're interested in experimenting with writing. What do you write about? How do you go about it? Starting with freewriting in groups can be a good beginning.

Freewriting. Freewriting is a widely used technique that dates back to the 1930s.[2] In free-writing you take a preset amount of time to write whatever comes to mind on a given topic. I'd suggest fifteen minutes for the freewrite in the group. Set an alarm to go off at the end of fifteen minutes, and everyone is to stop writing at that point! There are many prompts that Jewish discussion groups can use to start writing about. I suggest some below, but first I want to make clear what to do when you actually free-write.

When you begin the fifteen-minute freewrite, *do not* think about what to write. Just start writing. Don't worry about grammar or punctuation or making sense. Just write whatever words come to mind. Here's the hard part: try to keep your pen moving the entire time! If nothing comes to mind about the topic, that's OK. Just write the prompt over and over until something comes.

If what you write feels irrelevant or meaningless, that's OK. At times freewriting is a great means of self-exploration; at other times it just tires out the hands! There is no right or wrong end product from a freewrite. After the fifteen minutes are up, each group member who is willing can read his or her freewrite aloud. After going all the way around the group, you can discuss what you've heard.

Here are some good writing prompts for Jewish discussion groups:

I first realized I was Jewish when...

My father's tallit...

When I hear Hebrew I feel...

The Shabbat candles in my home...

Sitting in temple during services, I feel...

My son's bar mitzvah (or My daughter's bat mitzvah)...

During my bar mitzvah (or bat mitzvah) I felt...

A moment as a Jew that I am particularly proud of is...
(This could be very long ago or as recently as today)

A particularly embarrassing or humiliating moment for me as a Jew was...

You can, of course, make up your own prompts. The point is that writing can be a useful way of expanding the stories and feelings available for discussion in the group.[3]

Pay attention to the connection of the group to the synagogue, if it is affiliated with one. Not all Jewish discussion groups are affiliated with a synagogue. If it is, however, be aware that discussion groups can also cut you off from the rest of the synagogue. This may happen both because you may become bonded as a small group vis-à-vis the rest of the congregation (which perhaps remains more anonymous) and because the rest of the congregation may perceive a threat in this small group that meets separately.

For example, at the board meeting of one synagogue, the president turned to another member, who had recently joined a discussion group, and asked, "What's this about that exclusive group you joined in the temple?" The tone implied some strange rites and rituals happening in this "exclusive" in-group that was excluding other members. Yet at this very synagogue, announcements were placed in every bulletin inviting congregants to come to meetings. The anxiety and assumptions about what was happening in this group clearly threatened the synagogue president and touched on very potent issues in the *shul* about who's out and who's in, and where power lies. So, be aware of schisms and splitting that are part of every synagogue. There can be outsider-insider anxiety whenever a group forms, and as it evolves. Reaching out can help. In this case, the group member explained more about the Jewish discussion group and invited the president to come to a meeting, as announced in the bulletin!

NOTES

INTRODUCTION

1 The American Jewish Committee, *1998 Annual Survey of American Jewish Opinion* (New York: AJC, 1998). This is a fairly stable figure: AJC yearly surveys through the 1990s indicate that from 44% to 49% of the sample surveyed does not belong to a synagogue.

2 Barry Kosmin, et al., *Highlights of the Council of Jewish Federation's National Jewish Population Survey* (New York: CJF, 1991).

3 Steven Cohen and Arnold Eisen, *The Jew Within: Self, Community, and Commitment Among the Variety of Moderately Affiliated* (Boston: Wilstein Institute, 1998).

4 Bethamie Horowitz, in a recent large-scale study of Jewish identity, found only 34% of her sample could be considered to be "Intensively Engaged" with Judaism. However, among the entire sample (which included those who were "Assimilated Otherwise Engaged" and another group entitled "Mixed Jewish Engagement"), only 9% was truly "Really Indifferent" to their Judaism. In fact, 25% of the "Indifferent" group still fasts on Yom Kippur—a finding, Horowitz notes in her introduction, that "challenges us to wonder about the nature and depth of that indifference." Bethamie Horowitz, "Connections and Journeys: Assessing Critical Opportunities for Enhancing Jewish Identity,"

Report to the Commission on Jewish Identity and Renewal of the United Jewish Appeal—Federation of New York (New York: UJA, 2000).

5 Eric Yoffie, "The Worship Revolution," *Reform Judaism* (spring 2000).

6 While I make no claim to a scientific sample, I have attempted to be representative in talking with Jews from a range of family backgrounds, sexual orientations, religious preferences, and geographic areas. I have interviewed Jews and offered seminar and focus groups in New York, Boston, Washington, D.C., Philadelphia, Cleveland, California, Florida, and Texas, as well as parts of Canada and a number of more rural and suburban areas around the country.

7 Kevin Sack, "Gore and Lieberman Make Tolerance the Centerpiece," *The New York Times,* 9 August 2000, sec. A, p. 1. There is a certain irony in the Times reporter's words. The *Times* reporting of the 2000 election might itself be a marker of how much American Jews have come to feel at home in America. The Sulzberger family, owners of the American "paper of record" and assimilationist German Jews, for years were accused of underreporting on Jewish matters for fear of seeming biased and "too Jewish." Susan Tifft and Alex Jones, "The Family: How Being Jewish Shaped the Dynasty that Runs the *Times,*" *The New Yorker* (19 April 1999).

8 Samuel G. Freedman, *Jew vs. Jew: The Struggle for the Soul of American Jewry* (New York: Simon and Schuster, 2000).

9 Erik H. Erikson, *Childhood and Society* (New York: Norton, 1963). See also Lawrence Friedman, *Identity's Architect: A Biography of Erik H. Erikson* (New York: Scribner, 1999).

10 Joseph Reimer, "Towards a More Inclusive Jewish Identity: Reflections on Reading Erik H. Erikson," *Journal of Jewish Education* 65 nos. 1 and 2 (spring/summer 1999): 10.

11 Horowitz, "Connections and Journeys," vii.

12 Leonard J. Fein, *Where are WE?: The Inner Life of America's Jews* (New York: Harper and Row, 1988); Arnold Eisen, *Rethinking Modern Judaism: Ritual, Commandment, Community* (Chicago: University of Chicago Press, 1998).

13 Howard Nemerov, "Debate With the Rabbi," in *The Collected Poems of Howard Nemerov* (Chicago: University of Chicago Press, 1997).

14 Names and identifying details have in some cases been changed.

15 Daniel Levinson, et al., *The Seasons of a Man's Life* (New York: Knopf, 1978); Lillian B. Rubin, *Women of a Certain Age: The Midlife Search for Self* (New York: Harper and Row, 1979); Elliot Jaques, "Death and the Midlife Crisis," *International Journal of Psychoanalysis* 46 (1965): 502–513; George E. Vaillant, *Adaptation to Life* (Cambridge, Mass.: Harvard University Press, 1995).

16 Rodger Kamenetz, *The Jew in the Lotus: A Poet's Rediscovery of Jewish Identity in Buddhist India* (San Francisco: HarperSanFrancisco 1994); Sheila Peltz Weinberg, "Many Voices in One Mind," *The Reconstructionist* (fall 1994): 53–58.

17 One group of "spiritual orphans" is ostensibly the most dramatic: those whose Jewish past was hidden from them as children, only to be rediscovered when they were adults. Playwright Tom Stoppard and former Secretary of State Madeleine Albright are examples of men and women who discovered they were born Jewish but didn't know that growing up. See M. Dobbs, "Double Identity: Why Madeleine Albright Can't Escape Her Past," *The New Yorker* (2 March 1999): 50–57. Perhaps with anti-Semitism on the wane and Hitler gone for over fifty years, it is a time for secrets to emerge. Autobiographical and fictional stories of Jewish orphans are now abundant. See James McBride, *The Color of Water: A Black Man's Tribute to His White Mother* (New York: Riverhead Books, 1996); Stephen J. Dubner, *Turbulent Souls: A Catholic Son's Return to His Jewish Family* (New York: William Morrow, 1998); Susan Jacoby, *Half-Jew: A Daughter's Search for Her Family's Buried Past* (New York: Scribner, 2000); Martha Cooley, *The Archivist* (New York: Little, Brown, 1999). We have no reasonable estimate of how large a group this is, but the dynamic issues arising from the discovery in adulthood that one is Jewish without having known that growing up are likely complex. Susan Goldberg, a psychology graduate student at the Fielding Graduate Institute studying this group as part of her doctoral dissertation, writes, "For those who have found their way back, I'm interested in how they conduct a Jewish identity, without any of the cultural frameworks, structures, language, and history that those of us who grew up with something in it have. How

does one become Jewish from scratch? What supports do you look to? How do you make it meaningful?" (Susan Goldberg, personal communication, 4 September 2000).

18 Samuel Osherson, *Finding Our Fathers: How a Man's Life Is Shaped by the Relationship with His Father* (New York: Contemporary Books, 2000).

19 Salvadore Minuchin, *Families and Family Therapy* (Cambridge, Mass.: Harvard University Press, 1974).

CHAPTER ONE

1 The category of the "Jewish nose" is still used by plastic surgeons today, as reported by Aviva Preminger in her senior thesis at Harvard, "Saving Face: Plastic Surgery and Jewish Identity from 1880 to the Present," *The Harvard Mosaic: A Review of Jewish Thought and Culture* 24 (summer 1999): 57. See also Matthew Frye Jacobson, *Whiteness of a Different Color: European Immigrants and the Alchemy of Race* (Cambridge, Mass.: Harvard University Press, 1998); and Elizabeth Haiken, *Venus Envy: A History of Cosmetic Surgery* (Baltimore, Md.: Johns Hopkins University Press, 1997).

2 Peter F. Langman, *Jewish Issues in Multiculturalism: A Handbook for Educators and Clinicians* (Northvale, N.J.: Jason Aronson, 1999): 280.

3 Egon Fabian, "Concretism and Identity Aspects in the Jewish Joke," *Psychoanalysis and Contemporary Thought* 21, No. 3 (summer 1998): 423–41.

4 Fabian argues that historically within Judaism there has been and continues to be a profound tension between abandoning and returning to tradition. He sees this as the root theme of the Old Testament, particularly "the covenant with God the Father, with its ambivalence, its separation conflicts, with its dialectics between abandonment (also abandoning) and return (also reconciliation), in other words between submission and emancipation" (p. 437). The Jewish joke expresses liberation and rebellion. It allows us to depart from God the Father, and from our personal fathers, to seek our Jewish identity—it does so via a loving deflation of tradition: "the departing son is not so guilty, since the father is not so holy, so perfect" (p. 438).

5 Although, interestingly, Abraham did not take the elder generation with him. We learn in Genesis 12 that Abraham is instructed by God to go forth from his father's house: "The Lord said to Abraham, 'Go forth from your native land and from your father's house to the land that I will show you." He leaves with his wife Sarah and his cousin Lot to "set out for the land of Canaan." *The Holy Scriptures: A New JPS Translation According to the Traditional Hebrew Text* (Philadelphia: Jewish Publication Society, 1985). Judaism begins, then, with a leave-taking from one's father. The Jewish tradition, which is so much about the loyalties and continuities between the generations, originates in a departure. Rabbi Sheila Peltz Weinberg commented to me that one of the paradoxes of Judaism is that it begins with a separation from the past yet it is so much about our connection to the past.

6 David Remnick, "In the Clear," *The New Yorker,* 81. This was not the first time appeals to the pain and suffering of the Holocaust were used to try and silence Jewish self-questioning or those who believe "differently" as Jews. See Peter Novick, *The Holocaust in American Life* (Boston: Houghton Mifflin, 1999).

7 Remnick, "In the Clear," 82.

8 Cohen and Eisen point to the important role of women's initiative in developing "self-conscious Jewish behavior." Deborah Dash Moore, in commenting on their work, underlines the ways that many women's Jewish identity is woven into their family life: "the centrality of family and of food, which lies at the heart of the American Jewish Passover, reflects women's perspectives and experiences." (That said, it must be remembered, too, that many women want to be able to read from the Torah and feel at home in the sanctuary, just as many men's spirituality is very much expressed through their love of cooking and taking care of the home.) She also asks the question, Is it possible that "there also exists a revolt against male authority? We are increasingly aware of how few immigrants transplanted male gendered sacred knowledges and practices to the United States. Women, by contrast, replicated a wider repertory of Jewish behaviors even as they transformed their meanings." See Deborah Dash Moore, *Comments on Cohen, S. and Eisen, A. The Jew Within: Self, Community, and Commitment Among the Variety of Moderately Affiliated* (Boston: Wilstein Institute, 1998), 70.

CHAPTER TWO

1 For a general overview on shame see Donald L. Nathanson, *Shame and Pride: Affect, Sex, and the Birth of the Self* (New York: Norton, 1994); and Andrew P. Morrison, *Shame: The Underside of Narcissism* (Hillsdale, N.J.: Analytic Press, 1989).

No gender, ethnicity, or religious group has a monopoly on shame. For perspectives on Jewish struggles with shame see G. Kaufman and L. Raphael, "Shame: A Perspective on Jewish Identity," *Journal of Psychology and Judaism* 11, No. 1 (spring 1987): 30–40; Michael J. Bader, "Shame and the Resistance to Jewish Renewal," in M. Lansky and A. P. Morrison, *The Widening Scope of Shame* (Hillsdale, N.J.: TAP, 1997): 397–408; see also Peter Langman, *Jewish Issues in Multiculturalism*.

2 Shame has been part of the Jewish experience through the generations. Being in the out-group is enshrined in our humor, from the Jewish contribution to burlesque to Groucho Marx's famous observation "I wouldn't want to be part of any group that would have me as a member" to the ironic, self-deflating humor of the Borscht Belt to Woody Allen, Adam Sandler, and other contemporary humorists to the ironic observation of Jerry, the struggling Hollywood writer portrayed by Ben Stiller in the movie *Permanent Midnight,* whose pants split as he first encounters the attractive woman who will become his wife: "It's Jewish leather," he explains, "designed for humiliation."

Humor has traditionally been, and continues to be, a powerful way of expressing and defusing shame in Jewish life. As psychologist Donald Nathanson has observed, adopting the clown role is one way for the individual to manage shame. As a cultural group Jews have embraced humor as a way of dealing with the outsider role, with its sense of difference from the mainstream.

3 See also Preminger, "Saving Face." Some women I have spoken with remember that when they were growing up, in their communities, plastic surgery for "nose corrections" was offered as highly coveted prizes in synagogue raffles.

4 Novick, *Holocaust in American Life.*

5 Joy Schaverien, "Inheritance: Jewish identity and the legacy of the Holocaust mediated through art therapy groups," *British Journal of Psychotherapy* 15, No. 1 (1998): 65–79. Daphne Merkin explores as

well the implications of the Holocaust for postwar adolescents and contemporary adults in her essay "Dreaming of Hitler: A Memoir of Self-Hatred," in *Dreaming of Hitler: Passions and Provocations* (New York: Crown, 1997). The tensions between remembering and forgetting in the post-Holocaust generations are powerfully examined in Martha Cooley's novel *The Archivist*.

6 Schaverien, "Inheritance," 66.

7 Osherson, *Finding Our Fathers*; Daniel Gilmore, *Manhood in the Making* (New Haven: Yale University Press, 1990).

8 Edwin Black, "Could We Have Stopped Hitler?" *Reform Judaism* (fall 1999): 15.

9 The keystone of the *Oranienbergurstrasse* Synagogue in Berlin, once the largest in the world, is now in the United States Holocaust Memorial Museum in Washington, D.C.

10 Daphne Merkin, "Freud Rising," *The New Yorker* (9 November 1998), 55.

11 Peter Novick comments, "When the word 'guilt' surfaced after the war, it usually referred to not having been *able*, rather than not having been *willing* to effect rescue." He goes on to say, "Another kind of guilt—though, again, not guilt for cowardly inaction—was that of unmerited safety and privilege, a deeply felt, albeit unmerited, 'survivor guilt.' American Jews were acutely aware that only the accident of geography saved them from the fate of their European brethren." *Holocaust in American Life*, 75.

12 See, for example, R. F. Lazur and R. Majors, "Men of Color: Ethnocultural Variations of Male Gender Role Strain," in Ronald Levant and William Pollack, *A New Psychology of Men* (New York: Basic Books, 1995). Lazur and Majors show how what they call "the cool pose" among African-American male adolescents and gang behavior is very much related to their attempt to manage the self-doubt and loss associated with the economic and social realities that led African-American men to fail to provide for their families. Similarly, observers have written movingly of the way a Native American male may regard his father with "disgust and hatred," in the face of the father's inability to protect him (or himself) from the dominant American culture. Underneath this hatred lies a profound unresolved grief. This ambivalent relationship between fathers and sons among Native Americans is

332 REKINDLING THE FLAME

powerfully evoked in the movie *Smoke Signals* and the fiction of Sherman Alexis.

13 See Deborah Dash Moore, *Comments on Cohen, S. and Eisen, A. The Jew Within: Self, Community, and Commitment Among the Variety of Moderately Affiliated, op. cit.*

14 David M. Bader, *Haikus for Jews* (New York: Harmony Books, 1999).

15 Psychoanalyst Egon Fabian closes his article on contemporary Jewish identity struggles to separate from fathers by observing that "...the second separation, that from the mother, has not yet been achieved." Fabian, "Concretism," 439.

16 Gershen Kaufman and Lev Raphael have developed a perspective on Jewish shame as deriving in part from the emphasis on conformity in American culture: "The awareness of being Jewish inevitably translates into being different and hence, potentially inferior in a culture which prizes social conformity." Kaufman and Raphael, "Shame," 34. One successful New York lawyer, a powerhouse in court and a former college football star, told me that he "never felt ashamed" at being Jewish, but ever since high school he had taken off the *chai* he wore around his neck when dressing in gym locker rooms because he "wasn't sure how others would see it." He added, "My Judaism was more private. I'm not sure many people really knew I was Jewish, so I guess there *was* some discomfort." When I asked what it felt like to be a Jew in that high school locker room, he replied, "It felt special. I was different from my friends. I had something—being Jewish—that they wouldn't achieve." Then he went on to describe the other side of that "specialness." "Pride is good and part of self-esteem, but there's a way that being different as a Jew just seems hard to escape and that also cuts us off from each other." The lawyer's comments brought to mind Kurt Lewin's astute observation, "The feeling of inferiority of the Jew is but an indication of the fact that he sees things Jewish with the eyes of the unfriendly majority." Lewin, *Resolving Social Conflicts* (New York: Harper, 1948), 198.

17 Michael Bader, "Shame and Resistance," 404.

18 Ibid., 407.

19 American Jewish Committee, *1999 Annual Survey of American Jewish Opinion*. Bethamie Horowitz reports a similar finding. In her

study of over 1,500 Jewish men and women, 73% of her sample reported "Remembering the Holocaust" as a key element of being Jewish. Only 25% reported "Attending Synagogue" and 20% "Studying Jewish texts" as similarly important to their Jewish identity. Horowitz, "Connections and Journeys."

20 Novick raises a different dimension to the Jew-as-victim American Jewish self-presentation, particularly in the context of that jewel of contemporary American Jewish effort—the United States Holocaust Memorial Museum in Washington, D.C. "Finally, there is the question of how we present ourselves to, how we wish to be thought of by, that vast majority of Americans who are not Jewish. The principal 'address' of American Jewry—the representation of Jewishness and the Jewish experience visited by more Americans than any other, and for most the only one they'll ever visit—is the Holocaust museum on the Mall in Washington. There surely isn't going to be a *second* Jewish institution on the Mall, presenting an alternative image of the Jew. And there surely isn't going to be *another* set of legislatively mandated curricula about Jews in American public schools, besides the proliferating Holocaust curricula zealously promoted by Jewish organizations—something to balance the existing curricula, in which, for enormous numbers of gentile children (Jewish ones, too, for that matter), the equation Jew-equals-victim is being inscribed." Novick, *Holocaust in American Life,* 11.

21 In *Mourning and Melancholia,* Freud wrote about our human tendency to incorporate aspects of the lost person, place, or thing into ourselves. Psychoanalyst Alexander Mitschelisch wrote, back in the 1950s, in his classic study *The Inability to Grieve* (about, ironically, Germans' inability to face the meaning of Nazism and the Holocaust and what they lost in it) about the way we weave loss into our lives when we cannot adequately grieve the loss itself, carrying it along like a runner trying to sprint away from a muscle cramp.

22 Samuel Osherson, *Wrestling with Love: How Men Struggle with Intimacy* (New York: Ballantine, 1993); James Gilligan, *Violence: Reflections on a National Epidemic* (New York: Vintage Books, 1997).

23 Sylvan S. Tomkins, *Affect, Imagery, Consciousness,* Vol. 2 (New York: Springer Publishing Co., 1963), 132.

24 A friend of mine, tired of the emphasis on Chanukah every December, perhaps intuiting her synagogue's attempt to inflate a minor

Jewish holiday simply to counter the overwhelming presence of Christmas, got an announcement trumpeting an upcoming "Chanukah service" and exclaimed wearily, "Oh, Chanukah! It really is just another
war story."

CHAPTER THREE

1 *"Remembering the Holocaust: Until What Generation?"* a sympo-
sium presented by the Boston Psychoanalytic Society and Institute and
Facing History and Ourselves, 30 October 1999, Pine Manor College,
Chestnut Hill, Mass.

2 Freud, who struggled with his own wounded father, having been
greatly shamed as a boy by his father's passive acceptance of having his
hat knocked off his head by anti-Semites on the street and then being
told to leave the sidewalk, compared the son's understanding of his father to the mystery of the sphinx, an oracle that spoke in codes and
ambiguities. There are many ways in which grown sons and daughters
struggle throughout their lives with the mystery of their fathers, and
find creative, poignant ways to come to terms with them. See Osherson, *Finding Our Fathers,* particularly chapters 1, 2, and 7.

CHAPTER FOUR

1 Mary Catherine Bateson, *Composing a Life* (New York: Penguin,
1989), 16, 18.

2 Leon Wieseltier, *Kaddish* (New York: Knopf, 1998), vii.

3 Jonathan Rosen, *The Talmud and the Internet: A Journey between
Worlds* (New York: Farrar, Straus and Giroux, 2000), 28–29.

4 Ibid., 58.

CHAPTER FIVE

1 This theme is explored in detail by James Carroll in *Constantine's
Sword: The Church and the Jews* (Boston: Houghton-Mifflin, 2001).

2 Robert Kegan, *The Evolving Self: Problem and Process in Human
Development* (Cambridge, Mass.: Harvard University Press, 1982).

3 Kamenetz, *Jew and the Lotus,* 254.

4 Joseph Goldstein, *Insight Meditation: The Practice of Freedom* (Boston: Shambhala, 1994), 34.

5 In Sheila's chapter on "Meditating as a Practicing Jew," in Avram Davis's edited volume, *Meditation from the Heart of Judaism* (Woodstock, Vt.: Jewish Lights Publishing, 1997), she discusses in depth such matters as "Blending Judaism and Meditation Practice" and "Blending Judaism and Dharma."

6 Sylvia Boorstein, S. Lebell, and S. Mitchell, *That's Funny, You Don't Look Buddhist: On Being a Faithful Jew and a Passionate Buddhist* (San Francisco: HarperSanFrancisco, 1997). See also Alan Lew, *One God Clapping: The Spiritual Path of a Zen Rabbi* (New York: Kodansha International, 1999).

7 See David A. Cooper, *God Is a Verb: Kabbalah and the Practice of Mystical Judaism* (New York: Riverhead Books, 1997). See also Aryeh Kaplan, *Jewish Meditation* (New York: Schocken Books, 1985) and Davis, *Meditation from the Heart of Judaism.*

8 Reimer, "Towards a More Inclusive Jewish Identity," 9–16.

9 Ibid.

CHAPTER SIX

1 Paul Cowan, with Rachel Cowan, *Mixed Blessings: Overcoming the Stumbling Blocks in an Interfaith Marriage* (New York: Penguin, 1987). Current estimates are that approximately 52% of Jews are in interfaith marriages, although there is a debate among researchers as to whether definitional ambiguities make the actual figure closer to 42% than 52%. See Steven Cohen, "Why Intermarriage May Not Threaten Jewish Continuity," *Moment* (December 1994): 54–57.

2 Cowan, 269.

3 Marcia Falk, *The Book of Blessings: New Jewish Prayers for Daily Life, the Sabbath, and the New Moon Festival* (San Francisco: Harper-Collins, 1996), 288.

4 I. H. Fishbein, *Rabbinic Participation in Intermarriage Ceremonies.* Summary of Rabbinic Center for Research and Counseling 1995 Survey (29 December 1995).

5 Interfaith marriages need to be put in their larger social context, as Sylvia Barack Fishman has done. She points out that traditional American values emphasizing romantic individualism and autonomy support an ethic of intermarriage. "From Bambi and Thumper and the forest creatures on upward, the American birthright is the right to make erotic life choices individualistically and freely" (p. 147). Even so, compared to white ethnic Americans and Americans of Asian heritage, Jews have a comparatively lower rate of intermarriage. Sylvia Barack Fishman, *Jewish Life and American Culture* (New York: SUNY Press, 2000).

6 The Ethical Humanist Society is a national humanist religion movement with chapters in many urban centers.

7 Robert Bellah, "Competing Visions of the Role of Religion in American Society," in *Uncivil Religion: Interreligious Hostility in America,* Robert Bellah and Frederick Greenspahn (New York: Crossroad, 1987).

8 The shroud of silence about the Holocaust was so complete in Yvette's family during her childhood that to this day she is uncertain which camp her father was in, although she suspects it was Auschwitz.

9 Such advances are not without their costs. Yvette wonders, too, if the stress of exploring and loving Judaism, which she had for so many years also hated, might somehow be connected with back and neck ailments that have bothered her since the bat mitzvah. "It's not so easy to remember that you love something you're used to being angry at," she observed.

10 Paula Vogel, *Desdemona* (New York: Dramatists Play Service, 1999).

11 Reimer, "Towards a More Inclusive Jewish Identity," 14.

12 Cowan, *Mixed Blessings,* 269.

13 The scornful, distancing image of some rabbis is all the more poignant when set against the internal struggles many of them have with the question of intermarriage. In their study of rabbis' attitudes and behaviors toward intermarriage, reported in *Rabbis Talk about Intermarriage,* Rabbi Gary Tobin and Katherine Simon observe that the best place to initiate a discussion of feelings aroused among rabbis by intermarriage is with their "feelings of anguish and alarm." They note that rabbis "visibly ache when reflecting on the topic."

Tobin and Simon found that rabbis talked with considerable feeling about members of their immediate families who have intermarried. Some rabbis refuse to marry their own sons or daughters; others welcome into their families members of other faiths. A significant number of the rabbis expressed taking *pleasure* in interfaith marriages—believing that they often result in a reaffirmation of Judaism. Other rabbis talk of developing moving and authentic ceremonies by which Jewish ritual is kept alive in an interfaith marriage. One rabbi commented that "whether or not intermarriage is a problem depends, of course, upon one's point of view....I empathize with distraught parents. But one of the worst consequences of intermarriage is that violent opposition to it can tear families apart. Wanting our children and grandchildren to marry Jews is fine and reasonable. Wanting them to be happy is more important" (p. 23).

Tobin and Simon's work gives a human face to rabbis' struggles; reading it we remember there is a person in the rabbi role, struggling with his or her own attempts to walk what they call "the anxiety of the tightrope," trying to both discourage *and* embrace the choices members of their congregation (or family) are making.

All of which makes some rabbis' reticence to show their uncertainty all the more poignant and disturbing. One sentence in Tobin and Simon's book casts a shadow over the discussion: "Many rabbis did not want to be quoted" (p. xiv). The intermarriage question is such a lightning rod, polarizing communities and congregations, that many rabbis keep a low profile. No wonder Tobin and Simon conclude their book with the observation that rabbis are central to how communities think and rethink the question of intermarriage. They comment, "The need for a forward-thinking, creative, charismatic rabbinate is an essential ingredient in building the Jewish community of the future" (p. 151). We may need less charisma and more forward thinking. Gary A. Tobin and Katherine G. Simon, *Rabbis Talk about Intermarriage* (San Francisco: Institute for Jewish and Community Research, 1999).

CHAPTER SEVEN

1 Donald Winnicott, *Playing and Reality* (New York: Penguin, 1980); see also M. Miller, "Winnicott Unbound: The Fiction of Philip Roth and the Sharing of Potential Space," *Int. Rev. Psa.* 19, No. 4 (winter 1992): 445–56. Miller explores Winnicott's concept of "potential space"—the play world of fantasy and imagination (a blending of the

349

real and not-real) that exists and is co-created by mother and child. This is often what is happening in a synagogue service as well.

2 For more extensive discussion, from a different viewpoint, of how the Jewish year itself is a psycho-spiritual journey, see Joel Ziff, *Mirrors in Time* (Northvale, N.J.: Jason Aronson, 1996).

3 Shoshana Silberman, illustrated by Katherine Janus Kahn, *A Family Haggadah: In Every Generation* (Rockville, Md.: Kar-Ben Copies, Inc.), 3.

4 Paul Johnson, *A History of the Jews* (New York: Harper and Row, 1987).

5 Jordan Lee Wagner points out in his book *The Synagogue Survival Kit* (Northvale, N.J.: Jason Aronson, 1997) that anyone can lead the community in worship and that traditionally the rabbi served as a resource to the community for worship, not necessarily the leader of the service. Traditionally, the rabbi's role was as settler of disputes and as teacher-scholar to the community. Wagner comments, "A rabbi is a repository of Jewish learning, functioning as a resource to the community and as a judge in disputes between Jews. Traditionally, the title 'rabbi' is a credential, not a job description. Although anyone may educate or preach, only a rabbi can issue a definitive ruling to answer a question in a binding way or formally resolve a legal dispute" (p. 22).

6 Sheila Peltz Weinberg, "Many Voices in One Mind," *The Reconstructionist* (fall 1994): 55.

7 Elliot Jaques, "Death and the Midlife Crisis," *International Journal of Psychoanalysis* 46 (1965): 502–514. See also an expanded version of this paper in G. Pollack and S. I. Greenspan, *The Course of Life*, vol. 5, *Early Adulthood* (Madison, Ct.: I.U.P., 1993): 201–231.

8 Jaques, "Death and the Midlife Crisis" (1965): 503.

9 Ibid.

10 Jaques, in Pollack and Greenspan, 214.

11 Thomas Cahill, *The Gifts of the Jews: How a Tribe of Nomads Changed the Way Everyone Thinks and Feels* (New York: Doubleday, 1998).

12 In his magisterial effort, *Kaddish,* Leon Wieseltier explores the role
of Jewish mourning rituals in grieving the death of his father and the
use of the Kaddish to express what could not be said directly. Similarly,
Morton Kissen, in his paper "The Morning (Mourning) Minyan:
Group Therapeutic Aspects," discusses the beneficial role of the ritual-
istic recitation of the Kaddish in an ongoing early morning prayer
meeting, following the death of his mother. Morton Kissen, "The
Morning (Mourning) Minyan: Group Therapeutic Aspects," *Group*
21, No. 1 (March 1997): 29–37.

13 Erik Erikson's notion of the "generative" backdrop to the middle
years is relevant here, as is his last stage of the life cycle: "ego integrity
versus despair," in which the task is to find an "acceptance of one's
one and only life cycle as something that had to be and that, by necessity, permitted of no substitutions; it thus means a new, a different love
of one's parents." Erikson, *Childhood and Society,* 268.

14 Jaques, "Death and the Midlife Crisis," 228.

CHAPTER EIGHT

1 The tendency to view *Tikkun Olam* in terms of planting trees in Israel rather than where one lives is still a powerful tendency in Jewish
thinking. For example, the American Jewish Committee conducts an
annual survey of American Jewish opinion, "detailing the views of
American Jews about a broad range of subjects." The lists of questions
to respondents in their surveys from the late 1990s start: "To begin,
how close do you feel to Israel?" Many questions about Israel follow
(e.g., "Do you agree or disagree with the following statement? 'Caring
about Israel is a very important part of my being a Jew.'"), after
which other subjects are explored, including attitudes toward American political issues, the nature of Jewish identity, intermarriage, and
the education of children. By choosing Israel as the very first subject,
the survey (likely without intending to) shapes a response set for what
follows (New York: American Jewish Committee).

2 The Playing for Peace Project has been supported by the U.S. State
Department and U.S. embassies in the Middle East and elsewhere in
the world, as the project has expanded to include other troubled regions, including Northern Ireland, Transcaucasia, and China.

3 Kathryn Watterson, *Not by the Sword: How the Love of a Cantor and His Family Transformed a Klansman* (New York: Simon and Schuster, 1995).

4 At the 1998 Union of American Hebrew Congregations Bienniel, for example, the Reform movement committed itself to an emphasis on socially responsible investing—adopting a resolution committing 1.8% of the UAHC endowment to investment in low-income community development institutions, partly at the urging of TZEDEC. In an open letter outlining the UAHC's rationale, Leonard Fein stressed that community investment fulfills Jewish teaching about *tzedakah* at its highest level: "These teachings stress partnership and investment over mere charity." In the letter Fein estimated that if Jewish agencies, federations, foundations, and institutions were to follow the lead of the TZEDEC campaign, "roughly one billion dollars could be made available" and noted that "against a backdrop of disinvestment and terrible income polarization, community development is a 30-year, self-help success story."

5 Lawrence Bush and Jeffrey Dekro, *Jews, Money, and Social Responsibility: Developing a "Torah of Money" for Contemporary Life* (Philadelphia: The Shefa Fund, 1993). For more information on The Shefa Fund, see www.shefafund.org.

6 Available from JeffRaz@aol.com.

7 Jeff the playwright is also working on understanding the role of Judaism in his own father's suicide, through the play. He wrote to me, "Connecting my dad's suicide to his time in the war is my leap. The family story has always been that his manic-depression came on due to the pressures of academia. He was apparently a very good teacher, which wasn't credited in Universities in the late 50s, early 60s. I suggest the connection with the war in 'Father-Land' and my mother and father both found it credible."

8 Available from JeffRaz@aol.com.

9 Felice Yeskel and Chuck Collins, *Economic Apartheid in America* (New York: The New Press, 2000). See also http://www.ufenet.org.

10 Felice Yeskel, "You Didn't Talk About These Things: Growing Up Jewish, Lesbian, and Working Class," in *Twice Blessed: On Being Lesbian, Gay, and Jewish,* eds. Christie Balka and Andy Rose (Boston: Beacon Press, 1989), 40.

11 Ibid., 41.

12 Ibid., 43.

13 Ibid.

14 The Responsible Wealth project is composed of wealthy individuals (those in the top 5% of income earners and wealth holders) who support economic reform, recognizing that the quality of life that results from a fairer distribution of wealth in this country overrides their narrow economic self-interest. Felice observed, "They understand that living in a country with gated communities and guards on every corner does not contribute to an increased quality of life."

15 Isaiah 57:17–58:14.

16 Genie Zeiger is also the author of *How I Find Her: A Mother's Dying and a Daughter's Life* (Santa Fe, N.M.: Sherman Asher, 2000) and *Leaving Egypt: Poems* (Lakeview, N.Y.: White Pine Press, 1995).

17 Gerald Stern, "Behaving Like a Jew," in *Telling and Remembering: A Century of American Jewish Poetry,* ed. Steven Rubin (Boston: Beacon Press, 1997); Yehuda Amichai, *Open, Closed, Open: Poems,* trans. Chana Block and Chana Kronfeld (New York: Harcourt, 2000).

CHAPTER NINE

1 A rabbinical student, reading the story of the three-D Haggadah, pointed out that the word for "teach" in the Shema ("and you shall teach [these words that God commands you this day] to your children, and discuss them..." is *v'shinantam*. This is not the usual word for "teach." *V'shinantam* is from the same root as *repeat* or *render again*. This suggests that the most sacred meaning of teach is to "make it meaningful"—teach it as it was taught to you (not as obvious). Transmit it to them; don't present it blindly and expect them to take it. Real teaching—at the seder and elsewhere—may require massaging the material as you teach it. For this is the same root as that of the word *Mishnah,* the name of the compiled contributions of the rabbis to understanding and re-receiving the Torah. Moreover, the Shema exhorts us, *v'shinantam...v'dibarta.* Repeat *and* discuss.

2 David Sobol, *Children's Special Places* (Tucson, Ariz.: Zephyr Press, 1993).

3 Jeff's favorite Esther reference is *The Torah Anthology, The Book of Esther,* translated by Rabbi Aryeh Kaplan from the *MeAm Lo'ez,* originally written in Ladino by Rabbi Raphael Chiyya Pontremoli (1825–1885) or Rabbi Yaakov Culi (1689–1732)—both are cited (New York: Maznaim Publishing Corp., 1978). To obtain copies of *Esther,* contact Jeff Raz at JeffRaz@aol.com or at the San Francisco School of Circus Arts: http://www.sfcircus.org.

4 The Jewish Women's Archives in Brookline, Mass., directed by Gail Reimer, is a wonderful source of updated and alternative ceremonies for weddings, festivals, and other occasions. See http://www.jwa.org.

5 Wayne Muller, *The Sabbath: Restoring the Sacred Rhythm of Rest* (New York: Bantam Books, 1999).

6 Abraham Joshua Heschel, *The Insecurity of Freedom: Essays on Human Existence* (New York: Farrar, Straus and Giroux, 1996); see also Heschel, *The Sabbath: Its Meaning for Modern Man* (New York: Farrar, Straus and Giroux, 1975).

7 Writing and the use of texts are central to the Jewish experience. Our own writing can be a vehicle for the exploration of our spirituality, building community, and creating a shared vision of Judaism and ourselves, both inside and outside the synagogue. Writing together in small groups in a focused way can be a prayerful means of attending to our place in the universe, calming the self, connecting to others, affirming what our hearts deeply value, and learning from each other. See Samuel Osherson, *The Hidden Wisdom of Parents: Real Stories That Will Help You Be a Better Parent* (Holbrook, Mass.: Adams, 1999) for more discussion and examples.

    In *The Talmud and the Internet,* Jonathan Rosen captures the special meaning words and writing can have for Jews: "I grew up believing that writing is the voice that continues after death, and in Judaism, where God never borrowed a body and walked among men, words are even more than that. They're the Divine medium of revelation. Long after the burning bush burned out and the pillar of smoke dispersed, words were still God's messengers. Even if you lived in a secularized home, words were like the stars in the sky—you were never sure if their source was still on fire somewhere far away or had gone cold long ago . . ." Rosen, *Talmud and the Internet,* 26.

8 Wieseltier, *Kaddish.*

9 Despite the myth of the lonely spiritual seeker, in reality most of us work out our spiritual struggles *in relationships*. Consider an example from a tradition known for its lonely spiritual quest: the traveling beggar tradition of Japanese haiku poets, such as Basho and others. Among the most famous and revered of such modern haiku poets was Santōka (1882–1940), who is said to have walked more than twenty-eight thousand miles in his travels as a wandering monk. His life was a study in ascetic living and renunciation, trying to find and express in haiku verse the Zen philosophy that he lived. Yet Santōka returned again and again to a group of friends and poets, including those who found him a home during a particularly difficult time in his life, a retreat in the mountains that he loved and from which he hosted poetry gatherings, wrote verse, and edited a literary magazine. Santōka's solitude was nourished and supported by a loose-knit group of people he cherished. See John Stevens, trans., *Mountain Tasting: Zen Haiku by Santōka Taneda* (New York: Weatherhill, 1980).

10 Arthur Waskow, *The Seasons of Our Joy: A Celebration of Modern Jewish Renewal* (New York: Bantam, 1982).

CHAPTER TEN

1 "Sh'ma: Communal Declaration of Faith," M. Falk, *The Book of Blessings: New Jewish Prayers for Daily Life, the Sabbath, and the New Moon Festival* (San Francisco: HarperCollins, 1996): 172.

2 W. S. Merwin, "Sheep Passing," *The New Yorker* 73, Aug. 4, 1997.

3 M. Oliver, *New and Selected Poems* (Boston: Beacon, 1992): 292.

4 See Kissen, "The Morning (Mourning) Minyan." See also Saul Scheidlinger, "The Minyan as a Psychological Support System," *Psychoanalytic Review* 84, No. 4 (August 1997): 541–52.

5 Rabbi Hayim H. Donan, *To Pray as a Jew: A Guide to the Prayerbook and the Synagogue Service* (New York: Basic Books, 1980).

6 There is a real difference between writing and talking. We Jews so value being articulate. Often when we talk we may hardly listen to ourselves. "When I talk sometimes it feels like the words just go out of me. I lose ownership of them," one writing workshop participant observed. "Whereas when I write I stay focused on what I'm saying."

When we write we often focus more on the experience. We stay in it longer; we can't just send it "out there," away from us. There are special possibilities when we take pen in hand, whether we consider ourselves "good writers" or not.

7 For information see http://www.danceexchange.org.

8 *From Tanakh: The Holy Scriptures, The New JPS Translation According to the Traditional Hebrew Text* (Philadelphia: Jewish Publication Society, 1985): 417–18.

9 See the collected works of Rainer Maria Rilke.

CONCLUSION

1 Among the best of the former is Gil Mann's book *How to Get More Out of Being Jewish Even If: A. You Are Not Sure You Believe in God, B. You Think Going to Synagogue Is a Waste of Time...* (Minneapolis, Minn.: Leo and Sons, Pub., 1997), which demolishes every intellectual argument against being Jewish. Among the best of the latter is Ari Goldman's book, *Being Jewish: The Spiritual and Cultural Practice of Judaism Today* (New York: Simon and Schuster, 2000), which offers a companionable and reassuring entry into modern Jewish observance.

2 Several Jewish parents I interviewed who had children with different kinds of developmental delays spoke of the pain of raising children in a culture that so values achievement and "success," feeling often "invisible" or in the out-group. The issue of how to make welcome those who feel in some way "different" is real in any group, and feeling welcomed in the synagogue can make a big difference in the lives of those who feel marginalized in our society at large.

3 Donald Winnicott, *The Maturational Processes and the Facilitating Environment* (New York: International Universities Press, 1965).

4 Kamenetz, *Jew and the Lotus.*

5 Falk, *Book of Blessings.*

6 Osherson, *Finding Our Fathers.*

7 Minister Diane Tennis, in a provocative article, explores women's resistance to the "feminization" of religion. Writing about Catholic

liturgy and ritual, she argues that paternal images in prayer are so powerful for women because they offer the one and only experience of a reliable, available father in women's lives. The resistance within Judaism to more feminine imagery and ritual may also be rooted in the sense of loss associated with giving up a paternal sense of the divine. Diane Tennis, "The Loss of the Father God: Why Women Rage and Grieve," *Christianity and Crisis* 41, No. 10 (June 1981).

8 Horowitz, "Connections and Journeys."

9 Yoffie, "Worship Revolution," 24.

10 Horowitz, "Connections and Journeys," 149–50.

11 J. Rolando Matalon, "Is Everything Kosher in Kashrut?" *Pardes* 12 (New York: Congregation B'nai Jeshrun, summer 2000).

12 In fact, the use of churches (rented by smaller communities) as sanctuaries is likely relatively recent and is limited to parts of this country. Halls, stores, homes, have indeed been used. But always— from ancient times to the building of each medieval town and each colonial settlement—there has been an attempt by Jews to create a special space for communal worship. Churches historically have been neither welcoming nor tolerant of Jewish worship, nor welcoming to Jews for worship.

APPENDIX

1 One example is the chavurah movement in Judaism, begun in the 1960s. Chavurot can operate either within, or independently of, a synagogue. In either case, Jewish discussion groups may be part of the chavurah's activities. For chavurah that are independent of a synagogue, there is usually an emphasis on the direct experience of Judaism in a more hands-on way. Members participate in and lead Shabbat, holiday, and educational events. Chavurot may also be sponsored by synagogues so that members have a more intimate group in which to meet. In such chavurot, discussion groups are often self-led and center on Torah study or Shabbat observance, or any of a variety of topics, including identity issues. Waskow, *Seasons of Our Joy,* and "Reconstructionism: From 'Heresy' to 'It's What Most Jews Are,'" *Moment* (30 June 1997). See also the Internet for more information

about the varying nature and number of chavurot (e.g., http://www. chav.net).

2 Dorothea Brande, *On Becoming a Writer* (Los Angeles: Tarcher, 1934).

3 For more on the use of writing and storytelling in groups, see Osherson, *Hidden Wisdom of Parents.*

ACKNOWLEDGMENTS

One of the delights of working on this book has been the number of welcoming, thoughtful people I have met. I've had the good fortune to spend many enjoyable hours in conversation with a number of concerned and engaging rabbis, including Carl Perkins, Julie Greenberg, Sheila Weinberg, Hayim Herring, Sally Finestone, Ben-Zion Gold, Bruce Lustig, Yael Lavi-Romer, Barry Krieger, Noah Kitty, Michael Lukens, Harry Skye, and Paul Gordon. In addition, Professor Joseph Reimer of Brandeis University provided invaluable support and discussion at several important points. While whatever errors in fact and interpretation are entirely mine, this book has benefited enormously from the generosity and goodwill of these rabbis and teachers.

I am indebted, too, to my dear friends in my Jewish Discussion Group for their unflagging support, openheartedness, and confidence in me: Joe Shapiro, Lynn Bergman, Yvette Yeager, and Ceil Goff. Our Sunday conversations have sustained me through many hard moments of self-questioning and doubt.

One of the special treats of being a writer is meeting individuals who are willing to share their struggles and thoughts with you. Listing people is tricky; my apologies to anyone I have unintentionally left out, but I do want to particularly thank: Meredith Barber, Sarah Barrett, Daniel Behr, Eric Bluestine, Marlene Blumenthal, Tom Brasserer, Henry Braun, Brian Cohen, Johnathon Cohen, Jody Comart, Nikki Demarest, Debbie Dunkle, Jeannine Earlbaum, Ted Englander, Irene Fallenborgen and Bill McBride, April Fallon, Susan Goldberg, Sharon Gordetsky, Cindy Greenburg, Jim Herzog, Allen Hollander, Steve Hollman, Saul Hopper, Jerry Jacobs, Amanda Joseph, Ruthellen Josselson, Marsha P. Kalina, Rob Kantar, Nick and Peggy Kaufman, Will Kouw, Steve Krugman and Suzanne Fournier, Nancy Leffert, Mark Lipman, Paul Neustadt, Rob Okun and Adi Bemak, Laura Orgel, Dr. Anna Ornstein, Adele and Louis Osherson, Dan Osherson, Arielle Parker, Saralee Perel and Bob Daley, Bill Pollack, Deborah Reiger, Adam Russo, Robin Savitz, Judith Schoenholtz-Read, Jill Ann Schwartz, David Sharken, Sherry Sherman and Jeff Raz, Dara Silverman, Malcolm Slavin, Eric Stumacher, Ilana Tal, Dr. Maurice Vanderpol, Abby Weinberg, Rob Wilson and Marion Abrams, Mark Wisan, Janet Yassen, Felice Yeskel, and Genie Zeiger.

Many thanks to my fellow congregants at Synagogue Achavas Achim in Keene, New Hampshire, including Judy Olson, Arthur and Ruth Cohen, Rick and Jan Cohen, the Kapiloff family, Malcolm and Selena Katz, Paul Teitelman, Bill Medvidofsky, Jack Fabian, Jerry and Deborah Kaufman, and Jane Taylor.

All my friends at the Northfield Conference—true seekers and mavericks all—have been sturdy companions on this journey, particularly Connie Walsh, Mickey and Mike Friedman, Betsy Stout, Len Fleisher, Lucy and Alan Katz, and Jill Ann Schwartz.

Thanks, too, to all the members of the Philadelphia Group Psychotherapy Association who stayed after for more discussion late one sunny November afternoon, and the many parents at the Washington Hebrew Congregation who have come to my lectures and discussions over the years.

My agent, Jim Levine, continues to meld the best features of savvy business adviser and true friend, a combination for which I am most grateful. And to my editor, Jane Isay—you are a gift in my life. Many thanks for your warmth, sense of humor, keen intelligence, and commitment to Judaism. This book would never have happened without both Jim and Jane's faith in the project.

And, finally, this book could not and would not have been written without the love, companionship, and teachings I've received from my family: my wife, Julie, son Toby, and daughter Emily.

INDEX

abba, 58
Abraham, 8, 31, 43, 291, 295–96, 304
adolescence
  Jewish identity and, 6, 16, 18, 39, 231
  rebellion in, 39, 112
  See also bar/bat mitzvah
Adonai, 314
aggression
  childhood shame and, 70–72
  male hiding versus, 90–93
Aleynu, 138
alienation from Judaism, 10, 16–18,
  162, 166–67
aliyah, 163, 196
aliyot, 155
Allen, Woody, 120, 122
ambiguous religious identity, 148–49
American Jewish Committee, 1
American Jewish Congress, 69–70
Americans for Peace Now, 217
Amichai, Yehuda, 237, 273
Amidah, 193
anti-Semitism, 50, 154
Apple Hill Chamber Players, 206–11
Argentina, 99–101
ark, 279
Art for a Fair Economy, 232
assimilation, 2–3, 5, 18
  historical tensions of, 30–31
  interfaith marriages and, 2–3, 5, 20,
    160

Jewish history and, 27, 29
Auschwitz, 81–82
authenticity in Judaism, 42–43, 64
authority
  demystifying the sanctuary, 278–91
  Jewish identity and, 173–87, 231
  mindfulness of attitudes toward,
    263–64
  Passover seder and, 176–80
  tension between creativity and,
    173–76, 270
  See also Internal Pharaoh
Avinu Malkenu, 247

Babi Yar, 56
Bader, Michael, 66–67
bar/bat mitzvah, 16, 26, 35, 91–92,
  112, 119–20
  and children of interfaith marriages,
    138–39, 146, 147, 149–50, 153,
    155–57
  community connections and,
    188–90, 194–97
  Internal Pharaoh of parents and,
    181–85
  Internal Pharaoh of self and, 185–86
  timing of, 309–10
Becket, Robin, 273
bedikat chametz, 177–78
Bellah, Robert, 148
Bellow, Saul, 30

Bergen-Belsen, 55
Berle, Milton, 30
bimah, 279, 281, 283
Birth Mark (Raz), 227
Black, Edwin, 58
blintzes, 35–36
b'nai mitzvah, 65
b'not mitzvah, 16
Book of Blessings, The (Falk), 274, 306
Boorstein, Sylvia, 133
Boston Combined Jewish
    Philanthropies, 213
Brokaw, Tom, 225
Buddhism, 5, 13–14, 117–18, 125–33,
    183, 305
    interfaith marriage and, 149–58
    Theraveda, 150
    Tibetan, 150
    Zen, 126–33

Cahill, Thomas, 193
calendars, 159, 181–82
careers, 204–40
    community development funds,
        211–22
    music and, 206–11
    social justice and, 204–6
    social status and, 228–34
    in theater, 222–28
    writing, 234–40
Catholicism, 123–25, 149–51, 167–69
challah, 36
Chanukah, 77–79, 134–35, 142, 143,
    165–66, 266
children
    gender differences and, 183–87
    healing harsh childhood images,
        275–76
    of interfaith marriages, 5, 138–39,
        142–49, 152–58
    Jewish education of, 3
    Jewish identity and, 139–40
    launching stage, 12
    Passover and, 179–80, 242–44
    providing with broader Jewish
        identity, 133–36, 166–69
    separation from parents, 139–40,
        159–61, 304–5
    shame of, and adult aggression,
        70–72
"chosen people" notion, 207, 209
Christianity
    Catholicism, 123–25, 149–51,
        167–69

Christmas and, 47–49, 74–75,
    77–79, 133–35, 141, 142, 143,
    145, 146
    music and, 47–48, 49, 118–21, 134
    spirituality in Judaism and, 116–25
Christmas, 47–49, 74–75, 77–79,
    133–35, 141, 142, 143, 145, 146
chuppah, 36–37, 253–54
civil rights movement, 39, 57, 240
Clinton, Bill, 232
Cohen, Arthur, 140–49
Collins, Chuck, 232
commitment ceremonies, 252–53
community, 102–3
    attitude toward intermarriage, 167
    bar/bat mitzvah and, 188–90,
        194–97
    good-enough Jews and, 31–33, 37
    holidays and, 162, 198–99
    in midlife years, 188–90
    synagogue and, 147–48, 291–93,
        301–2
concentration camps, 54–56, 57–58,
    80–84, 87–93, 152, 222–25
Conservative Judaism, 4, 5, 28
    interfaith marriages and, 138
    rabbis in, 42, 43
contemplative pessimism, 191–92
conversion to Judaism, 197–202, 246,
    285–86
Cowan, Paul and Rachel, 137–38, 167
creativity and play, 98–115, 175–76
    anniversaries and, 252–53
    in approaching traditional rituals,
        242–60
    awareness of resistances and, 268–69
    cultivating, 260–61
    in demystifying the sanctuary,
        278–91
    discomfort in, 267
    family history and, 267–68
    funerals and, 258–60
    High Holidays and, 244–49, 263,
        295–96, 297
    humor in, 30–31, 76–77, 225–26,
        249, 269
    impact of shame on, 67
    importance of, 175
    Internal Pharaoh and, 173–76, 270,
        274
    in midlife years, 187–92
    Passover seder and, 176–80,
        242–44, 261, 262–63, 264–66
    in prayer, 272–78

creativity and play (*continued*)
    precipitate, 191
    Purim and, 249–52
    Rosh Hoshanah and, 287–88,
        295–96, 297
    sculpted, 191–92, 202–3
    Shabbat and, 254–58, 261, 269–70,
        312–17
    starting small, 266–67
    synagogue affiliation and, 180–87
    tension between authority and,
        173–76, 270
    weddings and, 252–54
    writing and, 239, 266–67, 280–88
    Yom Kippur and, 289–91
cremation, 259–60
cross-gender relationships, 61–63,
    159–60

Dachau, 223–25
dance, movement choir, 293–96
davening, 17, 35, 122
Dayenu, 127, 261
"Debate with the Rabbi" (Nemerov),
    8, 41–42
Dekro, Jeffrey, 211
Desdemona wish, 160–61
DeWolf, Ada, 140–49
Diaspora, 204
di Donato, Pietro, 32
difference
    lesbianism and, 230
    and resistance to being Jewish,
        46–51, 56, 57, 67, 70–72, 73–77,
        112
    social status and, 229–30
discontented Jews, 2, 26
    See also good-enough Jews
discussion groups, 318–24
    forming, 318–20
    guidelines for, 320–22
    synagogue and, 323–24
    writing and, 321–24

Easter, 141, 145, 152, 162
Economic Apartheid in America
    (Yeskel), 232
Elat Chayyim, 130, 134, 271
Ellison, Ralph, 32
Erikson, Erik, 5, 6
Esther (Raz), 228, 249–52
ethical humanism values, 66, 140–41
Exodus, 177
extended family

bar/bat mitzvah and, 188–90, 194–97
holidays and, 194–95
interfaith marriages and, 163, 166

Fabian, Egon, 30–31
Falk, Marcia, 138, 273–74, 306
family life in Judaism, 4, 9–21
    alienation and, 10
    cross-gender relationships, 61–63,
        159–60
    exploring family history, 267–68
    extended family, 163, 166, 188–90,
        194–97
    generational threads, 34–37
    interfaith marriages and, 2–3, 5,
        143, 152–58
    lesbianism and, 230
    wounded fathers, 58–61, 85, 87–93,
        119
    wounded mothers, 60, 61–63,
        85–86
    See also children; parents
Father-Land (Raz), 223–25
feminism, 41, 249–52
Fiddler on the Roof (play), 209
Finestone, Rabbi Sally, 282
First Jewish Catalog, The (Siegel),
    245–46
Flowers, Harvey, 112–13
food
    keeping kosher and, 28, 29–31, 48,
        51, 311
    ritual and, 35–36, 61, 62–63, 67,
        144, 262–63
Freedman, Samuel, 4
Freedom Hagadah (Waskow), 231
freewriting, 11, 237–38, 255–58,
    287–88, 322–23
Freud, Sigmund, 59, 73
Frost, Robert, 28
"frozen" Judaism, 18–20
funerals, 258–60

Gandhi, Mahatma, 135
Gardner, Howard, 227–28
gays and lesbians, 186–87, 228–34,
    252–53
gefilte fish, 35–36
gender, 16
    access to the Torah and, 183–87
    cross-gender relationships, 61–63,
        159–60
    good-enough Jews and, 35–38,
        40–41

integration of masculine and
  feminine sides and, 197–202,
  272–75
rabbis and, 183–87
recovery from Holocaust and, 80–93
role of male and female images in
  Judaism, 305–7
separation of sexes and, 215
spirituality in Judaism and, 107–8
women as rabbis, 39–41, 130–33,
  183, 200, 273–74, 282, 306
wounded fathers, 58–61, 85, 87–93
wounded mothers, 60, 61–63,
  85–86
See also feminism; patriarchy
Gibran, Kahlil, 156
Gifts of the Jews, The (Cahill), 193
Ginsberg, Allen, 125, 273
Girardi, Judah, 167–69
Gold, Rabbi Shefa, 273–74, 306
Goldstein, Joseph, 131
Goodbye, Columbus (Roth), 32
good-enough Jews, 25–44
  assimilation and, 30–31
  community and, 31–33, 37
  conformity to rules and, 27–30
  doubt and uncertainty of, 38–43
  feeling of inadequacy and, 26,
    27–33
  gender and, 35–38, 40–41
  generational threads and, 34–37
  Jewish identity and, 33–38, 43–44
  rabbis as models of, 39–43
  synagogue involvement and, 37–38
  time in Israel and, 38–41
Gordon, Mary, 275
"gray" Judaism, 16–17
Greenberg, Cindy, 204–6
grief, 69

Haggadah, 29, 149, 177, 178–79, 241,
  242–44, 245, 262–63, 265–66
Hannah, 297, 300
Hashomer Hatizair camp, 215
Havdalah, 269–70
Hebrew calendar, 159, 181–82
Hebrew free loan societies, 213
Hebrew language, 2, 67, 129, 155, 194,
  196
Hebrew school, 119, 145, 146, 149,
  153, 166, 194, 215–16, 219
herring, 36
Heschel, Rabbi Abraham Joshua, 220,
  240, 254–55, 292

High Holidays, 17, 36, 62–63, 127–28,
  143, 174, 215, 244–49, 263,
  295–96, 297, 299
Hillel, 311
Hinduism, 151
historical Judaism, 7, 8–9, 18–21, 108
Hitler, Adolf, 58–59
holidays, 15
  Chanukah, 77–79, 134–35, 142,
    143, 165–66, 266
  Christmas, 47–49, 74–75, 77–79,
    133–35, 141, 142, 143, 145, 146
  community and, 162, 198–99
  Easter, 141, 145, 152, 162
  High Holidays, 17, 36, 62–63,
    127–28, 143, 174, 215, 244–49,
    263, 295–96, 297, 299
  interfaith marriages and, 141–46,
    149, 152, 153, 158–59, 162,
    165–66
  Passover. *See* Passover
  Purim, 228, 249–52
  Rosh Hashanah, 34, 158–59,
    244–49, 263, 287–88, 295–96,
    297
  Yom Kippur, 15, 34, 133, 193,
    233–34, 235, 263, 289–91
Holocaust, 28–29, 204, 234–35
  concentration camps and, 54–56,
    57–58, 80–84, 87–93, 152,
    222–25
  impact on contemporary Judaism,
    69, 151–52
  role in American life, 70
  shame and difference and, 51–58, 67
  wounded fathers and, 58–61, 85,
    87–93
homophobia, 233
Horowitz, Bethamie, 6–7, 307, 309
humor, 30–31, 76–77, 225–26, 249,
  269

individualism, community versus,
  32–33
Insight Meditation Society, 130–33,
  158
interfaith marriages, 2–3, 20, 137–69
  anxiety concerning, 137–39
  Buddhism and, 149–58
  challenge and opportunity of,
    158–66
  of children, 37
  children and, 5, 138–39, 142–49,
    152–58

interfaith marriages (*continued*)
  cultural continuity and, 138–39, 154
  deeper roots of, 159–66
  extended family and, 163, 166
  family life in Judaism and, 2–3, 5,
    143, 152–58
  good-enough Jews and, 26
  holidays and, 141–46, 149, 152, 153,
    158–59, 162, 165–66
  loneliness and, 165–66
  rabbis and, 138, 145, 146–47,
    154–55, 168–69
  respect for other beliefs and, 166–69
  separation from parents and,
    139–40, 159–61
  single-faith marriages versus, 163–65
  spiritual issues in, 147–49, 154–55,
    158–66
  wedding ceremonies for, 253–54
Internal Pharaoh
  defined, 173
  of gays and lesbians, 186–87
  Passover seder and, 176–80
  rabbis and, 181–85
  synagogue and, 180–87, 270, 274
  welcoming, 173–76, 270, 274
irony, 76–77
Isaac, 8, 291, 295–96
Isaiah, 233–34
Israel, 53, 204, 216–17, 221
  army and air force of, 72, 92
  Jewish identity and, 39–41
  kibbutz movement, 17, 40, 85–86
  Playing for Peace Project, 206,
    207–8, 237
  relationship between God and,
    66–67

Jacob, 237, 294
Jaques, Elliot, 190–92
Jesus Christ, 47–49, 159
Jew in the Lotus, The (Kamenetz), 13,
  125, 305
Jewish calendar, 159, 181–82
Jewish features, 50, 51
Jewish feminist theology, 41
Jewish identity, 5–7
  appearances and, 33–38
  aspects of parents and grandparents
    in, 98, 104–8
  assimilation and, 2–3, 5, 18
  authority and, 173–87, 231
  bridging disparate experiences and,
    214–22

careers in. *See* careers
  conformity to rules, 27–30
  creativity and play in, 242–70
  effects of resistance on, 63–73
  as emotional phenomenon, 303–4
  felt experiences of childhood and,
    98–104
  fluidity of, 11–12
  Holocaust and, 51–58
  inclusive sense of, 43–44
  interfaith marriage and, 139–40,
    144–49, 152–58
  Interior Journey and, 309
  Jewish myopia and, 310–11
  joy and liberation in, 242–60
  key adult relationships and, 98,
    108–9, 123–25
  marker experiences and, 98, 103,
    110–14
  in midlife years, 187–90, 192–97
  minority status and, 5–6, 27, 32,
    76–77, 145–46
  as mosaic, 26
  movement and, 293–96, 311–17
  multiple pathways to, 307–8
  observable behavior versus, 308–9
  through opposition, 14
  of parents versus self, 18–21
  providing children with broader,
    133–36
  resilience of, 114–15
  searching process and, 8
  as tapestry, 97–115
  time in Israel and, 39–41
  tipping events and, 98, 108, 109–10,
    114–15
  top-down versus bottom-up
    approach to, 26
  vibrant sense of, 80–87
  work in. *See* careers
Jewish question, ambivalence about,
  10–11
Jewish Social Justice Network, 204–6
Jewish values, 205, 211
Jew v. Jew (Freedman), 4
Job, 235
Joseph, Amanda, 211–22
JuBus (Jewish Buddhists), 125–33
Judaism
  conversion to, 197–202, 246, 285–86
  cultural continuity and, 138–39, 154
  historical, 7, 8–9, 18–21, 108
  internal undertow and, 7–9
  music in, 121–23, 178

nature of, 7
outside the synagogue, 5
resistance. *See* resistance to being
    Jewish
sculpted and foreclosed, 202–3
shades of religious belief, 4–5
social action versus faith and, 105–8
tensions between groups of Jews, 4
Judgment at Nuremburg (movie), 56

Kabbalah, 129–30
Kaddish (Wieseltier), 113, 260
Kamenetz, Rodger, 13, 125, 305
Kaplan, Abraham, 278
kashrut, 28, 311
kavanah, 282, 291
keeping kosher, 28, 29–31, 48, 51, 311
kevah, 282, 291
kibbutz movement, 17, 40, 85–86
kiddushim ceremonies, 37, 252–53
King, Martin Luther, Jr., 240
kippot, 55
klezmer music, 254
Kligler, Rabbi Jonathan, 293–94
Kol Nidrei, 247–49, 260–61
Kripalu Institute, 134
Kunitz, Stanley, 273
Kushner, Harold, 121

Landsmeinschaften, 213
Langman, Peter, 27
late adulthood, 15
Laws of Gifts to the Poor
    (Maimonides), 212
Lerman, Liz, 294–96
lesbians and gays, 186–87, 228–34,
    252–53
Lester, Julius, 277
Levinson, Daniel, 13
Lieberman, Joseph I., 4
life stages, 12–18
    adolescence, 6, 16, 18, 39, 112
    key events of life cycle, 98, 103,
        110–14
    late adulthood, 15
    marker events and, 98, 103, 110–14
    midlife years, 13, 16, 187–97
    normal transitions in, 12, 38
    separation from parents, 139–40,
        159–61, 304–5
    young adulthood, 13, 14–15, 18
lived experience of Judaism, 4
Lot's wife, 68
lunar cycle, 200

Maimonides, 212
Male Choir of the Great Synagogue
    (Moscow), 121–22
marker experiences, Jewish identity
    and, 98, 103, 110–14
Matalon, Rabbi Rolando, 311
materialism, 3, 49–51, 141
matrilineal descent, 26
matzoh, 49
meditation, 126–27, 129–33, 150, 152,
    158
megillah, 249
menorahs, 51, 75, 214
Merwin, W. S., 274–75
mezuzah, 277
midlife years, 13, 16
    awareness of fragility of life and,
        190–97
    contemplative pessimism and,
        191–92
    Jewish identity and, 187–90, 192–97
    mourning process and, 192
mikvah ceremony, 201
mindfulness, 130–33
minority status of Jews, 5–6, 27, 32,
    76–77, 145–46
Minuchin, Salvadore, 20
mitzvah, 86–87
    time in Israel as, 39–41
Mixed Blessings (Cowan and Cowan),
    137–38, 167
Modeh Ani, 220
Mormonism, 141, 150
Moses, 48, 179, 180
motzi, 314
mourning process
    funeral, 258–60
    grief and, 69
    in midlife years, 192
movement, in embodiment of
    spirituality, 293–96, 311–17
Moving Jewish Communities Dance
    Institute, 294–96
music
    Apple Hill Chamber Players, 206–11
    Christian, 47–48, 49, 118–21, 134
    Jewish, 121–23, 178, 254
    Playing for Peace Project, 206,
        207–8, 237
    spirituality and, 118–23

naming ceremony, 201, 210
National Jewish Population Survey, 1
Nazi Germany, 32, 58–59, 99–100

Nemerov, Howard, 8, 41–42
New Israel Fund, 217
Noah, 132
Northfield Conference, 312–17
Not by the Sword (Watterson), 208
Novick, Peter, 54–58, 70

100 Acres Monastery, 123–25
Ornstein, Anna, 80–84, 86, 87
Orthodox Judaism, 2, 3, 4, 5
    community and, 32–33
    interfaith marriage and, 161
    keeping kosher and, 29–30
    patriarchy of, 40, 156–57, 215–16
    rabbis in, 43
    synagogue affiliation and, 37–38
outmarriage, 167. *See also* interfaith
    marriages

pagan beliefs, 134–35, 200
Paley, Grace, 273
parents
    aspects of, in Jewish identity, 98,
        104–8
    funerals of, 258–60
    Jewish identity of, 18–21. *See also*
        Jewish identity
    in midlife years of children, 188–90,
        195–97
    mixed messages from, 29
    negative feelings toward faith, 65–66
    questions about faith, 165
    separation of children from, 139–40,
        159–61, 304–5
    wounded fathers, 58–61, 85, 87–93,
        119
    wounded mothers, 60, 61–63, 85–86
Pascal, Blaise, 199
Passover, 19, 29, 30, 37, 67, 121, 127,
    142, 143–44, 146, 153, 162,
    195–96, 198, 235
    creativity in seder, 176–80, 242–44,
        261, 262–63, 264–66
    Haggadah and, 29, 149, 177,
        178–79, 241, 242–44, 245,
        262–63, 265–66
patriarchy, 40
    of Orthodox Judaism, 40, 156–57,
        215–16
    segregation of women and, 62–63
    wounded fathers and, 58–61, 85,
        87–93
    wounded mothers and, 60, 61–63,
        85–86

Pawnbroker, The (movie), 89
Pesach, 241
play. *See* creativity and play
Playing for Peace Project, 206, 207–8,
    237
pork, 30–31, 48
prayer, 272–78
    communal sharing in, 291–93
    davening, 17, 35, 122
    healing harsh childhood images
        through, 275–76
    patchwork prayerbook, 272–75
    power of, 297–98
    tactile, 277–78
    visualization and, 276–77
    writing and, 239, 266–67, 280–88
precipitate creativity, 191
Purim, 228, 249–52

Rabbinical Assembly, 138
rabbis
    authority of, 180–83
    Buddhism and, 130–33
    as human, 30–31, 41–43, 183–87,
        200
    interfaith marriages and, 138, 145,
        146–47, 154–55, 168–69
    responsive, 129
    women and, 183–87
    women as, 39–41, 130–33, 183,
        200, 273–74, 282, 306
Raz, Jeff, 222–28, 249–52
Reconstructionist Judaism, 4
    interfaith marriages and, 138
    music in, 122–23
    rabbis in, 43
Reform Judaism, 2, 3, 4, 5
    interfaith marriages and, 138
    keeping kosher and, 29–30
    rabbis in, 43
Reimer, Joseph, 6, 135, 166
resistance to being Jewish, 45–79
    adult Jewish identity and, 63–73
    awareness of, 268–69
    exploring Judaism, 10–11
    Holocaust and, 51–58, 67–70, 73
    managing, 73–79
    overcoming, 80–93
    rejection of victim stance, 57, 60–62,
        72, 209
    resistance to talking about, 45–46
    shame and difference in, 46–51, 56,
        57, 67, 70–72, 73–77, 112
    wounded parents and, 58–63

rituals, 29, 269–70, 307–8, 309–10
  food and, 35–36, 61, 62–63, 67,
    144, 262–63
  See also creativity and play; holidays;
    Shabbat; synagogue *and specific*
    holidays
Rosen, Jonathan, 113–14
Rosh Hashanah, 34, 158–59, 244–49,
    263, 287–88, 295–96, 297
Roth, Michael, 59
Roth, Philip, 30, 32–33, 225
Rothenberg, Martin, 232

Sabbath. *See* Shabbat
Samuel, 297
sanctuary of synagogue, 278–91
  psychology of, 279–80
  writing and, 280–91
Sarah, 304
scapegoating, 77
Schaverien, Joy, 55
Schindler's List (movie), 84, 88
Schwartz, Jill Ann, 293–96, 313,
    314–17
sculpted creativity, 191–92
sculpted Judaism, 202–3
searching process, 8
seders, 19, 29, 37, 67, 127
  creativity and play in, 176–80,
    242–44, 261, 262–63, 264–66
Seinfeld, Jerry, 30
self-esteem, 46, 51, 74
self-hatred, 27
Senish, Hannah, 201
S'ferot, 129
Shabbat, 157–58, 220–21, 233
  approaches to, 254–58, 269–70,
    312–17
  candle lighting, 98–99, 261
shame, 11, 43
  of childhood, and adult aggression,
    70–72
  defining, 46–47
  feeling different and, 67
  opportunity for growth in, 73–77
  and resistance to being Jewish,
    46–51, 56, 57, 63–77
  social status and, 229–30
  wounded fathers and, 58–61, 85,
    87–93, 119
  wounded mothers and, 60, 61–63,
    85–86
Shavuot, 107
Shechinah, 201

Shefa Fund, The, 211, 219–20
Shehecheyanu, 256, 282
Shema, 157, 199–200, 274, 306,
    313–17
shul, 118, 120, 122, 129–30, 184, 186,
    196, 220, 308
Siegel, Richard, 245–46
silence, 296–97, 298–301
Silverman, Dara, 240
single-faith marriages, interfaith
    marriages versus, 163–65
Sobol, David, 244
spirituality in Judaism, 10, 12–13, 14,
    16
  Buddhism and, 5, 13–14, 117–18,
    125–33
  children and broader Jewish identity,
    133–36
  Christian contemplation and,
    123–25
  Christianity and, 116–25
  gender and, 107–8
  Holocaust and, 28–29
  interfaith marriages and, 147–49,
    154–55, 158–66
  movement and, 293–96, 311–17
  music and, 118–23
  not-knowing in, 300–301
  organized religion versus, 164
  search for, 25, 105–6
  shame and, 65, 120–22
  See also prayer
Stern, Gerald, 237
Stiller, Ben, 30
Stumacher, Eric, 237
success of Jews, 4, 19, 49–51, 60
suicide, 222–23, 224
survivor guilt, 29, 53, 90
survivor syndrome, 81
synagogue, 2, 32, 35, 36, 271–302
  active involvement in, 37–38
  community and, 147–48, 291–93,
    301–2
  discussion groups and, 323–24
  institutionalized homophobia and,
    233
  Internal Pharaoh and, 180–87, 270,
    274
  movement and, 293–96
  overemphasizing importance of,
    307–8
  prayer and, 272–78
  sanctuary of, 278–91
  talking and, 288, 291–93, 296–302

tactile prayer, 277–78
talk
  discussion groups, 318–24
  encouraging, 288, 296–302
  personal presentation format, 301–2
  resistance to addressing resistance,
    45–46
  silence and, 296–97, 298–301
  in synagogue, 288, 291–93,
    296–302
tallit, 35, 55, 103, 104, 124, 253
Talmud and the Internet, The (Rosen),
    113–14
Tashlich, 263
tefillin, 35
Terezin, 89
teshuvah, 132–33
Theraveda Buddhism, 150
Tibetan Buddhism, 150
Tikkun, 185
Tikkun Olam, 204, 212, 231
tipping events, Jewish identity and, 98,
    108, 109–10, 114–15
To Life (Kushner), 121
Tomkins, Sylvan, 77
Torah, 102–3, 279, 281
  as current events, 296–99
  female access to, 183–87
  male observances and, 36
Trapp, Larry, 208–9
trust, 301
tzedakah, 212, 219
TZEDEC, 211–22
tzitzit, 35, 253

uncounted Jews, 1–2, 26
  See also good-enough Jews
Union of American Hebrew
    Congregations, 2
Unitarianism, 152, 164–65
United for a Fair Economy (UFE),
    228–29, 232–34, 240

Vanderpol, Maurice, 87–93
victim cycle, 57, 60–62, 72, 209
Vipassana, 130–33
visualization, in prayer, 276–77
Vogel, Paula, 160

Waskow, Arthur, 231
Watterson, Kathryn, 208
wealth, shame and, 49–51
weddings, 36–37, 252–54
Weinberg, Rabbi Sheila Peltz, 130–33,
    183
Weisser, Michael, 208–9
Western calendar, 159, 181–82
Wieseltier, Leon, 113, 260
Winnicott, Donald, 175, 304
winter solstice, 134–35
Wise, Stephen, 58
Women in Black movement, 217, 218
women's movement, 41
Woodstock Jewish Congregation,
    293–96
work. *See* careers
World Union of Jewish Students, 217
World War II, 16–17, 19, 28–29, 32,
    54, 59, 99–100, 222–23, 225. *See
    also* Holocaust
wounded fathers, 59–61, 85, 87–93
wounded mothers, 60, 61–63, 85–86
writing
  careers in, 234–40
  discussion groups and, 321–24
  freewriting, 11, 237–38, 255–58,
    287–88, 322–23
  poem-prayers, 266–67
  in the sanctuary, 280–91
  Shabbat and, 255–58
  "Top Secret" game, 289–91

yarmulkes, 28, 124, 155, 268–69, 279
Yeshiva University, 32–33
Yeskel, Felice, 228–34, 252–53
Yizkor, 133
Yoffie, Rabbi Eric, 2, 307–8
yoga, 129, 130
Yom Kippur, 15, 34, 133, 193,
    233–34, 235, 263, 289–91
young adulthood, 13, 14–15, 18

Zeiger, Genie, 234–40, 280–88
Zen Buddhism, 126–33